Raise Happy Children Through A Happier Marriage!

By

Mary Ann Budnik

R.B. Media, Inc

Springfield, IL

IMPRIMATUR: Most Reverend George J. Lucas
Bishop of Springfield in Illinois
June 20, 2001

The Imprimatur is a declaration that a book or pamphlet is considered to be free from doctrinal or moral error.

First Edition: June 26, 2001

For additional copies of *Raise Happy Children Through A Happier Marriage,* or for copies of Mary Ann Budnik's other books, *Raise Happy Children...Raise Them Saints!, Raise Happy Children...Teach Them Virtues!, You Can Become A Saint!, You Can Become A Saint! Workbook* and *Looking For Peace? Try Confession!* contact:

R.B. Media, Inc.
154 Doral
Springfield, IL 62704
Phone: (217) 546-5261 Fax: (217) 546-0558
Website: www.rbmediainc.com
E-mail: MABudnik@worldnet.att.net

Library of Congress catalog card number: 2001117920
R.B. Media, Inc.: ISBN 0-9700021-4-9

This book is dedicated to Father Mike, a priest of the Holy Cross and Opus Dei, who has painstakingly taught me theology, writing skills, the importance of "tone" in addition to giving me editorial help for six books and hundreds of articles and columns over the last eighteen years.

He has acted as confessor and advisor in difficult situations. He has kept me persevering in the face of almost insurmountable obstacles and at times provided solutions to impossible problems.

My favorite memory of Fr. Mike is the day he officiated at the wedding of our youngest daughter, Mary Terese, the bride on this cover, to Jeffrey Wills.

My deepest gratitude goes out to him for all of the above, but most of all for opening my eyes to the depth of our Catholic Faith. You see, the degree of happiness we experience on earth depends on the intenstity of our love for God.

Acknowledgements

Steve Wood quotes his mother as saying, *By the time you're an expert you are unemployed.* As an "unemployed mother," I now have the time to share with you what Bob and I found invaluable in our marriage and family life. I would like to thank the following for their help:

- My husband, Bob, who sacrificed himself in countless ways so that this book could now be in your hands.

- Reverend Michael Giesler of the Prelature of the Holy Cross and Opus Dei who acted as my chief editor, theologian and coach.

- Christine Mack for her beautiful illustrations and graphic design help with the book cover.

- Anna Betzelberrger who made the book cover a reality with her computer and layout expertise.

- My copy editors, Nancy and Jim Hanlon, Carol Kelly, and Mary Kate Budnik Stangel. Their input and editing skills added the polish.

- Mary Magnor, my sister-in-law, for writing the Preface and providing four of the five children on the cover: (l-r) Patrick, Kathryn, Anne Marie, and Elizabeth Magnor. My daughters: Marianne for suggesting the book be broken into a series; Mary Terese for the use of her wedding picture and her two older daughters on the back cover; Mary Kate for editing and all our daughters for allowing me to use their youth for examples. (Katie's son, Michael, is the little boy pictured front right on the cover.) This series on the family has been a family affair!

- Dr. David Isaacs of the University of Navarre in Pamplona, Spain, for permitting me to quote extensively his course material on family and marriage as well as his book, *Character Building.*

- Mr. James Stenson for allowing me to quote his books at length.

- Dick and Lou Prince who audiotaped Dr. Isaacs' course, "Marriage Relationships" for us in Spain.

- Other resource material that I was permitted to use freely.

- Fr. Mark Schulte, for permitting me to use his homily on "Fatherhood." Drs. Bushholz and Follmer for allowing me to quote their lecture.

- Scepter Publishers, Inc. for allowing me to freely quote many of their publications; Leaflet Missal for allowing extensive quotations from *The Catholic Family In The Modern World* by John A. Hardon, S.J.; Doubleday for permission to quote from Bill Cosby's book, *Fatherhood*; the office of Family Life, of the Diocese of Peoria, for allowing me to quote their book, *We Are Family.*

- My readers who suggested this book, then sent audio tapes, videos, books and prayers. The latter kept me writing!

In writing this book I found inclusive language awkward. For this reason I use the traditional meaning of he/him as including men and women, boys and girls.

Table of Contents

So Why Is Holiness Important?

We are all called to be saints. Discover how you can become a saint through your vocation to marriage. People truly living the Catholic faith influence culture, science, history, music, art, politics, etc. Learn why. How does one grow holy? Summary of a plan of life is given. Personal holiness requires generosity but how does one live this generosity in the vocation of marriage?

Marriage Creates Future Saints!

What is a Catholic marriage? The mystery of marriage, the Sacrament of Matrimony and its primary purpose are discussed. The powerful graces of the sacrament are explored as well as how to utilize these graces for a happier marriage. What is meant by unity in marriage? When couples deviate from God's plan for marriage serious problems erupt. The personal cost of doing it *my* way rather than God's way is explored. The universal call to holiness includes not only us but also our children. You are called to raise your children saints!

What's So Important About Virtues?

The three theological virtues, the four cardinal virtues and the natural virtues are necessary for happy marriages and for raising responsible, happy children. How does one obtain them? How does one cope with the defects in one's spouse?

Life In The Married Lane

"I Do" is simply the beginning. Discover the secret of a happy marriage and how it can be achieved by developing the characteristics of empathy, appreciation, congruence, and character. Learn how to improve communication in your marriage. Have fun as you grow in married love...and holiness. Study how to resolve problems. Find out why happy marriages need good memories. Discover how to grow happy and holy by utilizing suffering rather than fleeing from it. The stages of marriage are explained as well as mid-life "crisis."

What is a family and why is it important? Why is the family called the Domestic Church? What are the duties of each parent? How does one raise a child? Are working moms a problem? Issues of upbringing are explored, such as bonding, the role of parent/leader, and the setting of family goals. Using the examples of the saints, discover how to develop a Catholic family culture. Learn how to teach your children the value of suffering.

Why are a male and a female necessary as parents? The important role of both mother and father is explored in depth. The question of equality is addressed as well as the authority of the father. What can single parents do to parent successfully? The secret to successful parenting is explained through the example of the saints as well as the example of the parents of saints.

Introduction

As my husband and I walked into my parent's country home on Christmas day, shouts and squeals of *Grandma! Grandpa* greeted us. What followed was mass confusion as four little ones, ages five, three, two, and one laughingly hugged us while trying to out shout each other for our attention. It was delightful bedlam.

Since that experience, my mind keeps wandering back to Christmas. Why did their greeting make such an impression on me? When I dissected the event, what I discovered was jarring. What was unique about these children were the smiles on their faces indicating their joy in being alive. This is how children *should* be. This is how I remember children acting in the past. Why is it *so* rare today to see a child smile or hear a child laugh? Everywhere I look I see sullen, surly faces from little ones to teenagers. Rarely will children or teens even greet an adult with a simple *Hello* or *How are you?* What has *happened* to our children?

I began to look deeper. Was "sullen childhood" limited to dysfunctional families or abused children? Surprisingly, I found sullen, surly children in families with strong marriages, even in married couples striving for holiness themselves. Is it our culture that is destroying the joy of our children? Possibly. Is it materialism? Maybe. Yet, as Christians we are to carry our environment within us so as to positively influence those we deal with rather than being negatively influenced by the world. As Blessed Escrivá writes: *Children of God—like yourself—cannot be afraid of living in the professional or social surroundings which are proper to them. They are never alone! God Our Lord, who always goes with you, grants you the means to be faithful to Him, and to bring others to Him.*[1]

Closer observation convinced me that "sullen childhood" is a spiritual disease. Why? *Joy is the echo of God's life in us,* according to Abbot Marmion. St. John Vianney adds, *It is always springtime in the heart that loves God.* While each of us longs for happiness, a large segment of society refuses to acknowledge that our degree of happiness solely depends on how closely we are united to God. These people seek happiness in atheism, humanism, and consumerism. To make matters worse, we have the non-directive method of education, which has permeated the majority of our schools on all levels. This method allows our children to make their own choices without ethical or moral guidelines. This results not only in the loss of their Catholic faith, but makes them part of the New Age Movement in which they think that they are self-contained gods and goddesses. This attitude is intensified when children read the best selling Harry Potter books based on the occult.

We cannot be happy without a growing relationship with God and this means more than just spending 45 minutes at Sunday Mass. Our relationship with God has to permeate every minute of every day. Marcus Grodie relates how he asked a gentleman what he did. Smiling, the man replied, *I'm a disciple of Christ cleverly disguised as a plumber.* This has to be our identity as well. Only then will our happiness spill over to our spouse and children. The closer we are to God, the more joy we possess. This in turn is reflected by our smiles and laughter. As the convert G. K. Chesterton noted: *It is the obligation of all Christians to be happy.* St. Francis of Assisi worried when he met a sad friar. *He felt that the gloomy brother was not in the grace of God. Hence, he one time told a dyspeptic-looking friar, point-blank, to go to confession, saying that only man, with his free will, could disturb the harmony that God wants in the world. "Then," he said, "return*

---

[1]Blessed Josemaría Escrivá, *The Forge* (New York, Scepter, 1988) #724.

and join once more in the chorus of praise to God.'''[2] St. Francis knew that without love of God there could be no joy, happiness, nor peace. Peter Kreeft believes that *happiness is goodness.* Mother Teresa came to the same conclusion. She told everyone who would listen, *Spread love everywhere you go: first of all in your own house. Give love to your children, to your wife or husband, to a next-door neighbor...Let no one ever come to you without leaving better and happier. Be the living expression of God's kindness; kindness in your face, kindness in your eyes, kindness in your smile, kindness in your warm greeting.*

Are our children sullen because they do not know God and therefore cannot love Him? It's a disturbing thought. Paul Claudel points out that *Man is only happy when he lives according to his nature and when he strives to accomplish his end.*[3] In talking further with parents who are striving for holiness themselves, I discovered much to my dismay that many were not teaching their children the faith. They are abdicating this job to the Catholic schools. These parents do not realize that the Catholic faith of their children needs to be nurtured by *them.* Parents are the **primary educators** of their children...not the school. Sadly, many parents discover this fact too late when their teens no longer attend Sunday Mass or when their adult children join the ranks of the fallen away Catholics.

The spiritual disease of "sullen childhood" correlates with what I heard years ago at a Day of Recollection. That Day of Recollection was a turning point in our parenting modus operandi. The words of the priest had a profound effect on how we have raised our three daughters. Originally I thought that if we taught our three daughters the morals and teachings of the Catholic Church, kept them out of sex education classes, and encouraged them to receive the sacraments regularly, when they became adults, they would *naturally* want to deepen their faith and strive for holiness. Our

[2] Hyacinth Blocker, O.F.M., *Walk With The Wise* (Cincinnati, Ohio, St. Francis Book Shop, 1950) p. 150.
[3] Quoted by Henri Morice in *The Apostolate of Moral Beauty* (St. Louis, MO: B. Herder, 1961) p. 88.

job was to give them the basic tools. When they grew up they would do the rest on their own. This view of parenting is only partially correct.

That day **the priest told us that if we were *not* raising our children to be saints, they *would* lose their faith in our pagan culture.** I sat there in a state of shock. This not only was a jolt of reality but it was also a call to arms. Raised within a family where the Catholic faith is considered the most prized possession, the thought of one or all of my daughters losing their faith was chilling. My husband and I redoubled our efforts. We took Family Development Courses that taught us how to teach our children virtues. Our daughters were enrolled in private schools that supported the faith and morals we were teaching them at home. Naturally the schools were located quite a distance from our home. In the primary grades it was a forty mile round trip twice a day with an infant. As the girls grew older, the ride lengthened to eighty miles round trip twice a day. When a job change relocated our family to Springfield in Central Illinois, we sent our daughters hundreds of miles away to board with family and friends so that they could attend a private high school that values the Catholic faith and morals as strongly as we do.

We took advantage of the spiritual formation offered by Opus Dei for young people. Our daughters attended leadership camps, girls' clubs, retreats, high school weekend meditations, doctrine classes and youth trips to Rome to see the Holy Father. They went on pilgrimages. We prayed the family rosary daily. All of this has been financially draining, physically exhausting, time consuming *but* morally exhilarating. By the time our daughters reached adulthood they were firmly planted on the narrow path Our Lord talks about in the Gospels. They know the Way and the Truth. They were taught to strive for holiness. The rest of the journey depends on their free will. However, they do not journey alone. Daily we accompany them with our prayers for their perseverance to be holy in mind, body and soul, and...being a mother I still give advice in conversations and by letters.

Friends found our conduct ridiculous and extreme. Living in a small city, I learned that complete strangers discussed "our weird ways" and us. One couple actually invited us over yearly just to check to see if we still believe in the same things we did a year ago. People dismissed our objections to sex education classes until their daughters had children out of wedlock, were living with someone, or became pro-abortion. The bulk of our income went to pay tuition at the private school while my friends enjoyed lavish vacations and purchased upscale homes. These same women declined invitations to send their children to any activities that would reinforce their children's faith...that was until it was too late and their children had left the faith.

As our daughters became parents, rather than breathing a sigh of relief, my concern increases. As I watch the population of "sullen children" growing it concerns me that parents in general remain indifferent to this spiritual disease. For example, several years ago a group of mothers, concerned that their teens were not being taught the faith in their Catholic schools, approached me for help. Could I find a priest who would teach the teens? A priest who lives in St. Louis, a 200 mile round trip away, agreed to give the teens a class once a month. From a list of 25 teens, we only averaged about 10 teens per class. The parents' excuses for their teens missing the classes exposed their misguided priorities. Helping their children to know, love and serve God better was *not* a priority. If it worked into their schedule that month, the teens attended the class. If not, so what if the priest gave of his time, made the long drive but only a few came? Listening to the silly excuses of some of these parents was maddening. I was tempted to shake them and shout, *Your child's soul is at stake! Wake Up!* Instead, I pray for them since talking to them did not seem to help. Hopefully they can be reached through prayer before their children's souls are lost.

Sadly, when it comes to sports or other extracurricular activities these same parents undertake great hardships. Some get up at 3:00AM to take their child to hockey or ice-skating practice. Others drive hundreds of miles for basketball, soccer games, riding competitions. What effort and expense parents put forth to equip their children for football, music, dance, tennis and a host of other activities and sports. Yet these same parents are unable to make the effort to drive them to a retreat house, leadership camp, to daily Mass, to Saturday afternoon confession or even an organized class given by a priest.

On the other hand, the parents who did make an effort to bring their teens to the class gave their children an example of heroic virtue. One drove 60 miles round trip in snowstorms to bring her two teens. Another mother told her son that on the evening of class, he could not work at his part-time job. He scheduled his work around the class. When a mother sets such a priority, she is teaching her child that God comes first...no matter what. That child in turn will pass on this lesson to his children. In essence, the message that is taught is that our *faith is more precious than anything else...even money.*

As parents we tend to forget that once high school is over and the teens go on to college, tennis, soccer, music, and ice-skating are usually forgotten and the equipment is sold in a garage sale. These extracurricular activities rarely have a lasting influence on our children. Yet, a thought, an inspiration, a question answered or heard in a catechism class or on a retreat may save our child's faith, chastity and soul. Maybe even his or her life will be saved in this age of spiraling teen suicide.

No child is born a mathematician, doctor, or figure skater. A child may have talents in one of these areas but to be able to perform these skills he must be educated and trained. Likewise, no person can become a saint without developing virtues, growing in holiness, knowing the truths of our faith and living the moral teachings of the Catholic Church. While we may be striving for holiness ourselves it's spiritually impossible for our children to become holy through osmosis, inheritance or by "catching" it from us like the flu. God expects us, as parents, to raise our children saints!

For those who have not read my previous books, sanctity may seem an *extreme* notion. Yet sanctity, which is striving for holiness, is the only thing that gives life meaning. Neither our children nor we were created for the main purpose of achieving great wealth, prestige nor power. We were created to become saints![4] If this sounds like an outlandish idea, consider the Mystical Body of Christ. It consists of the *Saints* in heaven, the Souls in Purgatory, and the Church Militant on earth (that's us). The only people who populate heaven are the saints. If we plan to go to heaven and expect to see our children there also, we all have to strive for sanctity (holiness) while we are on earth. Heaven does not open its gate to just anyone. To get in that pearly gate at the moment of death we have to die in the state of sanctifying grace (our souls cannot be soiled by mortal sin), after living a life of heroic virtue on earth. On May 13, 2000, John Paul II beatified the two Fatima children, Francisco and Jacinta. In a press release on the beatification it was noted that *the honor is bestowed not for their being visionaries, but because they practiced virtue to a heroic degree.* Heroic virtue is not doing something "nice" when it's convenient or when we're in the mood. It's being heroic each day in every task we undertake or are asked to undertake. As St. Joan of Arc stated, to be holy is *to do God's will* every minute of every day of our life. Mother Teresa adds: *We are called upon not to be successful but to be holy.*

How we live our daily lives on earth determines whether we go directly to heaven, stop off in Purgatory or end up in Hell for eternity.

If we die in the state of sanctifying grace but have *not* lived a life of heroic virtue, we land in Purgatory until we do reparation. The Holy Father recently reminded us that nothing tainted can enter heaven. To enter Heaven we *must* be purified. If we die in the state of mortal sin, we risk spending eternity in Hell. (Read #1861 in the *Catechism of the Catholic Church.*) Some people deny the existence of Purgatory and Hell but remember...one does not have to believe in their existence to dwell there.

When I first began this book, my focus was to help you to teach

---

[4] For a deeper understanding of this concept read *You Can Become A Saint!* available from R.B. Media, Inc.

your children the natural virtues and the Catholic faith. But once the book began unfolding I realized that the happiness and quality of your marriage relationship profoundly affects the happiness of your children. For this reason, what I thought was one book suddenly became a series of three books. This book, the first in the series, concentrates on how to have a happier marriage, and happier children while growing in holiness. The second book teaches you how to raise your children saints. The final book in this series teaches you how to train your children in the virtues necessary for a happy, holy, and successful life. The quicker you apply what you read, the happier you and your family will become.

These books were written out of love for you, in your vitally important role as a Catholic parent, and for your children so that they may laugh and smile in the knowledge that God loves them with an everlasting love. Together may we give honor and glory now and forever to the God of mercy and love.

Mary Ann Budnik
June 26, 2001
Feast of Blessed Josemaría Escrivá

Foreword

By
Mary Magnor[1]

*First comes love, then comes marriage and then comes a baby
in the baby carriage*—so goes the familiar children's tune.
Sounds logical, right? Why, then are so many people putting
the baby carriage before marriage or even love? They are
searching for an elusive and ambiguous sense of happiness.
Elusive when sought in earthly possessions and ambiguous
when not thought of relative to God. True happiness is the
inner peace that comes from being in perfect union with God.

Malls cater to women searching for happiness in new clothes,
fancy cosmetics, jewelry or household goods. Professionals
climb the corporate ladder seeking happiness through power.
Thousands of dollars are spent by stressed out families on
dream vacations so they can find happiness by relaxing in
contrived surroundings. Sooner or later, however, we all
realize that the little black dress, incredible job promotion or
trip to Disney may bring pleasure but certainly not lasting
happiness.

The ancient Greeks differentiated between the notions of
pleasure and happiness. Pleasure, they maintained, is sense-
related and therefore fleeting. Happiness, on the other hand,

---

[1] Mary Magnor, a free-lance writer and the mother of eight children, lives in
Brookfield, Wisconsin. Impressed by how well Mary, and her husband, Tom, have
raised their children, ranging in age from a newborn to teens, I asked her to share her
insights on marriage and family life.

is eternal. Our culture treats the two synonymously. When lives are spent chasing pleasure in search of happiness, the result is a profound emptiness. A dramatic comparison can be seen in the lives of two twentieth century icons who ironically died the same week—Mother Teresa of Calcutta and Princess Diana. Mother Teresa had a physically demanding life, working with the poorest of the poor, the sick and the dying. Yet, her face radiated peace and happiness. Her eyes, which witnessed untold human suffering, sparkled with love behind her well-worn wrinkles. On the other hand, Diana, who was considered one of the most glamorous women in the world, lived an unhappy life battling eating disorders, thoughts of suicide and her husband's very public betrayal. While their interior dispositions are known only to God, the public lives of these women stand in stark contrast to show that pleasure and happiness are very different.

By examining the lives of Mother Teresa and the saints, we learn that happiness comes from doing the will of God. If Mother Teresa chose not to live the life ordained by God and instead decided to follow her own plan, she would have lost her serenity and the world her wonderful example.

The only way to achieve happiness is to seek the plan, which God has for our life, and to strive faithfully to live it. God's plan for our family's happiness is simple but certainly not easy. It is best summed up by the old catechism, which taught, *God made me to know Him, love Him and serve Him in this world and be happy with Him forever in the next.* Departure from His plan will ultimately bring us frustration. St. Thomas Aquinas said it most succinctly when he said, *God alone satisfies.* To know that God has had a plan for us from before the beginning of time is an awesome thought. No one else can fulfill that plan for us. God depends on our cooperation. Without us, His divine scheme cannot be fulfilled as it was originally intended. Our most noble vocation in this divine scheme is to pass this truth on to our children. Of course, they have free will and may decide not to live as we have taught but we must teach them nevertheless.

When we hear the word "vocation" the image of a priest or nun may come immediately to mind. However, a vocation is any calling from God to a particular state in life. Some are called to live in community as religious brothers, sisters or priests and others are called to live a single life of apostolic celibacy. Those so privileged are few in number but touch the lives of many people. Most are called to the vocation of marriage, to live united with a spouse for the purpose of raising a family. Realizing that marriage is a vocation and part of the plan that God has for us helps us to see its true eternal value.

St. Thomas More, the man depicted in the movie, *A Man for All Seasons*, said that marriage is arguably the most difficult vocation. The Catholic Church has always taught that heroic virtues are needed to keep marriages intact. In fact, Pope John Paul II has said he hopes to canonize a married couple to give witness to the vocation well lived. A Vatican official said, *In this period when marriage and family are being crushed under the stress of heavy burdens, there is a need for a convincing example.* He continued, *Staying together in good times and in bad, in sickness and in health, shows a heroic degree of virtue.* When parents live their marriage commitment fully, their example is far more eloquent than words could ever be.

To do this of course takes many virtues or good habits. Charity, patience, generosity, understanding, perseverance, fortitude and a spirit of service are several of the necessary virtues. In short, we need to be saints! By practicing these good habits, we will seek to make life more pleasant for others. We will choose the worst for ourselves and leave the best for the others. Overlooking small, annoying defects in others and helping without drawing attention to ourselves are small, concrete ways to grow in virtue.

Obviously, we need more than our own efforts to acquire virtues. Our marriages will not flourish without prayer. A couple should make time for prayer both together and individually. Together parents should attend Sunday Mass. Although it may seem easier to go to Mass separately when the children are little, it is more beneficial to attend as family. Because it requires great effort to get everyone dressed up and to church on time, we underscore the importance of the Mass in our lives. The very best things require and deserve tremendous effort. In a time when attendance at Sunday Mass is down, we must pass its value to our children. By emphasizing that Jesus is truly present in Holy Communion, we will teach our children to attend faithfully.

Another excellent way to pray together is by reciting the family rosary. We gain strength and insight into the lives of the Holy Family by meditating on the mysteries of the rosary. Older children can take turns leading each decade and the little ones can follow along in a picture book. By inviting, rather than insisting on daily attendance during the devotion, our children are more apt to come.

We must not neglect personal time for prayer and reflection. Mental prayer, a heart-to-heart conversation with God, spiritual reading and vocal prayers dispersed throughout the day will keep the presence of God in mind. As spouses develop strong individual relationships with God, their marital bond grows stronger. We can help each other go up the inclined plane too by encouraging and making it easy for each other to attend sacramental confession frequently, days of recollection, a yearly retreat, doctrine classes, and other means of spiritual formation. By respecting each other's relationship with God and their particular charism, mutual growth is assured.

The roles of father and mother are distinct yet complementary, each having its own area of expertise, struggle and the grace of its vocation to form children in very specific ways. When each parent takes seriously his vocation, the combination is unbeatable. No wonder God wanted His Son to be born into a two-parent family.

Today's prime time sitcoms portray fathers as bumbling, laughable and weak, a far cry from the all-knowing dad on *Father Knows Best*. Unfortunately today, Chevy Chase, with his pratfalls and roving eye for women is the modern, all-American dad. This characterization has damaged the family and society has a whole. In reality, men typically exude strength, perseverance, fortitude, a sporting spirit and an incredible single-mindedness that helps them tackle any project and see it through to the end. Men look at a job like a military general, making long-range plans and the tough decisions without sentimentality. Above all else, they seek to be respected personally and professionally by their peers and family.

As father, the man is the leader in the family. Not only does he provide financial resources but, more importantly, moral leadership. If the man is the primary breadwinner, he should be free to make decisions regarding his career and the family's financial stability. Of course a prudent leader relies on the input of others, and a good husband would discuss important job changes and moves with his wife. His final decisions, however, should be respected and supported by all, knowing he has the particular grace to lead.

Today's work environment is especially draining. With the advent of high-speed communications, across the board lay-offs and the longer workday, men come home from work exhausted. They need to come home to a place where they can regain their strength. A home where peace and order reign is essential. Without it, men find it difficult to work up to their potential thereby threatening the financial stability of their family. Rather than channel surfing to relax, dad can have fun by spending time playing or reading to the children or sharing a hobby with them.

By far the most important role for dad is that of moral leader of the family. His example of service to his family and others, along with a life of piety are powerful examples to his children. In one family the mother decided that her family should say the daily rosary before going to bed. While the husband did not object, he had to be prodded and reminded often. As a result, the children were also reluctant. After several difficult weeks, the wife gave up the idea. A few years later, the husband decided to institute the family rosary. The result was remarkable. The children attended enthusiastically and the tradition continues to this day, much to the delight of the mother. The father's leadership on this issue alone was the catalyst his children needed.

Perhaps the biggest struggle for the modern father is striking a balance between duties to professional work and his family. Demands from the workplace can easily seem more imperative than those of wife and children. Society also stresses that good fathers provide the highest quality of life for their families. Although food, clothing, shelter and education are the true basics, our materialistic society demands Happy Meals, Nike shoes, a private bedroom and horseback riding lessons on Saturdays as necessities for each child. Fathers, as leaders, need to teach the difference between wants and needs. This lesson is taught daily by the father's example. Good fathers keep work, and the money earned from their work, in proper perspective relative to their family life and their wife and children's true needs. St. Joseph, the foster father of Jesus, is a wonderful example and intercessor for men, having lived a balanced life of professional work and family life.

If a good father is the leader, a good mom is the heart of the home. Her warmth, tenderness, intuition, patience and attention to detail help her create a cheerful environment for her family. Her loving touch and hidden sacrifices transform her family and eventually society, setting a truly Christian tone to the world. Because she notices details and can see subtle differences, she is especially good in dealing with people. As a person, she values feeling cherished and appreciated.

She too has a multifaceted role in the family. Even if she holds a job outside the home, studies show she still does most of the household tasks and childcare. While housework is not particularly valued today, women must realize it is professional work and should be approached as such. Being a professional means working smarter not harder. Moms should keep a cleaning schedule and plan meals weekly or bi-monthly so shopping can be done more efficiently (that is, professionally). While homes should not look or feel like museums, clutter should not reign either. This monotonous, never-ending work can have eternal benefits if it is done well and offered up to God. Tasks can be dedicated for specific intentions and, this way, even laundry can become prayer.

By far the most rewarding part of a mother's job is caring for her children. Women are particularly suited for this job because they can sense changes in others. By combining this intuition with prayer, a mother can see the strengths and weaknesses of each child clearly. Then she can effect the necessary formation this book will explain in greater detail.

A woman's job is not without its struggles. It is a physically, emotionally and mentally exhausting, 24-hour a day job which demands total selflessness. A mother's greatest struggle is to strike a balance between the demands of her children and the needs of her husband. While a mom may reason that children are helpless, needy creatures and her husband is a capable adult, she must set her priorities right. She is first a wife and then a mother. She can best serve her children by maintaining a good relationship with her husband, their father. Children can survive a little "benign neglect" if they see their parents as best friends. The woman can nurture their friendship by learning about his business and other interests, keeping up with current events and maintaining her physical attractiveness.

A young couple once received a crucifix on their wedding day with a card, which read, *In marriage you will find the cross.* While they did not fully appreciate the message on that day, years later they began to understand. Our greatest joys, sorrows, triumphs and frustrations are found in marriage. Creating one life with another human being is bound to bring pain at some point. Not only do we deal with the basic differences between the sexes, temperamental differences cause us to see things in entirely different lights. Add to that the tremendously important work of forming the minds, bodies and souls of our children and it is no wonder conflict can come so easily at times. Parenting is a physically, emotionally and, at times, financially draining enterprise but we need to keep in mind that God designed it that way to bring us to perfection.

Sometimes, however, the conflicts can be very serious in nature. A spouse may not honor his marital commitment, another may get involved in drugs or alcohol and a third may abandon the faith altogether. Whatever the form, the cross is there. At times like this we need to embrace it joyfully and take God as our faithful, loving spouse and continue to live our vocation of marriage. It may be tempting to see oneself as a victim, but we need to remember that Jesus was the only truly innocent Victim. When God allows us to share in His cross, we should respond not with resignation but joy. The saints thanked God for their crosses because they understood how the cross showed God's love and confidence. Knowing too that our children always watch our reactions, we need to be especially careful not to complain about the cross we have been given. It is a good practice not even to allow ourselves to grumble interiorly.

Since marriage is both a vocation and a sacrament, we can be sure that God gives His grace in abundance to help during trying times. By relying on that grace, we can experience true Christian joy with the cross and our children will see our example of fidelity to commitment.

Virtues are not just "caught" by our example, they must also be taught. Before we teach the virtues, we need to have clear ideas of the kind of adults we want our children to be. New parents regularly tell their friends that their child will be a doctor, lawyer or other such professional. We don't hear them say that their child will be a person of integrity and self-control or that he should be of service to the world. Much less do they say their child should be detached from material goods, living easily in a mansion or a tenement. Such long-range plans help us realize what is truly important. Schooling children in the virtues begins at a very early age. Of course we are not going to teach loyalty to a one-year-old but it would be equally ridiculous to begin manners at age 12.

If you like buy-one-get-one free sales, you will love the bargain in teaching good habits. Virtues are closely related with one another. If you gain one, you acquire a few others besides. Some may say a program of teaching virtues sets out to control children. Controlling or micro-managing children should never be the objective. Rather, we want to create a culture within our homes, and living a life of virtue is the surest way to create that culture. The Holy Father has always believed that by influencing the culture, we can re-Christianize the world. Culture, he believes, is the engine of history. He practiced this belief as early as World War II when he was an actor during the Nazi occupation of Poland. By acting in and producing plays depicting Polish history and culture, he participated in the Resistance. Keeping the Polish culture alive was the key to defending the soul of the country. We can use this profound truth in our own homes. The culture we create within our home will eventually influence the world. Being comfortable with our God-given authority to limit and censor the reach of the popular culture into our homes is essential, realizing it is a genuine threat to our family life. While closely monitoring all television, magazines, movies, music and fashion that degrade human dignity, we can promote at the same time all the good that is currently available in terms of entertainment and culture.

In the **Raise Happy Children** series of books, Mary Ann Budnik provides practical tips on how to implement these ideas in your marriage and in your family. Then in our own small way we can build, what the Holy Father calls, "a civilization of love" one family at a time, beginning with our own while finding happiness along the way.

Prayer For Families

Lord God, from you every family in heaven and on earth takes its name. Father, you are Love and Life. Through your Son, Jesus Christ, born of woman, and through the Holy Spirit, fountain of divine charity, grant that every family on earth may become for each successive generation a true shrine of life and love.

Grant that your grace may guide the thoughts and actions of husbands and wives for the good of their families and of all the families of the world.

Grant that the young may find in the family solid support for their human dignity and for their growth in truth and love.

Grant that love, strengthened by the grace of the sacrament of matrimony, may prove mightier than all the weaknesses and trials through which our families sometimes pass.

Through the intercession of the Holy Family of Nazareth, grant that the Church may fruitfully carry out her worldwide mission in the family and through the family.

We ask this of you, who are Life, Truth, and Love, with the Son and the Holy Spirit. Amen.

Pope John Paul 11

Chapter 1

Is Holiness Necessary?

"Today's world...is in need of saints, that is, men of integrity who fulfill the will of God with fidelity, full of the spirit of service and concern for man; of honest men who love the truth, who give themselves in service of the common good, even paying the price of generous renunciation of their own interest."

John Paul II

When you were younger didn't you have a burning desire to do great things? You landed your first job, married and settled down. Life was great. Your future was filled with promise and dreams. Remember how excited you were at the news that you were going to be a mother or a father? Then, suddenly the doldrums set in. Now bills outnumber the junk mail. Your career may not be advancing as fast as you first hoped. The kids always seem to have either ear infections or the stomach flu. Laundry, dirty diapers, grocery shopping, doctor appointments and chaperoning kids take up the bulk of your days. There's rarely time to sit down to read a book, even less time to think. That vision of doing great things is packed away along with your college memories.

If this is the case, it's time to refocus...to realize that you have the potential to change the world right there in your *own* family. Life hasn't passed you by but rather changed directions in a most incredible way. Your true call to greatness began at baptism and increased when you exchanged vows with your spouse at your wedding. Let me explain. A story is told that when Pope St. Pius X was elected, his mother approached to pay him homage. As only a mother can at such a moment, she took his hand with the papal ring on it and said, *You would not have that ring, if I did not have this [wedding] ring.* Mrs. Sarto reminded her son that it was the sacrament of marriage, faithfully lived by his parents, that paved the way for his priestly vocation, which in turn led to his papacy and eventual sainthood.

As baptized Catholics, our purpose in life is to become saints. Nothing is more personally fulfilling than to strive for holiness…to become a saint! The fact that God created you means that He is calling you to great sanctity. St. Thérèse of Lisieux reminds us that *God is occupied with each soul as though there were no others like it.*

It's never too late nor is one ever too old to start down the path of holiness. Our past is never an obstacle to holiness. Look at St. Augustine who prayed: *Grant me chastity and continence, but not yet!* He confides: *I feared my pleas would be too quickly answered and I would be too soon healed of this sickness of concupiscence, for I preferred to satisfy it than to see it extinguished.* Finally "tomorrow" came for this man. He became the greatest doctor of the Western Church. So you see it is the present and future that counts. Why settle for being mediocre when you can strive for greatness in the daily circumstances of your life? Does personal sanctity sound too incredible? Remember, all things are possible with God. As Mother Teresa emphasized, *Give God permission!*

Besides being called to be saints, you, as parents, are called to procreate with God saints for eternity. Mother Teresa stressed: *Our Lord has the right to have a personal relationship with everyone He has redeemed.* That includes our children. Lying dormant within your family could be another John Paul II, a Thérèse of Lisieux, a Thomas More, an Elizabeth Seton, and a Katherine Drexel. What could be more exciting, more thrilling, or more ambitious? Granted, from your vantage point it may not look promising but remember, the Curé of Ars had difficulty in school and Augustine was every mother's nightmare. Cardinal Theodore McCarrick of Washington, D.C. *was thrown out of high school for disciplinary reasons.*[1] Besides, every saint's mother went through the frustration of trying to potty train him or her.

What could be more exciting, more thrilling, and more ambitious than being a saint and raising saints? **Saints do great things. They change the world.** As Cardinal Anthony Bevilacqua reminded his listeners at the Pro-Life Mass at the National Basilica of the Immaculate Conception on January 24, 2000: *We have no right to expect a holier world if we are not willing to become a holier people.*[2]

Consider the powerful impact saints, holy men and women, have on history, on culture, in politics, in business, in the arts and sciences. The first Christians, many of them martyrs, changed the world's culture from paganism to Christianity by their radical lifestyle, witness, and heroic deaths. It was because of the influence of the dignity of Our Lady that women were finally accorded similar dignity and placed on a pedestal. Christianity gave birth to the pro-life movement. It was through the influence of the first Christians that infanticide and abortion were abolished. Couples were taught to cherish children rather than considering them a burden, financial or otherwise. Before Christianity, contraception was universal in the Roman Empire. Fr. Hardon, S.J. explains: *Historians of contraception trace its practice to as early as 2800 BC. By the end of the first century BC, the Greeks and the Romans had become masters of the art of contraception. However, they never really distinguished between contraception and abortion. The drugs that a woman used were calculated to not only avoid conception, but to destroy whatever conception in the womb may have taken place.*[2]

---

[1] Zenit, March 14, 2001.

[2] John A. Hardon, S.J., *The Catholic Family* (MN: Leaflet Missal Company, 1991) pp.1-2.

RU 486 isn't anything new. What is remarkable is that our Christian culture was able to keep it off the market until now. Fr. Hardon continues: *Abortion was correspondingly widespread in the Roman Empire. There were no laws prohibiting abortion...Infanticide was commonplace...*[3]

John Paul II urges us to imitate the heroic example of the early Christians because tragically, our world has slipped from vibrant Christianity back into paganism with legal abortion and infanticide (partial birth abortion). In this area alone we, along with our children, can make a tremendous difference in our culture by the way we live, vote, socialize but most importantly, by practicing our faith. As Ronald Knox reminds us: *Christ has won the war but He has left us to mop up the debris.* To do that mopping up, we have to begin by changing ourselves. This means eliminating our defects by replacing them with virtues...by becoming saints.

During a trip to Austria in 1998, John Paul II stressed: *The persuasive power of the message...depends on the credibility of its messengers. Indeed, the new evangelization starts with us, with our life-style...The Church today does not need part-time Catholics but full-blooded Christians.*

To be full-blooded Christians we must be generous with God, to give to Him our lives, our talents, our time...in other words to become saints! *Hell is full of the talented, but heaven of the energetic* according to St. Jane Frances de Chantal. St. Francis de Sales counsels us: *Faithfully attend to your obligations, but know that you have no greater obligation than that of your salvation...*[4] We were created to be holy. Holiness perfects our nature and our abilities along with our personality. It makes us more successful in everything we do. It doesn't make us weird, but wise. We become mentally sharper, more aware of truth and how to implement it. We can grasp situations faster thereby responding correctly in a prudent manner. In striving to grow holy, we develop listening

---

[3] Ibid, p.2.

[4] St. Francis de Sales, *Thy Will Be Done: Letters to the Persons in the World* (Sophia Institute Press, 1995), pp. 48-49.

skills in our prayer, which in turn help us in our daily work and marriage. Since we do our work for the honor and glory of God we struggle to do it promptly, with attention to detail, as perfectly as humanly possible. If our goal is to please God, we actively work to acquire the natural virtues and increase the supernatural virtues through the infusion of grace we receive through prayer and the spiritual and corporal works of mercy, along with the worthy reception of the sacraments. As we grow in the Gifts of the Holy Spirit (wisdom, piety, understanding, counsel, fortitude, knowledge, and fear of the Lord) as well as hundreds of other virtues, we are spiritually helped to advance successfully in our daily work. The practice of these virtues positively impacts all we do. If we use the natural and supernatural means to grow holy we cannot help but become a success in this life and the next! This doesn't mean that if we strive for holiness we are going to become members of the "billionaire club" but rather a success in the area God places us. On the other hand, sin darkens our intellect, clouds our judgment while negatively impacting all we do.

The Impact Of Living Our Faith

"It is no longer the time for compromises! We, Christians, must be strictly dedicated to holiness." Bl. John Calabria

Let's briefly look at some Catholic men and women who made a tremendous impact on our world. This could be a book in itself...a very thick book. As Dr. Tom Dooley enjoyed saying, *It takes ordinary people to do extraordinary things.* These people loved their faith and infused it into their work. Unfortunately, we live in a country that has an anti-Catholic bias. The truth of the contributions of Catholics throughout the world are not found in our school texts nor portrayed accurately in books or in the media. Don't put too much credibility into revisionist historians. As a reporter I have personally witnessed the distortion of news. Take the negative you hear about Catholic historic figures with a grain of salt.

It was a Catholic, Christopher Columbus, who discovered the Americas. Despite his bad press, he was   striving to be holy. According to Italian historian Ruggero Marino, Columbus' first voyage to the Americas was *seven years earlier [than 1492] on a secret mission for the Pope...The aim was to use the gold of the New World to fund the Crusades and to gain souls for Christianity.*[5] The Servant of God, Queen Isabella of Spain, financed Columbus' return trip. St. Catherine of Siena brought peace to the warring nations of Italy. St. Joan of Arc, a seventeen-year-old peasant girl, united the armies of France under her banner thereby saving the national identity of France. St. Thomas More was one of the greatest statesmen in history. It was the Spanish monks who developed our economic system. Even today the Church is actively involved in every area that affects mankind but you will never know this if you limit yourself to watching CNN. Subscribe free to Zenit, (www.zenit.org) a news agency located in Rome.

Cardinal Merry Del Val, Secretary of State for St. Pius X, describes how the Church has been a patron, protector and supporter of the arts: *The Church has always granted generous patronage to art wherever her influence has extended. Rome bears eloquent testimony in that respect to the traditional munificence of her Pontiffs and to their enlightened efforts, not only to preserve the monuments of antiquity and the countless relics of past ages, whether pagan or Christian, but also to encourage the activity of artists who afforded proof of genuine talent. And this has been noteworthy even during troubled periods of history whilst Pontiffs were harassed by financial straits and overburdened by the cares of their apostolic ministry.*[6]

Tour the Vatican Museums and the Catholic churches in Europe. Non-believers come from all over the world to view the magnificent art collection of the Catholic Church in Rome and the murals in Assisi. John Paul II calls it a dialogue between faith and art. *It can truly be said that the Museums represent, culturally speaking,*

---

[5] Richard Owen, *London Times,* May 8, 2001.

[6] Cardinal Merry Del Val, *Memories of Pope Pius X* (Maryland: The Newman Press, 1951) p.43.

one of the Holy See's most important doors open to the world.[7] Most of our greatest artists, for example, Michelangelo and Blessed Fra Angelico, were Catholics. Fra Angelico, considered one of the greatest religious painters, was nicknamed Angelico because of his virtuous life and artistic capabilities. The famous Dutch artist, Johannes Vermeer, converted to Catholicism during a time of persecution for Catholics in Holland. It is said that his paintings have an *accent of Catholicism with moral and religious symbolism.* Count Balthazar Klossowski de Rola, known to the world as the great artist Balthus and former director of Villa Medici, said before his recent death at age 93, that he believed that *painting and praying are the same thing. I have never thought of painting in any way other than as a religious activity. To pray, if one is abandoned in this state, means one can create...I am a practicing Catholic; I have a very exacting spiritual life. Christianity is a religion that produces saints. It is a great elevation, which sustains us every day and makes us grow. The world is lost in rumor and furor, in speed and incompetence, in the denial of real values, in a flight that makes the end of all hope. It is necessary to rediscover the way the ancients worked, the patience of artisans, the art of living that spiritualizes men.* While ill he related that *God had spoken to me, that He told me my life had not ended, that I still had to work.* Balthus came from a renowned family. His mother was the famous Catholic poet Rainer Maria Rilke, and his father a famous painter, historian and art critic. His brother is the famous Polish author Pierre Klossowski.[8]

Most of the world's greatest composers were not only Catholics but their music was created to enhance the Mass. Handel's *Messiah*, written in six weeks, was composed to raise money for a charity. He noted: *Never was I so devout as when composing "The Creation." I knelt down every day and prayed to God to strengthen me for my work.* J.S. Bach wrote: *Like all music, the figured brass should have no other end and aim than the glory of God and the re-creation of the soul; where this is not kept in mind there is no true music, but only an infernal clamor and ranting.*

---

[7] Feb. 7, 2000 John Paul II at dedication of new entrance to museums.
[8] Zenit, Feb. 20, 2001.

Robert Schumann wrote to Felix Mendelssohn that a particular Bach chorale *was full of such beatitude that you yourself confessed to me that if life were to deprive you of hope and faith, this one chorale would bring it all back again to you.* The film *Amadeus* did a great disservice to Mozart. Rather than being the fool portrayed in the film, he was the chief founder of the opera and the greatest pianist in Germany at the time. His music is so powerful that psychologists have found that those who listen to his music before a test score higher than those who do not listen. Mozart writes: *I thank my God for graciously granting me the opportunity of learning that death is the key which unlocks the door to our true happiness. I never lie down at night without reflecting that—young as I am—I may not live to see another day.* Beethoven wrote to the Archduke Rudolph in 1819, *The day when a High Mass of mine shall be performed at the ceremonies for Your Imperial Highness will be for me the most beautiful day of my life, and God will inspire me so that my weak powers may contribute to the glorification of this solemn day.*

Just a glimmer of the faith and trust of the deaf musician Beethoven is revealed in his diary. He discloses: *Tranquilly will I submit myself to all vicissitudes and place my sole confidence in Thy unalterable goodness, O God! My soul shall rejoice in being Thy immutable servant. Be my rock, my light, forever my trust.* [9]

When Hayden was criticized for writing music that was too happy to accompany liturgy, he replied that his "heart leaped for joy" at the thought of God. He doubted God would reproach him for praising him "with a cheerful heart."[10]

We have great Catholic authors among them Dante, Cervantes, Evelyn Waugh, Tolkien, Chesterton and Clare Luce Booth.

Consider the innumerable works of mercy done by Catholic organizations such as Catholic Charities, Catholic Relief, and

---

[9] These quotes were taken from an article by Howard Reich in the *Chicago Tribune* (12/25/88) Section 6, p. 16.

[10] Julia Vitullo-Martin, "A Joyful Noise," *Wall Street Journal*, 12/15/2000.

countless other Catholic agencies and organizations. In the U.S. alone, Catholic hospitals last year cared for 85 million people.

Men of faith, to honor God and His Mother Mary, built most of the greatest architectural wonders in the modern world. St. Jerome translated the books of Scripture into Latin so that we could have the Bible. St. Elizabeth Seton was the foundress of our Catholic school system. Abbot Gregor Mendel discovered the law of heredity known as Mendel's Law. Louis Pasteur is the founder of the modern science of bacteriology. Madame Curé discovered radium trying to find a cure for cancer. Blessed Francis Fa'A Di Bruno was one of the greatest astronomers and mathematicians in the late 1800s. His writings can be found in the Catalogue of Scientific Papers of the Royal Society in London. Bl. Nicolaus Stensen, a doctor and convert to the faith lived in the 1600s. He discovered unknown aspects of glands, the circulatory system, brain, muscles, embryology and heart. He eventually gave up his science research to be come a priest and bishop. Bl. Peter Jamet, a Frenchman, developed sign language and a dictionary for the deaf people he cared for in the 1800s. Walt Disney created wholesome family entertainment. Bill Keane casts a positive glow on family life through his syndicated cartoon *Family Circus*. Marconi was inspired to invent the radio at the ancient shrine of Our Lady of Oropa in Italy. It was from this same shrine that Marconi sent the first ever radio message to the Holy Father at the Vatican. Blessed Faustino Míguez, a Piarist priest, teacher, founder of a religious teaching order, and renowned medical researcher founded the famous Míguez Laboratory in Getafe in Spain. He died in 1925. Look at the impact that Mother Teresa of Calcutta has had on the world. Mother Angelica, a cloister nun, had the vision and drive to develop the first international Catholic radio and TV network.

The current head of South Korea, President Kim Dae-jung, is not only the first Catholic president of his country, but he won the Nobel Peace Prize in 2000.[11]

---

[11] Zenit, March 22, 2001.

So dust off those dreams. Make your mark in the world by striving to become holy along with your spouse and children! As John Paul II emphasizes over and over, *Sanctity is the only force that can change the world.*[12] Bishop Gordon of Baltimore humorously adds, *If you don't stand for something in life, you'll fall for anything!*

The greater the mission entrusted, the greater the need to correspond to the grace of God. The sanctity of you, your spouse and children is one of the greatest missions. As Blessed Escrivá exhorts in his book ***The Forge*** (#1001) : *Keep going forward cheerfully and trying hard, even though you are so little--nothing at all! When you are with Him nobody in the world can stop you. Consider, moreover, how everything is good for those who love God. Every problem in this world has a solution, except death, and for us death is Life.* Besides, the greater our unity with God the happier we and our children will be. ***Psalm*** 16 reiterates, **Thou dost show me the path of life; in Thy presence there is fulness of joy, in Thy right hand are pleasures for evermore.**

Holiness Requires Generosity

"When Christ touches a life, He imprints a profound change in our perception and plans. It is a radical change that leaves no room for doubts and leads one on a path full of difficulties, but which is supremely liberating."
                                                                    John Paul II

We are children of God. The more we realize this, the greater peace, joy and happiness we will possess. As such, Our Lord is inviting you to be an instrument in His hands. Each soul who comes into contact with you should be warmed up and lifted up to God. Jesus tells us *[God] created you. He knows all about you and how best you can serve Him. And what your share is in the sanctification of the world; for each one of you has some special contribution to make. What sorrow for you if you were to fail! If*

---

[12] John Paul II in Slovenia at the beatification of Bishop Slomsek 9/19/99.

you didn't respond to the call![13]

During Christian Unity Week Cardinal Etchegaray told a legend from the Orthodox Church: *After Easter, when Christ was at the point of going up to heaven, He looked down on earth and saw it submerged in darkness, with the exception of a few small lights that illuminated the city of Jerusalem. In the process of his Ascension, He came across the Angel Gabriel, who was accustomed to going on terrestrial missions. The divine messenger asked Him: "What are those little lights?" "They are the apostles seated around my mother. My plan is that, once I return to heaven, I will send them the Holy Spirit so that these little fires become a great fire that inflames the whole earth with love." The angel replied intrepidly: "And, what will You do if the plan doesn't work?" After a moment of silence, the Lord replied: "I don't have any other plans!"*

Our families are part of God's plan to re-evangelize the world. We must be those sparks that set the world on fire. God is depending upon us.

Our God is such a loving, merciful Father. He wants us to be happy. He longs for our lives to be joyful. God gifted us with the Ten Commandments to safeguard our happiness along with the Church to guide us. While original sin is replaced with grace at Baptism, the effects are still visible in our deformed nature. How easy it is to get off track! How easy it is to be self-centered and selfish. Having foreseen this, God provides us with the sacraments to continually infuse our souls with graces. You see, Christ wishes to live in us so that we think like Christ, talk like Christ, act like Christ, and feel with the heart of Christ. Our transformation into Christ depends upon our interior disposition. Avoid putting obstacles in the way of God. It is you who must carry Christ to your family and to the world each day. If you don't, who will?

God loves you and your family so intensely, yet He will never force you to return His love. His love is so great that He actually risks losing your love by giving you the gift of perfect freedom.

---

[13] Gabrielle Bossis, *He and I* (Sherbrooke, Quebec, Editions Paulines, 1969) p.151.

Although He created you to become a saint, He will never force you against your will to love Him or to grow in holiness. You are perfectly free to cooperate with God's grace or ignore it. You are free to strive for heroic virtue or live a life of vice. The choice is up to you. As you go through the day making the choices that decide your place in eternity, stop periodically to remember how passionately God loves you! Fr. Leo Trese writes: *Life is purposeful...Day by day the world, and all who are in it, are moving forward towards the final fulfillment of God's plan. You and I are bristles on God's brush. Day by day we are adding our own little brush-strokes to the grand masterpiece, even though we shall not see clearly what our part has been until we see the finished product in heaven.*

If we refuse to cooperate we shall hurt ourselves, but we shall not hurt God's plan...God would not have made us if there had not been a special job that God wanted us to do...I think that surely one reason that God loves us so uniquely is because God saw that we could do a certain task for Him, and do it better than anyone else He might create.

...[I]t may be a very small thing, this special assignment that God has in mind for us...Perhaps it is some one person whom we have met or shall meet in the whole course of our life; some one person whom God had to reach (humanly speaking) through us or not at all. Indeed perhaps it is only one word which we have said or shall say; some one word which has to be spoken by us, or forever go unsaid.

That is why it is so important that we try to do well whatever we do, even our homeliest and dreariest tasks. That is why our personal relationships in particular must be motivated by great charity. We never know (in this life) the moment at which we are facing the task which is to be our special and exclusive contribution to God's plan. Everything which we do for God counts with Him, of course; everything is important. But there is some one thing that only we can do.[14]

---

[14] Leo. T. Trese, *More Than Many Sparrows* (Chicago: Fides Publishers Association, 1958) pp. 13-14.

Becoming The Light Of The World

Film and TV star, Ricardo Montalban, rightly believes that *The Catholic religion is a priceless jewel. In order to obtain a priceless jewel you must pay an enormous amount of money. You can get a zircon for considerably less. If we think of the Catholic Church as a zircon, then we are in trouble. We have to think of it as a priceless jewel, which is going to cost you a lot of concentration, devotion, and reflection on God and on His teachings.*[15]

In St. Louis, John Paul II addressed the effort needed to grow in holiness. Quoting St. Paul's instruction to St. Timothy: **Train yourself for devotion.** (*1 Timothy* 4:7) He continued: *These are important words for every Christian, for everyone who truly seeks to follow the Lord and to put his works into practice...and so, you need to ask yourselves what training am I doing in order to live a truly Christian life?*[16]

The training that the Holy Father is talking about involves several different areas. First of all, to train ourselves in devotion we need to follow a plan of life. We have plans to build our home, to pay for our child's college tuition, to advance professionally but do we have a plan to grow holy and pleasing to God? Drifting through life saying, "I want to be holy, I want to be a saint" is simply inadequate. We can't just waltz through life hoping somehow to grow holy without any effort on our part. God gives us the necessary graces; we have to cooperate with Him. *Holiness is God at work in our souls through grace.*[17] *[God] does not expect superhuman feats from us, but rather supernatural acts that are within our reach, thanks to grace.*[18] So to grow in holiness we have to have a "plan of attack," a plan of life.[19] In your prayer

---

[15] Ricardo Montalban, "In The Heart Of Tinseltown, A Faith Lived Deeply," *Be Magazine,* March-April 2000, p.7.

[16] Jan. 1999, Kiel Center address to youth.

[17] Francis Fernandez-Carvajal and Peter Beteta, *Children of God* (NJ: Scepter, 1997) p.29

[18] *Ibid.*

[19] To learn more about a "plan of life" read *You Can Become A Saint!* by Mary Ann Budnik. It can be purchased from R.B. Media, Inc.

time, write down what you are doing spiritually now. Then, consider in front of the Blessed Sacrament what Jesus is asking you to add to your plan. If you aren't doing anything but going to Sunday Mass, begin to say a daily Morning Offering so that you are offering up your prayers, works, joys and sufferings of the day and turning them into prayer. You can use the formal prayer or simply your own words. Sound too simple? Gabrielle Bossis, a French woman offered to Jesus the steep steps she was climbing one day. As she did so she asked, *Lord how can You accept such tiny things?* Within her heart she heard, *You call them tiny, yet you use your memory, your understanding, and your will; in other words, your entire being. No matter where you give yourself to Me, I take you. Do you understand?*[20]

The spiritual life of any saint is the story of the love of God.[21] It's difficult to love someone you never talk to so add mental prayer to your daily schedule. *A Catholic, without prayer? It is the same as a soldier without arms,* warns Blessed Escrivá.[22]   St. Rose of Lima maintained that *It is better to talk with God than about God.* St. Thérèse observed that *for me, prayer is an upward leap of the heart.* St. Teresa of Avila inisted that *anyone who doesn't pray doesn't need any devil to tempt him; while whoever prays, even if only for a quarter of an hour each day, will necessarily be saved.* Bl. Escrivá explains that *This is because our conversation with our Lord--who is so loving, even in times of difficulty or dryiness of soul--enables us to see things in their proper perspective and discover the true proportions of life. Be a soul of prayer.*

Prayer is a readily available source of grace. St. Ephrem, who lived in the fourth century tells us: *Prayer preserves temperance, puts a brake on anger, moderates high spirits, leads to modesty, accepts injury without hate, destroys envy, and facilitates piety. Prayer is strength for the body, and a sure guide in the good administration of family affairs, a foundation for rights and of laws, the upholder of society, the sepulcher for war and the guardian of peace.*

---

[20] *He and I* , *Op. Cit.*, p. 123

[21] *Children of God, Op. Cit.*, p. 35.

[22] Blessed Josemaría Escrivá, *Furrow* (NY: Scepter, 1987), #453.

Prayer is the seal of virginity, it guards matrimony, provides a great refuge for travelers, looks after those who are asleep, gives confidence to those on guard, gives fertility to the harvest, and provides a safe haven for sailors. Prayer is a protection to those in prison, a respite for those enchanted, consolation for those who are depressed, ...balsam for those in tears, a crown for spouses, rest for the dying.[23]

What is mental prayer? Mental prayer is simply sitting quietly and talking to God in your own words. Should you run out of what to say, use the book, *The Way* by Bl. Escrivá or *In Conversation with God*[24] by Fr. Francis Fernandez to stimulate your prayer. If you are not doing any mental prayer now, begin with five minutes in the morning and five in the afternoon. The reason we split our prayer time up is to keep our mind and heart coming back to God throughout the day. If we do all our prayers in the morning we tend to forget God the rest of the day. Increase your prayer time until you can give God 30 minutes in the morning and 30 minutes in the afternoon. During the same talk in St. Louis, John Paul II reminded us that *[Y]ou will get to know...[Christ] truly and personally only through prayer. What is needed is that you talk to Him and listen to Him...Prayer enables us to meet God at the most profound level of our being. It connects us directly to God...Believe in God: Father, Son and Holy Spirit, in a constant exchange of love.*

Through prayer you will learn to become the light of the world, because in prayer you become one with the source of our true light, Jesus Himself.

The Holy Father speaks from experience. Although incredibly busy, he spends long periods of time, both day and night, in prayer. It is the Holy Father's prayer that gives him the power to accomplish all that he does.

Fr. John Hardon, S.J. explains why we should imitate the Holy Father's example: *[P]art of the divine plan...is that we should*

---

[23] Claire Russell, Ed., *Glimpses of the Church Fathers* (London: Scepter, 1994).

[24] These books can be purchased from Scepter Publishers, Inc. (800)322-8773.

obtain many of the things that we need only by asking God to grant them. There is no question here of informing God what we need, as though we have to tell Him, or otherwise He would not know. We do not have to pray in order to persuade God, or convince Him, that we need help... Prayer is necessary for our sake, so we might humbly admit before God how blind and weak, and in fact, helpless, we are without the constant support of His help...

We have no choice; either we pray or we do not get the divine light and strength we need. Either husbands and wives pray or they will not receive the grace to even sustain their married love...Either they pray and become patient husbands with their wives and wives with their husbands or their marriages are weakened and finally break down...The most common failure in marital love is due to a failure in prayer...The Church's history has seen the most humanly impossible marriages succeed. Thus Monica, the mother of St. Augustine, converted her unfaithful pagan husband and her immoral genius of a son, because she prayed.[25]

Every member of the family must be faithful to the daily practice of prayer. It is not too much to say that the members of a family will remain united if they pray. There are so many divisive forces at work, and human nature is too selfish to hope for a stable family life without constant light and strength from God, to be obtained from devoted prayer. Without prayer, grace will not be available. Without grace, stable family life is impossible.[26]

In addition to our mental prayer, how can we as lay people pray constantly? We are to do the same as the first Christians. St. Ephrem explains: *Do pray, whether you are in church, or in your home or in the countryside; whether you are tending to your flocks, constructing a building or attending a meeting. Wherever you can, get down on your knees; and when this is not impossible, call on God mentally, in the afternoon, in the morning, or at noon. For if you put prayer ahead of any other activity, and when you get out of bed in the morning you direct your first thought to God, then sin will have no power over you.* Develop the habit of praying

[25] *The Catholic Family In The Modern World, Op. Cit.,* pp. 45-47.
[26] *Ibid.,* p. 18.

as you walk upstairs, answer the phone, cut the grass, pump gas, fold laundry, wait for appointments, stand in check-out lines, or run errands. Say short aspirations such as, *Jesus, I love you, save souls; Sacred Heart, save sinners; Most merciful and Sacred Heart of Jesus, grant me peace!; or Mary, help of Christians, come to my aid.*

Show gratitude toward God. Thank Him for your spouse and the pleasure of married love that you both share. Thank God for family members, friends, your job, home, car, heat, food, the change of seasons, and all the continuous gifts God sprinkles throughout each day of your life. If you only look for big manifestations of God in your life you will be disappointed. Delight in the little joys that God sends your way like the hug from your child, a call from a friend, a close parking spot, a delicious strawberry, a sunny day. Use each little joy as a moment to lift your heart to God in thanksgiving, praying as Mother Angelica does, *Thank you, Jesus!*

As concerns come up throughout the day send up short prayers of petition such as: *Jesus, end the scourge of abortion*; *Help the suffering people in Africa*; and *Lord, give us moral political leaders.* Pray daily for the continual protection of your spouse and children. Did you know that *eight out of every ten entertainers in Italy said that they "never forget to pray before going on stage or on the air," a survey finds?*[27] We can learn to pray before, during, and after our work as well.

It's likewise difficult to love someone we don't know. The Holy Father emphasizes: *You are children of light! You belong to Christ, and He has called you by name. Your first responsibility is to get to know as much as you can about Him.*[28] Read three minutes of the **New Testament** each day. It's not long and can be done over lunch, in the bathroom or right before bed. Put yourself into the scene and become a silent observer. Apply what you read to your life. If you read Scripture slowly and analyze what is happening in each scene you will be amazed at the insights

---

[27] Zenit, Feb. 22, 2001.
[28] Jan. 1999, Kiel Center address to youth.

you receive. Having trouble motivating yourself to read the Gospels? Get the novel **A Philadelphia Catholic In King James's Court** by Martin De Porres Kennedy.[29] When you finish this intense novel not only will you have a good grasp of scripture but also a desire to make it a part of your day.

Spiritual reading is also important. Read the spiritual masterpieces to fuel your prayer and grow in knowledge of the Catholic faith. Solid Catholic magazines and newspapers are great but do *not* constitute spiritual reading.[30]

Say the rosary daily. If you are not in the habit of saying it now, begin with a decade a day and keep adding a decade until you are saying all five decades of the rosary each day. This can be said while driving to work or taking the kids to school, waiting for an appointment, before bed, before work, or with your family after dinner. The family rosary is a tremendous source of grace for each member. Make the effort to include it daily, even if you have to say it at breakfast before everyone goes his or her separate ways.

Deepen your devotion to the Blessed Eucharist. When running errands, stop in and make a visit to the Blessed Sacrament. If you are not presently going to daily Mass, add an extra day a week until you are able to get to daily Mass. St. Peter Julian Eymard writes: *Yes, we were present at the Last Supper, and Jesus stored up for us not one Host but a hundred, a thousand, one for every day of our life. Do we realize that? Jesus wanted to love us superabundantly. Our Hosts are ready; let us not lose a single one of them.*[31] Holy Mass gives us tremendous strength. While Wheaties might be called the breakfast of champions, the Eucharist is the breakfast of saints! Years ago there was a commercial for Wonder Bread that claimed that the bread built muscles. The Holy Eucharist, the bread of life, builds spiritual

---

[29] The book can be ordered from Lilyfield Press at (270-325-5485).

[30] See *You Can Become A Saint!* By Mary Ann Budnik for a recommended list of spiritual reading books

[31] St. Peter Julian Eymard, *The Real Presence* (Cleveland: Emmanuel Publications) p. 38.

muscles/strength. If we skipped eating for a week, how physically weak we would become. Without the Eucharist we become spiritually weak. Let's take this comparison a little further. How weak you would become if you had to work without any food for a whole week. Likewise, how can one function spiritually without receiving the Bread of Life daily? If you are not already going to daily Mass, I encourage you to give it a try. You will discover that daily Mass and Communion will have a profound effect on your life. St. Eymard explains: *Jesus works a threefold miracle in the one that receives Him. A Miracle of reformation. Jesus gives the communicant an assured mastery over his passions...And the communicant feels stronger...Man finds greater difficulty in correcting or overcoming himself than in performing some exterior good deed, be that deed heroic. Habit is second nature. The Eucharist alone...gives us the power to reform the bad habits that lord it over us.*

A miracle of transformation. There is only one means of changing a natural life into a supernatural one; that is the triumph of the Eucharist, in which Jesus Christ Himself sees to the education of man.

The Eucharist develops faith in us. It elevates, ennobles, and purifies love in us. It teaches us to love. Love is the gift of self.

The Eucharist transforms even our exterior. It imparts to the body a certain charm and beauty which is a reflection of the beauty within. There is in the countenance of the communicant a certain transparency of the divine; in his words a gentleness and in his actions a sweetness that indicate the presence of Jesus Christ. This is the good odor of Jesus.

A miracle of strength, which leads one to self-forgetfulness and self-sacrifice...In the midst of adversity, calumny, and worries the Christian finds peace and calm in the Eucharist. The faithful soldier of Jesus overcomes temptation and the assaults of men and of hell through Holy Communion.[32]

You will notice that the days you are unable to go to Mass

[32] *Ibid.,* pp. 46-47.

seem purposeless. Besides, John Paul II insists, *[t]he Eucharist is the very source of Christian marriage.* Fr. Hardon explains: *He means that except for the Holy Eucharist...Christian marriage would not survive. Why not? Because the heart of Christian marriage is the practice of Christian charity; but Christian charity is a bad dream unless sustained and nourished and enlightened and protected by the constant flux of supernatural grace whose principal divinely instituted source is the Holy Eucharist..*

Believing married people must be devoted to the Holy Eucharist if they want their marriage even to survive, let alone to thrive...this is not piety. It is factual reality...

Do you know one reason why in the early Church the family was such a spectacle of admiration to the pagans...Christians in the early Church went to Mass and Holy Communion every day.[33]

Love toward God is shown in deeds. Sprinkle little sacrifices and mortifications into your day to strengthen your will and develop the different virtues. Sacrifices could include being cheerful when you really feel crabby or listening patiently to a long story you have heard before. Stand up for the faith when it is attacked. Make a delicious dinner for your family even when you are tired. Drink a glass of water rather than a cup of coffee or pop when you are thirsty. Do something you know *God* wants you to do rather than something *you* want to do. Talk to your wife when you would rather watch a football game. Do an activity with your family that they enjoy but you dislike. Visit the sick when it's inconvenient. Offer to help someone when you would rather not.

These are some of the ways to get to know God and to grow holy. Remember, *Only in holiness do we find happiness. The holier, the happier.*[34] Sound too hard? It really can't be because tens of thousands of people around the world are doing these pious practices daily. They can be incorporated into *every* lifestyle. Sure it's a struggle but along with the struggle comes happiness and

---

[33] *The Catholic Family In The Modern World, Op. Cit.*, pp. 47-48.
[34] *Children of God, Op. Cit.* p.13

joy. Personally I find it's well worth the effort! You will too.

Archbishop Sheen wisely noted: *In order to reform the world we must reform man...The revolutions of which we read daily in our papers are easy. It is easy to topple thrones, upset palaces, and dethrone rulers; but to bomb our selfishness, to upset our pride and to dethrone our egotism—that takes the courage of a man modeled upon Him who rose from the dead by the power of God.*[35]

This leads into the next area in which we need training—the development of virtues, which are simply good habits: *To seek God we must first rebel against the enemies of our holiness. It will be a struggle; a Christian's is not an easy path. "Get used to saying No," advised Blessed Josemaría, as a means to rein in our caprices and thoughtlessness. We're to say "No" to laziness and apathy, to self-indulgence and comfort. The "law of sin," of which Paul speaks (Rom. 7:23), in many souls means the "law of whims or getting one's own way." It leads to "that disease of character whose symptoms are a general lack of seriousness, unsteadiness in action and speech, foolishness—in a word, frivolity."*

A frivolous person is inconstant, moody, dislikes standards and justifiable motives. By virtue of such uncertainty and lightheadedness, he can easily end up hollow, unprincipled—the very opposite of holiness. Saying "No" to many things permits saying "Yes" to what God is asking...A determined pledge to second God's will in everything is what alone can weather life's ups and downs.[36] In Chapter 3 we will cover the virtues in depth.

Just before the battle of Orleans, Joan of Arc learned from her saintly voices that the sinfulness of her soldiers was the cause of her army's defeat. She decreed that no soldier would be allowed to participate in the Battle of Orleans, or any other battle under her banner, unless he first went to confession the night before the battle and Holy Mass the day of the battle. St. Joan was not interested in general absolution for her soldiers. Each of the tens of thousands of men had to make a private confession. These

---

[35] *Apostolate of the Little Flower*, Vol. 66, #2, March-April 1998, p.15.

[36] *Children of God, Op. Cit.*, pp. 32-33.

confessions began during the day and continued throughout the night. The French won the Battle of Orleans and preserved their country. Everyday we go into battle. The sins of each day blacken our souls. If we hope to win spiritually we need to make frequent use of the Sacrament of Confession. This is the sacrament, which makes saints out of sinners!

Likewise, to grow in virtue we need at the very least monthly confession and spiritual direction. To grow *holy* we need the constant infusion of God's graces into our soul through weekly confession and daily Mass. We are all sinners. As such, our souls pick up more dirt in a week than our body does. Why then do we wait so long for a spiritual cleaning? We wouldn't dream of going a week or more without a shower or bath. Besides, in addition to asking God's forgiveness, we have a chance to ask the priest for spiritual direction. As one great saint said: *Only a fool has himself as a spiritual director.* We need an unbiased outside observer to help us along the path of holiness. We cannot do it ourselves.

Confession becomes easier if you develop the habit of doing a nightly examination of conscience. Just briefly go over your day and consider: What good did I do? Where did I fail? How can I improve tomorrow? Spiritually we never stay stagnant. We either grow more holy or more evil. There's no holding pad on the path to sanctity. So if we aren't struggling to improve, we will be backsliding spiritually. John Paul II, so concerned for the stability of our marriages and the salvation of our souls stresses: *Repentance and mutual pardon within the bosom of the Christian family, so much a part of daily life, receive their specific sacramental expression in Christian penance. In the Encyclical **Humanae Vitae**, Paul VI wrote of married couples "And if sin should still keep its hold over them, let them not be discouraged, but rather have recourse with humble perseverance to the mercy of God, which is abundantly poured forth in the sacrament of penance." The celebration of this sacrament acquires special significance for family life. While they discover in faith that sin contradicts not only the covenant with God, but also the covenant between husband and wife and the communion of the family, the married couple and the other members of the family are led to an encounter with*

God, who is "rich in mercy," who bestows on them His love which is more powerful than sin, and who reconstructs and brings to perfection the marriage covenant and the family communion.[37]

Fr. John Hardon, S.J. asks, *Why do husbands and wives quarrel?... The fundamental reason is that either one or the other or both are not at peace. Sinners are not at peace. Either we recover peace inside of us or we are going to be a problem to others and maybe, humanly speaking, an impossible person to live with. Every troublesome person in the family needs to be relieved of his sin. That is why the Sacrament of Peace is necessary to restore peace to families that are in conflict.*[38]

As spouses and parents, we have specific duties and obligations to fulfill. When we ignore these, we commit sins of omission or commission. For example, as spouses the two sins against fidelity are adultery and **selfishness.** Marital intercourse is sacred, holy and a source of grace for the spouses. We sin mortally against fidelity should we have relations with someone other than our spouse. We also sin against fidelity with pornography and watching the sleaze on the Internet or cable stations. It's important to censor what we read, hear on the radio and see on TV. Otherwise we are placing ourselves in the occasion of sin. We also sin against fidelity when we put our job, interest, hobby, or even children before our spouse.

The final area in which we need training is in regard to the teachings of the Magisterium. We need to know the Church's teachings in regard to faith and morals to form our consciences. Only then can we evangelize first our children, then our friends. Get a copy of the *Catechism of the Catholic Church.* Read it from the beginning. It is not difficult reading. Read the encyclicals of the Holy Father. Our faith is being explained on TV, on the radio, in videos, on audiotapes, on the Internet, in books, magazines and newspapers. Use these means to learn more about the Catholic Church and your faith. The more you learn, the more fascinated you will become with Catholicism. A person can

---

[37] *Familiaris Consortio* #58.
[38] *The Catholic Family In The Modern World,* op. Cit., p.50

never know all there is to know about the faith.

Living The Will Of God

Again quoting the Holy Father: *[This is] ...the training that makes it possible for you to give yourselves without reservation to the Lord and to the work that He calls you to do!...Each one of you belongs to Christ and Christ belongs to you. At baptism, you were claimed for Christ with the Sign of the Cross, you received the Catholic faith as a treasure to be shared with others. Then in confirmation, you were sealed with the gifts of the Holy Spirit and strengthened for your Christian vocation. In the Eucharist, you received the food that nourishes you for the spiritual challenges of each day...Christ and the Church need your special talents. Use well the gifts the Lord has given you!*[39]

Let's consider the "Parable of the Talents" or gold coins. In this parable, the master hands over five talents to one servant, two talents to another and the final servant receives one talent. The Gospel tells us these talents were distributed **to each according to his particular ability.**[40] The master asked only of each servant what that servant could handle. God does the same for us. Prayerfully consider, how are you using your talent or talents for God? It isn't important how many talents you have. What is critically important is the "if" and "how" you are using the talent or talents in God's service. When the master returned, he asked his servants for an accounting. God, when He calls you before Him at the moment of death, is also going to ask you for an accounting. The first two servants doubled their talents while the master was away. If you are generous in your service to God, He will multiply your talents also. Look at Mother Angelica. She knew nothing about running radio and TV stations. She had no money. But what she does have is a burning desire to serve God. He has taken the simple talents she utilized in His service and multiplied them. As Venerable Fr. Solanus Casey, O.F.M. Cap., observed: *God condescends to use our powers if we don't*

---

[39] Jan. 1999, Kiel Center address to youth.
[40] Matt. 25:15.

spoil His plans by ours.

God will multiply your talents, just as He does in the life of Mother Angelica, but only if you faithfully use your talents in His service. The third servant was lazy. He just buried the talent and then tried to rationalize his action to his Master. The Master was no fool. He called the servant *wicked and slothful*, then had him *cast forth into the darkness outside, where there will be the weeping, and the gnashing of teeth.* This is a description of hell. Remember, that servant wasn't doing anything objectively evil. He was simply doing *nothing*. What a sobering thought to consider. Doing nothing with the talents God has given to you could land you in hell.

It's time to seriously consider if you are doing all within your power to spread the faith to others starting with your own family. If not, what is the cause of your apathy? Is it lukewarmness, fear or simply laziness? In the *Book of Revelations* Christ says He vomits the lukewarm from His mouth.

How many fallen away Catholics do you know? Invite them to return to the Church. Give them sound spiritual reading. Bring them to confession. Start classes to teach your children and friends the faith. But remember what the Holy Father said at the beginning of this chapter: *The persuasive power of the message...depends on the credibility of its messengers.* To bring others to God, we have to be striving to be saints ourselves.

The Holy Father speaks a great deal about the "new springtime" but it is conditional. Unless each of us becomes actively involved in bringing lapsed Catholics back to the fold, unless we live the faith in its totality, unless we reach out to our Protestant brethren, unless we bring Christ's light and truth to our government, rather than a "new springtime," we will grow deeper into a nuclear winter. God has placed a tremendous responsibility on our shoulders during this critical period of salvation history. What is your response to Christ?

John Paul II writes in *The Role of the Christian Family In The Modern World: The Christian family's faith and evangelizing mission also possesses this Catholic missionary inspiration. The sacrament of marriage takes up and reproposes the task of defending and spreading the faith, a task that has its roots in Baptism and Confirmation, and makes Christian married couples and parents witnesses of Christ "to the ends of the earth," missionaries, in the true and proper sense, of love and life.*

A form of missionary activity can be exercised even within the family. This happens when some member of the family does not have the faith or does not practice it with consistency. In such a case the other members must give him or her a living witness of their own faith in order to encourage and support him or her along the path towards full acceptance of Christ the Savior.

Animated in its own inner life by missionary zeal, the Church of the home is also called to be a luminous sign of the presence of Christ and of His love for those who are "far away," for families who do not yet believe, and for those Christian families who no longer live in accordance with the faith that they once received. The Christian family is called to enlighten "by its example and its witness...those who seek the truth."

The missionary aspect of the Church of the Home is being lived in an incredible manner in Ann Arbor, Michigan. It was there that I was introduced by Tom Monaghan, the founder of Domino's Pizza, to several couples, among them Steve and Janet Ray, and Al and Sally Kresta, who invite Protestants, atheists, and fallen away Catholics over for Sunday dinner for the expressed purpose of "arguing religion." These couples are converts to Catholicism themselves. In 2000 more than 20 families entered the Church due to the evangelization triggered by these dinners. In addition to these families, a Protestant minister, Alex Jones, and his congregation entered the Church Easter of 2001.

By corresponding to the grace of God you can change the world for the better. Let's briefly consider some examples. The blasphemous language used by film crews distressed the famous Catholic actress, Loretta Young. She took action by insisting on *one quarter each time anyone takes the Lord's name in vain.*[41] In the beginning of her campaign she raised hundreds of dollars for St. Anne's Maternity Home. Due to her campaign actors and crew members began watching their language. One day she received a bouquet of red roses with a card that read, *Dear Miss Young, these flowers are from my wife and three daughters. For many years, they have complained about my profanity. But I never realized how bad it was until you started that crazy Swear Box. Because of you, I have cleaned up my mouth, and we all just wanted to say thanks.* The card was simply signed, "Bill."[42] Even though she was under contract to a studio, she refused to do a movie that glamorized adultery. She went to Louis B. Mayer, the head of her studio, and told him courageously, *I find this script immoral. I don't want to do it.* She then asked if he had read the script. When he replied in the affirmative she asked, *Well, if your daughters, Irene and Edie, were actresses, would you want either of them to play this role?* Mayer thought for a moment then replied, *No, I wouldn't. And you don't have to either.*[43] When Miss Young ventured into TV her goal was to have a weekly show where she *could get one wholesome and positive idea into the mainstream of life each week.*[44] *She would then play the lead role, and return at the end to deliver "a thought for the evening," something patriotic, character-building or spiritual.*[45] Not only did she win an Emmy for *The Loretta Young Show,* but was named TV's Most Important Female Personality. Her sponsor Proctor and Gamble, was less than pleased. She was told by them *to tone down your moral standards, and stop doing shows involving priests and nuns.*[46] She refused, thereby losing them as her sole sponsor. Although things looked bleak, God sent her two sponsors to replace Proctor and Gamble so the show could go on.

---

[41] Joan Wester Anderson, *Forever Young* (TX, Thomas More Publishing, 2000) p. 165.

[42] *Ibid.*, p. 166.

[43] *Ibid.*, p. 170

[44] *Ibid.*, p. 183.

[45] *Ibid.*, p. 190

[46] *Ibid.*, p. 211

Each of us is called to act in a similar manner to positively influence our environment. In Springfield we have a community summer theatre. Most of the offerings are excellent family entertainment but it seems that each summer there is one play that is not. For the off-color play this season, rather than holding open auditions for one of the male leads, the part was offered to a young man who is a great vocalist and actor. He is also a recent convert to Catholicism. He flatly refused to take the part unless they change the script because *I'm simply not going to say those lines.* They changed the lines to accommodate him and his talents. My husband, Bob, was president of a local board. When a situation arose that he felt was unethical, he used all the means available to protest and change the situation. Unsuccessful, he resigned his position in protest. Imagine his surprise a year later when he was asked to join the state board of directors. From this position he is now in a position of influence to address the problems on the local level. There is another gentleman in town who chaired an important committee. When his term was up he received a letter thanking him for his services but letting him know that he was not going to be reappointed. He knew he was not being reappointed because he was "too Catholic." When his expertise could not be replaced, the organization, now very embarrassed, was forced to ask him back.

The *Wall Street Journal* described how 46-year-old Deby Schlapprizzi of St. Louis stopped the American Heart Association from endorsing research using embryonic stem cells. As chairman of the 2001 Heart Ball for the American Heart Association in St. Louis, Deby and her family are also large financial contributors to the Association. When she learned that the Heart Association not only endorsed embryonic stem cell research but also was going to underwrite the research, she withdrew from chairing the ball in addition to her family's financial pledges. St. Louis Archbishop Justin Rigali likewise denounced the Heart Association's decision and vowed "to discourage Catholics [and Catholic organizations such as the Catholic schools and Catholic hospitals] from supporting the AHA." Several board members threatened to resign while three nominees refused to join. When the AHA totaled up their potential financial losses nationwide, they rescinded their decision. What was disturbing is the fact that the chairman of AHA is *a Catholic but his father-in-law and brother-in-law died from heart disease and his wife suffers from it. That means his two children were at risk. "What if it turns out they could grow a new heart for my son when he's 40?"*[47] the chairman asked. As Catholics, personal considerations can never dictate our moral standards. Deby Schlapprizzi, Archbishop Rigali, and others involved in this situation exercised heroic virtue thereby winning a tremendous victory for the "culture of life."

Father Peyton, the apostle of the rosary, promised Our Lady that if he were cured of tuberculosis he would spend his life promoting the rosary. He was and he did. Someone donated a train ticket to Hollywood where he sought out Loretta Young. Could she help him get Catholic movie stars to lead the rosary on a national weekly radio show? *A month later, Loretta, Irene Dunne, Rosalind Russell, Ann Blyth, Bing Crosby, Jane Wyatt, Pat O'Brien, Ethel Barrymore, Don Ameche, and several more gathered to pray,* discloses Joan Wester Anderson in her book, **Forever Young.** Father Peyton took his rosary crusade all over the world; yet when he began it everyone agreed that not only was he a poor speaker but his thick Irish brogue made him difficult to understand. Actress Jane Wyatt recalls, *...Father Peyton...was a big gangly guy, a poor speaker, and he invited the congregation to come back that night, to hear his plans to start a Catholic radio show. I remember thinking that he was never going to succeed.* She went back that evening because *I was afraid no one will show up for this poor priest, and he'll be so disappointed.*[48] Imagine her surprise when there was standing room only at the church. See the wonders God works when we allow Him to use us as instruments?

As you grow in holiness, you will change...for the better. *You're relatives, colleagues and friends have noticed the change, and*

---

[47] Laurie McGinley, "Heart and Soul: Stem-Cell Debate Consumes A Charity," *The Wall Street Journal,* Friday, June 22, 2001, p. A16.

[48] *Forever Young, Op. Cit.,* p. 144.

realized that it is not a temporary phase, but that you are no longer the same. Don't worry, carry on. [I]t is now Christ that lives in me—that's what is happening.[49]

John Paul II reminds married couples: *By means of the sacrament of marriage, in which it is rooted and from which it draws its nourishment, the Christian family is...called and engaged by Him in a dialogue with God through the sacraments, through the offering of one's life, and through prayer.*

The Holy Father ended his talk in St. Louis with: *"Mary, Mother of Mercy, teach the people of St. Louis and of the United States to say yes to your Son, our Lord Jesus Christ!"*

Will you say yes?

 *Additional Helps*

✓ To start out on the path to holiness read **The Way** by Blessed Escrivá and **The Devout Life** by St. Francis De Sales.
✓ Consider reading **You Can Become A Saint!** and utilizing the **You Can Become A Saint! Workbook** as a means to learn how to grow holy.
✓ View the video, **The Meditation of the Passion of Christ**, by Radix. (St. Joseph Communications (800)526-2151).
✓ Check out www.rbmediainc.com for audiotapes to help you to grow in holiness.
✓ Check out Bud McFarlane's CatholicCity on the Internet as well as Catholicity. They both have tremendous Catholic resources.
✓ Check out www.vatican.va/ for the Vatican; www.masstimes.org to find churches and Mass times when traveling.

---

[49] *Furrow, Op. Cit.*, #424.

Chapter 2

Marriage Creates Future Saints!

"God created man in His own image and likeness; calling him to existence through love, He called him at the same time for love."
John Paul II

I bet when you read the title of this chapter you thought the "future saints" referred to were your children. You are partially correct. The future saints also include you and your spouse. It's impossible to raise your children saints if you are not striving for holiness yourselves. St. Peter counsels, **become holy yourselves in every aspect of your conduct, after the likeness of the Holy One who called you; remember, Scripture says, "Be holy, for I am holy"** (*1 Peter* 1:16). The worst way to raise children is to have the "do what I say, not what I do" attitude. It just won't work! Children are too sharp for that.

The first chapter gave a brief synopsis of the means Catholics should use to know, love and serve God more devoutly. The purpose of this chapter is to examine how you are living your vocation to marriage since this is your personally chosen path to holiness. Msgr. Peter J. Elliott of the Pontifical Council for the Family explains: *Marriage is one specific incarnational way in which the saving work of Christ enters people's lives. In the bond of this sacrament, the spouses minister grace to one another in daily life. As spouses, they will be judged ultimately on their fidelity to the sacramental covenant. As spouses, they will enter, God willing, into the eternal saving union with God which will replace the union of the earthly sacrament which signified and even foreshadowed it.*

*Marriage, a sacrament among sacraments, is one response to God's call. As the Second Vatican council teaches, we are all called to holiness. But this universal vocation, and each specific vocation, including Marriage, is ultimately a call to divine union. In their union as "one flesh," spouses anticipate the blessed union in heaven, described by...John with mystic insight, as the nuptials of the triumphant Lamb of God (**Revelation** 19, 21, 22).*[1]

Let's Talk Marriage!

"A love that is faithful, exclusive and generous presupposes an intense spiritual life, deep doctrinal convictions, and the courageous exercise of asceticism and charity."

John Paul II

Moses Mendelssohn, the hunchback grandfather of the famous German composer, loved a beautiful young woman. Frumtje, the object of his affections, was repulsed by his appearance. One day he asked her, *Do you believe marriages are made in heaven? Yes, and do you?* responded Frumtje.

Yes I do. You see, in heaven at the birth of each boy, the Lord announces which girl he will marry. When I was born, my future bride was pointed out to me. Then the Lord added, "But your wife

---

[1] Peter J. Elliott, *What God has Joined...The Sacramentality of Marriage* (NY: Alba House, 1997) p. xvii.

will be a hunchback."

Right then and there I called out, "Oh Lord, a hunchbacked woman would be a tragedy. Please, Lord, give me the hump and let her be beautiful." Frumtje became his wife.

For those called to the vocation of marriage, the selection of a spouse is mysterious. Haven't you sometimes wondered why certain individuals married? Why would a beautiful woman marry a seemingly homely, boring man? Or why did a short man marry a tall wife? The answer is simply that each discovered something unique and tremendously lovable in the other.

Isn't it interesting how couples meet? One friend is from Ireland. Her husband is from Rumania. They met in Boston and married. One of my grandfathers was from New York while my grandmother was from Wisconsin. They met in Chicago and married. Another grandfather was from Canada. He came to the Chicago World's Fair, met my grandmother from Pennsylvania and married. God goes to a great deal of trouble to bring couples together!

How does marriage relate to God's plan? Rev. Thomas J. Gerrard wrote almost one hundred years ago this beautiful explanation:

The institution of matrimony was to be a kind of prophecy of His Incarnation and a figure of His Church. As Adam was made weak so that Eve might be given to him to be his strength, so the Son of God became weak, emptying Himself of Himself so that He might take upon Himself the form of a servant and, clothed in flesh, might accomplish the strong victory over sin and death. As Eve was taken from the side of Adam as he slept, and became the mother of all the living, so was the Church taken from the side of Christ as He slept upon the Cross, and became for Him His chosen spouse, the Mother of all those to whom He had come to give life.

The state of marriage, therefore, as reflected in the mysteries of the Incarnation and the Church is seen to have the high function not only of procreating human beings to replenish the earth, but also of training them in the higher life of grace and thus preparing them for the still higher life of glory. Christ came into the world solely to save sinners. The end of the Church is merely the salvation of souls. If, therefore, matrimony is a figure of the Incarnation and the Church, then its chief end is the population of heaven with immortal souls.[2]

Baptized Christians receive the Sacrament of Matrimony. This sacrament infuses our souls with continuous graces throughout our marriage so that we can carry out our vocation and duties as married men and women, as well as parents. These sacramental graces are infused into our souls the day of our wedding (if we are in the state of sanctifying grace) and continue to be lavished on us throughout our marriage as long as we are in the state of grace. Fr. Gerrard insists, *The grace conferred on the wedding morning [or afternoon] remains with them when they leave the church, remains with them in their home life, fortifies them in their discouragements, and steels their wills to the emergencies of every difficult situation.*[3]

What happens if a person marries while in the state of mortal sin? That person does not receive the sacramental graces of matrimony until he/she makes a good confession. During our married life, each time we commit a mortal sin we cut off the sacramental graces of matrimony thereby negatively impacting our marriage. In addition, we lose all sanctifying graces, destroying our relationship with God. For the sake of our souls and the health of our marriage we must get to confession immediately so that God can restore these necessary graces to our souls.

What About An Unbaptized Spouse?

Few couples realize that if a Christian marries an unbaptized

---

[2] Rev. Thomas J. Gerrard, *Marriage and Parenthood, The Catholic Ideal* (NY: Joseph F. Wagner, 1911) pp. 11-12.

[3] *Ibid.*, p.16.

person, the marriage is valid but you do not receive the Sacrament of Matrimony, nor its sacramental graces. Fr. John Hardon, S. J. explains the importance of the sacramental graces of Matrimony: *Having received the sacrament, the couple receive a title to all the graces they need to know what God wants them to do as husband, wife and parents; and how they are to do His will. They also receive a claim to all the strength they need for their wills to live a faithful married life and raise a Christian family according to the plan of God for them. No one else except two baptized Christians when they marry receives the Sacrament of Matrimony. If either or neither is baptized, they may be validly married, of course, but they do not receive the sacrament of marriage nor the lifetime guarantee of graces which the Savior confers on His married followers.*

Since Christian marriage is a sacrament, the whole family benefits from the graces...Not only husband and wife, but the children share in the graces.[4]

Msgr. Elliott softens this seemingly harsh stand toward marriage with unbaptized spouses: *Writing to the Corinthians, Saint Paul said:* **For the unbelieving husband is consecrated through his wife, the unbelieving wife is consecrated through her husband** (*1 Cor.7:14*). He then explains, *Saint Paul discerned a true Marriage in this union, if consent to cohabit peacefully is granted in some way. The family is blessed through the Christian partner...[T]he way the marriage is raised to some special status is through the Christian partner...*

The unbaptized partner is "consecrated" through his or her Christian spouse...Thus the Christian partner is the minister of Grace in this Marriage, the Grace of Christ...Therefore, at least from the side of the Christian, we are looking at a Marriage well beyond a natural union...

Let us not forget the unbaptized partner...stands to gain much in terms of the ministry of Grace which the Christian can, and

---

[4] *The Catholic Family In The Modern World, Op. Cit.,* p. 31.

should offer. But, in return, in loving and cherishing one who is "in Christ," the unbaptized person is able to love Jesus. This love may not be given with any conscious faith in Christ, or even belief in God, but it is "graced" by God...

The salvation of both partners may well be worked out in terms of how each of them lived their covenant of love in this Marriage which is an effectual sign of God's universal salvific will. But salvation is always and only mediated through Christ and His Church, that is, through the "great mystery." By being consecrated in a union of "one flesh" with a Christian, the unbaptized partner is associated with the mystery of the Church. Under the Old Covenant, "strangers and sojourners" enjoyed the spiritual hospitality of Israel. Under the new Covenant, the unbaptized are brought into the hospitality of the Church by way of Marriage to a Christian.

So much depends on the quality of the nuptial ministry of the Christian partner, because this association with the mystery of the Church is a call to enter the Church, to receive the gift of Faith in Baptism. Through the words and deeds of the Christian spouse, we would hope for this complete response to the call of the Bridegroom and His spouse the Church. But in His hidden ways, God may offer salvation as a Baptism of desire, in living the Marriage covenant. Fidelity to that covenant is always fidelity to God.[5]

Living Those Vows

Marriage is that incredible sacrament in which you and your spouse are given graces so powerful that if you cooperate with them, it's your sure path to holiness, to sainthood. Even more exciting is the fact that you aren't required to walk this path alone. You have a helpmate, your spouse, walking with you along the path to sanctity. Your spouse helps you in several ways—through spiritual and natural support and/or through the cross of unbelief or difficult personality traits. By cooperating with the

---

[5] *What God has Joined...The Sacramentality of Marriage,* Op. Cit., pp.200-203.

graces of matrimony, everything that occurs in your marriage can be used to help you grow holy. Even in the worst situations a person can grow holy according to John Hardon, S.J.: *Our English word "patience" comes from the Latin verb pati, which means to "suffer." It is impossible to practice patience unless you suffer. Christ taught that families must be patient. The husband must be patient with his wife, the wife with her husband; the parents must be patient with their children; and the children with their parents. Do members of families cause each other some suffering? That is what life is all about. Every human being suffers. We come into the world crying and, unless we are totally anesthetized, we leave the world in pain. Jesus taught patience and He taught patience not only by word, but especially by example.*[6]

Well-formed Christian spouses realize that in the vocation of marriage they will have to shoulder the cross. It's a daily reality. There will be periods of illness, financial or job problems, misunderstandings, marital problems and family problems. In addition there will be disappointments, disillusionments, personality conflicts, even boredom in day-to-day routine living. These are the daily crosses that arise in every marriage from the sloppiness of one spouse to the tardiness of the other. It's these little irritations and sufferings that are instrumental in leading us to develop the different virtues that we all need to grow holy...virtues such as patience, perseverance, generosity, temperance, sociability, fortitude, self-control, humility, charity, hospitality, thoughtfulness, kindness and even long suffering.

Now all this involves much trouble and anxiety both on the part of the husband and of the wife. With the former lies the paramount obligation of working for the sustenance of the household; with the latter lies all the cares of childbearing; with both lies that anxiety for the temporal and spiritual well-being of each other and of the children...

Those who enter this state, therefore, should do so with the eyes wide open to the fact that it is a life fraught with difficulty and that both man and woman are supposed to be willing to bear grave

---

[6] *The Catholic Family In The Modern World, Op. Cit.*, p.17.

inconveniences. When a man complains of his loss of liberty or the increased burden on his pocket; or when the woman complains of the troubles of children, there has evidently been some radical misunderstanding as to the end of the institution of marriage and of its burdens. What is needed on those occasions is the consideration that marriage is a Sacrament—a Sacrament which is a channel of divine strength to bear the burden, of divine light to see the way out of the difficulties, of divine refreshment for the constant renewal of conjugal life and love.[7]

In the movie *RUNAWAY BRIDE*, the male character had a rather realistic way to propose marriage. He didn't go for the clever, romantic or emotional proposal. Instead he says, *I think the most anyone can honestly say is…"Look, I guarantee there will be tough times. I guarantee that at some point one or both of us will want to get out of this thing. But I also guarantee that if I don't ask you to be mine, I will regret it for the rest of my life…because I know in my heart you are the only one for me."*

Living married life according to the plan of God is at times difficult but God did not give us His divine law then leave us to muddle through on our own. His grace is sufficient for our needs. By cooperating with His graces we can handle any situation that arises in our marriage. If we prefer to rely on our own strength we will fail. There will be moments in our marriage when God will ask us to be heroic. Consider it a test of your virtue remembering that sanctity requires heroic virtue.

Catholic Christian spouses realize that their hierarchy of values is different from the world's values. Rather than seeking "me," they seek first of all God, then their spouse, children, others, and themselves last. In the musical, *Playing Our Song,* the male lead ends his relationship because he's too selfish to completely give himself. He sings, *…You were everything good. I know that you love me…[But] in loving you I was losing me…Was I less…were you more?*[8] This tendency toward selfishness destroys too many marriages today. Did we realize at the time, or have we forgotten

---

[7] *Ibid.*, p. 17.

[8] Casablanca Record and FilmWorks, Inc., 1979. Lyrics by Carole Bayer Sager.

that in our vows we made a total self-donation to our spouse?

In **Familiaris Consortio**, John Paul II explains: *Like each of the seven sacraments...marriage is a real symbol of the event of salvation, but in its own way.* "The spouses participate in it as spouses together, as a couple, so that the first and immediate effect of marriage is not supernatural grace itself, but the Christian conjugal bond, a typically Christian communion of two persons because it represents the mystery of Christ's incarnation and the mystery of His covenant...[C]onjugal love involves a totality, in which all the elements of the person enter—appeal of the body and instinct, power of feeling and affectivity, aspiration of the spirit and of will. It aims at a deeply personal unity, the unity that, beyond union in one flesh, leads to forming one heart and soul; it demands indissolubility and faithfulness in definitive mutual giving; and it is open to fertility. In a word it is a question of the normal characteristics of all natural conjugal love, but with a new significance which not only purifies and strengthens them, but raises them to the extent of making them the expression of specifically Christian values.*[9]*

The social role that belongs to every family...is based on the sacrament of marriage...[T]he sacrament gives to Christian couples and parents a power and a commitment to live their vocation as lay people and therefore to "seek the kingdom of God by engaging in temporal affairs and by ordering them according to the plan of God."[10]

Everyone loves a wedding. The word itself conjures up images of an elegant reception, gorgeous flowers, happy people and *love*. Yet, there is more to a wedding than the gifts and romantic honeymoon. While many couples do not articulate their concept of marriage, they look at marriage as the joining together of two different, self-seeking individuals who anticipate through their marriage the fulfillment of their own desires.

Catholic marriage is a completely different concept. It is a

---

[9] *Familiaris Consortio. #13*
[10] *Ibid., #47.*

dynamic, permanent covenant between a man, a woman and God. A contract can be broken. A covenant cannot. In this covenant, the couple put aside their own self-interests to serve the one they love, their spouse, with understanding, forgiveness, spirit of service, thoughtfulness, charity and flexibility. John Paul II stresses that this concept of self-donation is key to marriage. The couple realizes that due to original sin they are living in an imperfect world and dealing with imperfect people...each other. While all married couples are compatible, none are perfectly compatible. From this imperfection flows the disappointments and problems of life, and yet, couples are courageous enough to say, "*I do.*"

In the early years of marriage, couples can become frustrated trying to seek the elusive ideal of perfect happiness on earth. Let's face it, "*It ain't going to happen.*" **Committed Christians will persist in working together to overcome the difficulties and natural frictions that arise.** This persistence will not only deepen their marital love, but will form them into mature, caring people of substance. It is not an easy job. It takes a thick skin, perseverance, daily prayer, trust in God and the frequent reception of the sacraments, that we talked about in the first chapter. These ingredients will turn the daily frustrations from a cross into a plus (+).

Pope Paul VI points out in ***Humanae Vitae****. Conjugal love reveals its true nature and nobility when it is considered in its supreme origin, God, Who is love...*

Marriage is not, then, the effect of chance or the product of evolution of unconscious natural forces; it is the wise institution of the Creator to realize in mankind His design of love. By means of the reciprocal personal gift of self, proper and exclusive to them, husband and wife tend towards the communion of their beings in view of mutual personal perfection, to collaborate with God in the generation and education of new lives...

This love is first of all fully human, that is to say, of the senses and of the spirit at the same time. It is not, then, a simple transport of instinct and sentiment, but also, and principally, an act of the free will, intended to endure and to grow by means of the joys and sorrows of daily life, in such a way that husband and wife become one only heart and one only soul, and together attain their human perfection.

Then, this love is total, that is to say, it is a very special form of personal friendship, in which husband and wife generously share everything, without undue reservations or selfish calculations. Whoever truly loves his marriage partner loves not only for what he receives, but for the partner's self, rejoicing that he can enrich his partner with the gift of himself.[11]

Couples who are unwilling to deepen their faith or unable to accept the fact that their vocation is to handle disillusions by working out problems together for the good of the spouse, may come to the realization that while the wedding was great, the marriage is not what they expected. Growing divorce rates indicate that only 50% of married couples today realize their vocation to marriage is for life. Only one out of two couples realize that when they said, **"I do," it means forever.** This statistic holds for Catholics as well as for the rest of the population. This is a recent development for Catholics. Writing in 1911, Fr. Gerrard quotes Sir John Bigham, then President of the Divorce Court in England: *My experience shows me that members of the Roman Catholic Church seldom come to our court, and I attribute that fact to the great influence of their priesthood, and to the respect which is inculcated amongst Roman Catholics for the marriage vow.*[12]

Fr. Gerrard continues: *What is the cause of this grand steadfastness amongst Catholics and of weak changeableness amongst their Protestant neighbors? A member of the Council of the Eugenics Society shall make an answer...[H]e says: "Marriage, like other natural and necessary relations, is sacred. Only in Catholicism is it a Sacrament; in scientific sociology the term is meaningless...Protestantism will have none of it. The Reformation, in this as in other points a revolt from Catholicism, expressly declared that marriage is not a Sacrament, that it is*

---

[11] Pope Paul VI, *Humanae Vitae,* 1968, #8-9.

[12] *Marriage and Parenthood, The Catholic Ideal, Op. Cit.,* p. 2.

essentially a secular matter."

For the present disastrous state of affairs [divorce, falling birthrate, white slave traffic, the break-up of society], then, we have to thank the system which for three hundred years has proclaimed the denial that marriage is a Sacrament. But, we have seen, the leaven of truth is still working. The preaching and the practice of the sacramental ideal with all its implications is to be the leaven of the whole mass...

It is also hoped that a re-statement of the Catholic ideal, in the face of modern ideals to the contrary, will tend to increase the happiness of Catholic family life. We cannot shut our eyes to the many failures. In all cases they are due either to ignorance of the ideal or to a refusal of its graces. They may be traced largely to the fact that false views of marriage and parenthood do make their way into Catholic homes.[13]

The Question Of Unity

The union of married couples is not only one of body, but also of soul. D'Ascoli writes in **Family and Marriage**: *In order that the state of marriage may be enjoyed to the full, the first necessity is that the minds of the partners be united, as completely as is humanly possible to them, in the possession of eternal truth. The unity between two rational creatures is likely to be the more profound and living, as their grasp of truth, and their sharing in that supreme good of the mind, is more complete...There will arise from the very depths of their natures an intellectual need for the same ideas, the same modes of feeling, the same respect for the truth—the same faith...The flame of feeling tends of its nature to penetrate to the most secret recesses of the other's soul and mind, and to clothe with its own ardor the entire personality of the loved one; if the feeling meets with no response, but only with a cold and obstinate resistance, it will die.*

Differences of opinion, different ideas, doubt, even error and false reasoning, may invade the home, and these things may well

---
[13] *Ibid.*, pp. 3-4.

become powerful dividing forces, walls of the spirit, built for the separation of souls.[14]

This is the reason that the Catholic Church stresses the importance of marrying another practicing Catholic. Marriage, being a union of body, mind and soul is more easily achieved when the spouses are united in faith as well as values. More important than sexual compatibility is spiritual and intellectual harmony. This is why many mixed marriages result in the loss of faith. Unless the Catholic partner is deeply grounded in the faith, receives the sacraments frequently, and perseveringly raises the children in the faith, the longing to be united in soul with one's spouse will result in the loss of faith for the Catholic spouse and the children. It is either the partner with the stronger faith who will prevail or the one who is the most stubborn. Former President Ronald Reagan's father was an indifferent Catholic, so Reagan was raised a Protestant by his mother. Ted Turner's father was anti-Catholic so his Catholic mother was forced to leave the faith. Dr. Laura Schlessinger's mother was a fallen away Catholic. In the case of a mixed marriage where both spouses have strong opposing faiths or the Catholic has a strong faith and the spouse is stubbornly anti-Catholic there will be a perennial tension in the marriage. Fr. Hardon, S.J. points out that *Jesus taught that a family should be a lifelong union of persons who are united by profession of the same divine faith as He revealed to the human race. It should be a lifelong union of persons who are obedient to the teachings of the Church founded by Christ... We are not saying that all Christian families either fully reflect these standards of Christ or always remain faithful to His expectations. But we should know what the standard is.*

...How many people, without a second thought, will marry someone who does not share their faith. The price they pay and the risk they take are known to God alone.

As envisioned by Christ, a family is a lifetime union of two persons who are obedient to the teachings of the Church which He founded and which alone is divinely authorized to tell

[14] Emidio D'Ascoli, OFM, Cap., *Family and Marriage* (Chicago: Scepter, 1961) p.29.

Christians how they are to live their married lives. This includes the Church's teaching on marital morality and, with emphasis, **her unchangeable doctrine on fidelity and procreative love in marital intimacy.**[15]

The inability to be united in our souls with our spouses is an intense suffering for partners in mixed marriages or in marriages where a spouse is a lapsed Catholic. F. J. Sheed adds: *[A] union of bodies is not the fullness of sexual union. It is valid only as an expression of the union of two personalities. Apart from that, it is a meaningless acrobatic...When, into the union of bodies, all the shared life and shared love of a man and a woman are poured, then you have the sexual union in its fullness ...**The completer the self-giving, the richer the bodily union.** The giving of one's self to another is the decisive act, the act that transforms. While the self is ungiven, one remains isolated, singular, single. Those who have never made the gift of self retain, through any number of bodily unions, a sort of unclean virginalness.*

...But in marriage...the sexual union has more to utter; and there is not the certainty of ultimate boredom which goes with all purely bodily pleasures. For while one soon comes to an end of what the body has to give, there is no end to the exploration of a personality. So that an act which must become stale when repeated for its own sake need never become stale when it is regarded as the expression of a profounder reality that is always growing.

...[P]utting a man and woman together does not of itself constitute the true human compound: something else must happen, something electric perhaps. **There must be that real giving and receiving...free-will offering of the self by each to the other. Obviously you can have a marriage where this mutual giving is at the barest minimum; but it is not marriage at its best, and it does not bring the enrichment of personality that each needs. In some marriages it comes quickly, in some slowly, in some hardly at all.** *But the quality of the marriage is measured by it.*[16] (Editorial emphases)

---

[15] *The Catholic Family In The Modern World, Op. Cit.,* pp. 13-14.

[16] F. J. Sheed, *Marriage And The Family* (New York: Sheed & Ward, no date) pp. 18-20.

In the early years of marriage, the lack of personal virtue along with little spiritual and intellectual harmony causes tension. Until children enter the picture, couples tend to be self-centered. His goals are different from her goals. She sees the purpose of life as people oriented. He sees it as business oriented. Young couples who together seek out spiritual formation, develop a prayer life, frequent the sacraments, especially the Sacrament of Reconciliation at least monthly, soon reconcile their differences and achieve close intellectual and spiritual harmony. Other couples may struggle a lifetime and never reach that ideal of harmony. This may be their cross, which in turn can be used for their own spiritual growth besides being offered for their spouse's sanctification.

Primarily, marriage is a union of wills. Marriage is not made by co-habitation but rather by the consent of the man and the woman. Rebuttati writes in *Matrimonio*: **It is only the perfect union of two souls—the fullness of communication in sympathy, made sacred by convictions of duty and of religion—which constitutes the basis and the perfection of the married state**, *ennobles it, and carries it to the heights which are sublime; bestowing great reserves of strength for the fulfilling of its obligations, and removing every limitation to the spirit of sacrifice, which will be necessary to the partners if they intend to build up the new family on a solid foundation.*[17]

D'Ascoli writes that marriage *is thus a relationship which involves the whole of a human being as an intelligent, and free person, having a sensibility which is exquisitely spiritual, ordered towards and centered in something that is of its nature sacred.*

A union of man and woman who marry only for the satisfaction of their [sexual] instinct is contrary to the order of nature and to the rational sequence of feelings and affections...Sexual union is, as it were, taken out of the context of human life and made an end in itself. **The sexual union is of its nature only licit between a man and a woman who have by mutual consent**

---

[17] Rebuttati: Art. *Matrimonio,* in *Nuovo Digesto Italiano,* v. VIII, p. 247, Torino, 1939.

entered into the married state with the right intentions.
(Editorial emphasis)[18]

The words "obligation" and "spirit of sacrifice" bring new images to the wedding scene. As Dr. John M. Haas, former Episcopal priest and convert to the Catholic Church, points out: *To embrace with abandon and without equivocation the Catholic vocation to marriage is to embrace the cross; it is to enter freely and joyfully into the mystery of Christ's paschal sacrifice; it is to declare one's readiness to sacrifice all for the beloved, even to the point of one's own life.*[19]

These words need to be given careful consideration by all couples considering marriage as well as those already married. Through the media we are deluged by daily exhortations to be happy, to live life to the fullest, to be self-fulfilled. The media has no use for the concepts of *"obligation," "responsibility," "fidelity," "chastity,"* and *"spirit of sacrifice"* in their exhaustive search for paradise on earth. Many couples are caught up in this philosophy of individualism, the *"I have to be me"* syndrome of current songs. If not grounded in the Christian philosophy of service towards others and abnegation of self, when conflicts and disappointments surface, the couple divorces to follow the elusive rainbow of happiness that has eluded them so far. This changing of partners is even shakier than original marriages, with 65% of second marriages ending in divorce. This endless quest for complete happiness is rooted in selfishness and the avoidance of the cross. As Bl. Escrivá reminds us, *Cross, toil, anguish—such will be your lot as long as you live. That was the way Christ went, and the disciple is not above his Master.*[20]

Previous to the explosion of the *"me generation,"* businessmen would meet for lunch and inquire of each other, *"Are you married?"* Now the standard question is, *"What's your situation?"* One executive confides that people are surprised when they learn he is still married to his *"first"* wife.

---

[18] *Family and Marriage, Op. Cit.*, p. 39.

[19] John M. Hass, "Marriage and the Priesthood" (NY: Scepter, 1987) p. 9.

[20] Blessed Josemaría' Escrivá, *The Way*, #699.

Yet Associate Judge John Ryan of Chicago claims that marriage is coming back because the Christian definition of marriage is the only one that works. It is the only institution that brings maturity to two different individuals. Ultimately it brings peace, harmony, and contentment, not only to married couples, but to society as well.

The Primary Purpose Of Marriage

"Perhaps the greatest social service that can be rendered by anybody to the country and to mankind is to bring up a family."
George Bernard Shaw

The purpose of marriage is to have babies and then educate them. Marriage is not legalized lust. *God blessed them* [Adam and Eve], *saying to them "Be fruitful, multiply, fill the earth and conquer it. Be masters of the fish of the sea, the birds of heaven and all living animals on earth"* (Genesis 1:28-29). This was the first command given to the human race by God...to be fruitful, to have children. If you are not ready to have children, you are not ready to marry! When the conception of children is put on hold either through the use of Natural Family Planning (NFP) without a good reason, or contraceptives we are saying to God, *I'm going to do my will, not yours.* Children are not a commodity to be acquired at our convenience.

God has a plan for each married couple. When a couple thwarts this plan they will later learn to their grief the suffering they have brought upon themselves. Couples that contracept run the risk of long-term infertility. Those who use NFP to avoid children until they can get a home, have their career more established, etc. weaken their marriage and run the chance of not having children due to fertility problems related to aging. We easily conceived three children rather close together. Following the birth of our last daughter, when I was twenty-eight, my subsequent pregnancies ended in miscarriages. If I had been a career woman waiting until my 30's to have children we would be childless today.

What a tragedy that would have been! God knows best when to send us children. Don't mess up your life by playing "God" in this manner.

Likewise we have to raise our children to value children, to know the importance of family life, to understand that marriage is for having children. When we make negative or disparaging comments about large families or with our tone of voice indicate that someone is having *another* child, or what a burden or bother children are, we teach through our words and attitude that children are an undesirable commodity...something to be avoided. With two of our daughters married we are expecting our eighth grandchild. Mary Terese has three daughters under three (by C-section) and Mary Kate is expecting her fifth making it five children seven years and under. My sister-in-law, Mary, just had her eighth child by C-section. While we are thrilled with each child and each new pregnancy, "good" Catholic women shock me with their negative, disapproving comments. One woman I ran into told me that her daughter was being married next month: *I told her not to get carried away with having babies.* She actually told me this on Mother's Day! In conversing with the daughters of these women, the young women have "caught" their mothers' negative attitude toward children. Remember, those who are open to life contribute to the "culture of life" while the others contribute to the "culture of death."

Fr. Gerrard explains, *The first duty is the bringing of children into the world and the educating of them in the service of God; the second duty is mutual love and service in the companionship of domestic life.*[25] How refreshing it is to hear engaged couples talk about their plans for children. On the other hand, many couples concentrate on their professional goals, others on their materialistic ambition. Little do they realize that they are creating their own crosses. Advancement and possessions do not bring happiness.

In **Humanae Vitae,** Pope Paul VI explains clearly, not only the responsibilities of married couples, but the reasoning behind

---

[25] *Marriage and Parenthood, The Catholic Ideal, Op. Cit.,* p. 16.

the law of God. While I apologize for quoting long passages verbatim, it is only by this method that you will discover the beauty and wisdom of the moral teaching of the Catholic Church on this controversial topic. It may even be the first opportunity for you to read this historic document. Note that this was written prior to the use of inclusive language. When the Holy Father uses the word "men" in the general sense he is speaking about both men and women except in #17 where he is specifically addressing men. On the 30th anniversary of *Humanae Vitae*, Archbishop Charles J. Chaput, O.F.M.Cap., of Denver, issued a pastoral letter, *Of Human Life: A pastoral letter to the people of God...on the truth and meaning of married love.*[26] I will be quoting his letter between sections of the Holy Father's encyclical. (The encyclical is in bold type.) Archbishop Chaput begins his pastoral by saying: *...I believe the message of* ***Humanae Vitae*** *is not a burden but a joy. I believe this encyclical offers a key to deeper, richer marriages. And so what I seek from the family of our local Church is not just a respectful nod toward a document which critics dismiss as irrelevant, but an active and sustained effort to study* ***Humanae Vitae****; to teach it faithfully in our parishes; and to encourage our married couples to live it.*

Excerpts From Humanae Vitae

Responsible Parenthood
10. ...[C]onjugal love requires in husband and wife an awareness of their mission of "responsible parenthood"...In relation to physical, economic, psychological and social conditions, responsible parenthood is exercised, either by the deliberate and generous decision to raise a numerous family, or by the decision, made for grave motives and with due respect for the moral law, to avoid for the time being, or even for an indeterminate period, a new birth.

Responsible parenthood also and above all implies a more profound relationship to the objective moral order established by God, of which a right conscience is the faithful interpreter...In the task of

[26]This was a ***Catholic World News Feature*** July 20, 1998. Copies of this pastoral letter can be obtained from: Archbishop Chaput's Website or Family Life Council, Inc., E-mail: familylifecouncil@compuserve.com

transmitting life, therefore, they are not free to proceed completely at will...but they must conform their activity to the creative intention of God, expressed in the very nature of marriage and of its acts and manifested by the constant teaching of the Church.

Respect for the Nature and Purpose of the Marriage Act
11. These acts, by which husband wife are united in chaste intimacy, and by means of which human life is transmitted...must remain open to the transmission of life.

Archbishop Chaput comments:
*13. That is why the Church is not against "artificial" contraception. She is against **all** contraception. The notion of "artificial" has nothing to do with the issue...[T]he Church teaches that all contraception is morally wrong; and not only wrong, but seriously wrong.* (Editorial emphases) *The covenant which husband and wife enter at marriage requires that all intercourse remain open to the transmission of new life. This is what becoming "one flesh" implies: complete self-giving, without reservation or exception, just as Christ withheld nothing of Himself from His bride, the Church, by dying for her on the cross. Any intentional interference with the procreative nature of intercourse necessarily involves spouses' withholding themselves from each other and from God, who is their partner in sacramental love. In effect, they steal something infinitely precious—themselves—from each other and from their Creator.*

Illicit Ways of Regulating Birth
14. In conformity with these landmarks in the human and Christian vision of marriage, we must once again declare that the direct interruption of the generative process already begun, and, above all, directly willed and procured abortion, even if for therapeutic reasons, are to be absolutely excluded as licit means of regulating birth.

Equally to be excluded, as the teaching authority of the Church has frequently declared, is direct sterilization, whether perpetual or temporary, whether of the man or of the woman. Similarly excluded is every action which, either in anticipation of the conjugal act, or in its accomplishment, or in the development of its natural consequences, propose, whether as an end or as a means, to render procreation impossible.

Licitness of Recourse to Infecund Periods

16. If...there are serious motives to space out births, which derive from the physical or psychological conditions of husband and wife, or from external conditions, the Church teaches that it is then licit to take into account the natural rhythms immanent in the generative functions, for the use of marriage in the infecund periods only, and in this way to regulate birth without offending the moral principles which have been recalled earlier.

The Personal Cost Of Doing It My Way

"On this road we cannot afford to be lazy, but strong, for on it abound the assaults of temptation. The devil lies in wait at the bends, trying by every means he can to arrest and gain mastery over the wayfarers. And once he succeeds in doing this, he leads his victim astray or detains him; he gets him to turn back, he hinders his advance, and even drags him off the road." St. Augustine

The quickest way to destroy our marriage, morally hurt our children, and lose our souls is to contracept. Although a harsh statement, I see the truth of this all around me—in young couples and older couples. The effects of this sin eventually catch up with the couples destroying their married love along with their living and unborn children. Let me explain. Contraceptive pills, I.U.D.s and many of the other devices used are abortifacients. This means they do not prevent a woman from becoming pregnant but prevent the embryo from implanting in the uterus. The embryo is then spontaneously aborted during menstruation. When the embryo is not aborted, the woman finds herself pregnant. My daughter, Mary Terese, knows of five women who became pregnant while on the pill, one of which became pregnant three years in a row.

Besides the moral aspect, the health of women who take contraceptives is also at risk. Zenit reports that the British Medical Journal (July 2001) found the newer "pills" are three times more likely to cause blood clots. Abortion and the birth control pill are linked to the almost epidemic problem of breast cancer in women. Contraceptives are also linked to the rapid growth of cervical cancer in the female population as well as choriocarcinoma, liver cancer, invasive hydatidiform mole, melanoma, and germ cell ovarian tumors. In addition to the elevated risks of breast, cervical, and hepatic cancer, OCP [contraceptive] use carries an increased risk of other major side effects that include:

- ✓ Heart attacks primarily in women with other risk factors such as diabetes, smoking, hypertension, or severe obesity.
- ✓ Blood clots and pulmonary embolism
- ✓ Hypertension
- ✓ Worsening of cholesterol levels
- ✓ Causing or worsening of depression
- ✓ Worsening of headaches, especially migraines
- ✓ Development of melasma (i.e., "dark skin spots") especially in the facial area.[27]

Dr. Chris Kahlenborn, concerned by the increased rate of breast cancer in women, spent six years analyzing medical data. She put the results of her research in the book ***Breast Cancer, Its Link to Abortion and the Birth Control Pill.*** Kahlenborn writes: *I have come to a definite conclusion. I believe that the evidence contained within this book will convince the lay person and the professional that both an induced abortion and the use of the birth control pill are independent risk factors for the development of breast cancer, especially if the woman has participated in either of these factors at a young age. The fact that few women have been informed of this is, in my opinion, a very, very serious "mistake"—one with worldwide implications.*[28]

Pharmacist Lloyd J. DuPlantis, Jr. compares the side effects of the pill as the same as radiation sickness which includes nausea, listlessness, *headaches, nervousness, depression, insomnia, hair loss, changes in menstrual flow, decreased fertility and susceptibility to disease because of immune system damage that prevents proper healing...The pill disrupts the basic self-regulatory function of every cell in a woman's body...Birth control pills cause "aging" of a woman's uterus. A general rule of thumb is that for*

---

[27] Chris Kahlenborn, MD, *Breast Cancer, Its Link to Abortion and the Birth Control Pill* (Dayton: One More Soul, 2000) p. 229. (One More Soul, 616 Five Oaks Avenue, Dayton, OH 45406)

[28] *Ibid.,* p. viii.

every year a woman takes the pill, her uterus ages two years...Increased rates of vascular diseases, cancers, and diabetes all suggest that our self-radiation with birth control chemicals is causing an overall life shortening.

Fibromyalgia, a disease identified in 1976, thirteen years after the pill was introduced, manifests itself by causing many "old–age" symptoms such as chronic pain, rheumatism, arthritis, chronic fatigue syndrome. Fibromyalgia occurs almost exclusively in women who have taken the pill (U.S. Pharmacist, December 1997).[29]

Another concern for Christian couples is the medical procedure known as amniocentesis. Many times doctors will recommend this procedure if there is any indication that a baby may have Down syndrome. This is to protect themselves from "wrongful birth lawsuits." Once the diagnosis is confirmed, the mother is given the option to abort the baby or carry the child to full term. Since abortion is not an option, be very reluctant to undergo this procedure since it can cause the miscarriage of healthy babies. A headline in Zenit claims "Down's Test Kills More Babies Than It Diagnoses." *A test in pregnant women to check for Down syndrome causes up to four healthy babies to be miscarried for every abnormality it detects, a study has shown...About 40,000 women a year undergo it. Only about 100 unborn babies are confirmed with the syndrome, but the study found that up to 400 healthy unborn babies are subsequently miscarried.*[30]

Fr. Paul Marx, O.S.B., founder of Human Life International claims that his research shows that parents who contracept are more likely to have children who fornicate, which means engaging in sexual relations outside of marriage. Fruitful married love, on the other hand, brings about the renewal of the world and the Church. Look at the example of the Martins, the parents of St. Thérèse. Without the generosity of Zelié and Louis, we would not have the Little Flower. In Fr. Marx's autobiography, *Faithful for Life*, he explains that he was one of 17 children. He was his mother's fifteenth pregnancy. Of the surviving 14 children, two

---

[29] Lloyd J. DuPlantis, Jr., P.D. "The Pill, A Human Time Bomb," *Celebrate Life,* May-June 2001.

[30] Zenit, April 1, 2001.

became priests and two became nuns. Fr. Marx has given his life to protect the unborn, to preserve families and to defend the Church throughout the world. He has touched millions of lives in 93 different countries. Only God knows how many hundreds of thousands of babies would have been aborted if his mother chose to contracept after her fourteenth pregnancy. Remember, the best gifts we can give our children are brothers and sisters.

Prior to the 1930s, contraception, abortion, and homosexuality were condemned not only by all Christian faiths but also by civil law. In 1966 only 10% of married couples in the world used contraceptives. Today figures claim that 60% contracept.[31]

In 1960 when "the Pill" hit the market, the Catholic Church was pressured to accept it as morally correct. This motivated Paul VI to pen **Humanae Vitae** in 1968. This encyclical was eagerly anticipated, not only by Catholics but also by the world in general. So eagerly was it awaited that John D. Rockefeller, Jr. had the audacity to offer to write it for the Holy Father. The media, population control groups, and even large segments within the Catholic Church were convinced that Pope Paul VI would modify the teachings of the Church. (If they had known their theology they would have known that Popes have no authority to change Divine Law.) When this encyclical was finally released the backlash was incredible.

How well I remember the day it was released. As a bride of seven weeks I was finishing up some theology classes at Marquette University. It was shocking to see the uproar in class when the Professor summarized the encyclical for us. The world and many Catholics echoed Satan's "non serviam" (I will not serve). Priests, religious and laity protested in newspapers, on TV, at conferences. They began their own organizations to promote contraception and abortion such as Catholics for a Free Choice funded by secular organizations such as the Rockefeller, Ford, Packard, and MacArthur Foundations. That was the "vocal protest." More insidious was the "silent protest" which simply ignored the teachings of this encyclical thereby extinguishing the light of

---

[31] Zenit, February 20, 2001.

Christianity within the world.

Not only is our world suffering the devastating fallout of dissension from **Humanae Vitae** but so are the individuals who refused to accept the teachings of the Church. On my flight to Cairo, Egypt, to cover the UN Population and Development Conference, I learned that Dr. Daniel C. Maguire, Professor of Ethics at Marquette University (Milwaukee) was on the same flight. Dr. Maguire was one of the leaders of the vocal protest against **Humanae Vitae**. His continuing protest against the moral teachings of the Catholic Church purchase him international fame and power but spiritual darkness. As President of The Religious Consultation on Population, Reproductive Health and Ethics, a group formed to change the beliefs of religions, he receives funding from the Ford Foundation. Maguire is a key player in population control activities at the UN. He is even accorded the honor of giving addresses to the Plenary Sessions. He and his first wife, Marjorie Reiley Maguire, met protesting **Humanae Vitae** at Catholic University in Washington, D.C. At the time, Maguire was a priest and Marjorie was a religious. He left the priesthood and she left her order. After he was laicized they married. They are the parents of two sons, one of whom is now deceased. Both were active in Catholics for a Free Choice. While Dan made the rounds on speaking circuits, Marjorie wrote the organization's promotional brochures including one which explains why Catholic women can utilize abortion(?!)

Dr. Maguire agreed to allow me to interview him on the plane. His interview is proof that it isn't possible to be a "pick and choose" Catholic and remain Catholic. See for yourself how rejecting the teachings of the Church leads to the loss of faith. Here is just part of the interview:

Q: As a moral theologian, what do you say are the criteria a Christian woman should use when contemplating contraceptives or having an abortion?

Maguire: First off the entire abortion question which is more difficult. I don't think abortion should only be done for life. The problem with the anti-choice [pro-life] people is that they look on life just in terms of the embryo. Life is a web of relationship so the criterion is to promote life. You may at times need to abort...

Q: You still consider yourself a Catholic?
Maguire: I'm not just a Catholic. I identify with certain/many elements of the Catholic tradition. I disagree with a great number of them....

Q: So you don't believe in Papal Infallibility?
Maguire: No. That's a 19th century dream that some people have...

Q: What are your views on Christ? Do you believe that He is God?
Maguire: No. I would go along with St. Paul that God was in Christ Jesus. But the identification of Him with divinity doesn't make sense to me....

Q: You don't believe in the resurrection?
Maguire: I think they are symbols.

Q: What about the doctrine of Transubstantiation?
Maguire: Again, it's taking a symbol and turning it into a physical thing. It was meant to be symbolic...

Q: How did your theology evolve?
Maguire: I got my degree from a Pontifical University in Rome. I got it right from the Roman source. The Second Vatican Council had a big influence on all of us.

Q: They actually taught you the doctrines we have been discussing?
Maguire: No, no. I was taught in a totally conservative way...

Q: In your view, what is the essence of the Catholic Church?
Maguire: You have to go to the essence of Christianity, the rethinking of the individual, the possibilities for the earth, hope for people, justice. There is a tremendous message there. The Church has become fixated in the pelvic zone. I've been calling it "Pelvic Orthodoxy" that they have been practicing...

After Cairo I had an opportunity to interview his wife, Majorie, shortly after their divorce. She confided that following her divorce she began to rethink her former positions. While she still defends abortion, she is fighting to stop Catholics for a Free Choice from using the materials she authored. As we ended our phone call, Majorie made an interesting comment referring to the vocal protests against **Humanae Vitae** in 1968: *We had no right to wreck havoc on the Church with our dissent.*

In The Face Of Dissent
"Whoever welcomes this child in my name welcomes me."
Jesus[32]

Pope Paul VI had tremendous pressure on him, yet he courageously stood firm. He knew instinctively what the world's response would be but he also knew what was at stake. He writes:

18.   It can be foreseen that this teaching will perhaps not be easily received by all..[T]he Church is not surprised to be made, like her divine founder, a "sign of contradiction,' yet she does not because of this cease to proclaim with humble firmness the entire moral law, both natural and evangelical. Of such laws the Church was not the author, nor consequently can she be their arbiter; she is only their depositary and their interpreter, without ever being able to declare to be licit that which is not so by reason of its intimate and unchangeable opposition to the true good of man.

Pope Paul VI was a visionary. He knew well the consequences for our families, society, and the world if we refused to accept Divine Law. Skillfully he points out:

Grave Consequences of Methods of Artificial Birth Control
17.   Upright men can even better convince themselves of the solid grounds on which the teaching of the Church in this field is based, if they care to reflect upon the consequences of methods of artificial birth control. Let them consider, first of all, how wide and easy a road would thus be opened up towards conjugal infidelity and the general lowering of morality. Not much experience is needed in order to know human weakness, and to understand that men— especially the young, who are so vulnerable on this point—have need of encouragement to be faithful to the moral law, so that they must not be offered some easy means of eluding its observance. It is also to be feared that the man, growing used to the employment of anticonceptive practices, may finally lose respect for the woman

---
[32] Luke 9:48.

and, no longer caring for her physical and psychological equilibrium, may come to the point of considering her as a mere instrument of selfish enjoyment, and no longer as his respected and beloved companion.

Slowly reread the above paragraph. Can't you see these effects spanning generations—from teens to adult politicians? The anti-family/anti-life mentality has created enormous social problems such as sexually transmitted diseases now epidemic among our youth; sex education programs which are pornographic; the selling of body parts from aborted babies; domestic violence; abortion; teen pregnancy; AIDS; pornography; homosexuality; sex crimes; single parent homes; and grandparents raising their grandchildren. *In Illinois, there are over 70,000 children, from infants to teenagers, currently being raised by a grandparent or grandparents*, according to educator and co-author Kay Mayberry of the University of Illinois Extension. Families are the first victims of contraception and its accompanying side effects.

If you want to see the visual effect of how fast our society collapsed when it succumbed to the contraception mentally, rent the video *Mr. Holland's Opus*. It begins in the mid '60s and ends in the mid '90s. Don't become so engrossed in the storyline that you miss the degeneration of the students. Bernard Asbell wrote a book entitled **The Biography Of The Pill: The Drug That Changed The World.** Not only did the pill change the world, it's destroying it. The Holy Father continues:

...[A] dangerous weapon would thus be placed in the hands of those public authorities who take no heed of moral exigencies...Who will stop rulers from favoring, from even imposing upon their peoples, if they were to consider it necessary, the method of contraception which they judge to be most efficacious? In such a way men, wishing to avoid individual, family, or social difficulties encountered in the observance of the divine law, would reach the point of placing at the mercy of the intervention of public authorities the most personal and most reserved sector of conjugal intimacy.

Again we see that Paul VI was a visionary. He could foresee the one-child policy of China that would usher in forced sterilization along with mandatory abortions. Look at the thousands of women forcibly sterilized in India and South America. In one UN Conference after another the battle is fierce between population controllers, who are determined to force sterilization and abortion on all countries, and the pro-life forces lead by the Vatican. Contraception is a dangerous tool in the hands of the state. Archbishop Chaput comments:

7. *...Pope Paul warned that contraception would mislead human beings into thinking they had unlimited dominion over their own bodies, relentlessly turning the human person into the object of his or her own intrusive power. Herein lies another irony: In fleeing into the false freedom provided by contraception and abortion, an exaggerated feminism has actively colluded in women's dehumanization. A man and a woman participate uniquely in the glory of God by their ability to co-create new life with Him. At the heart of contraception, however, is the assumption that fertility is an infection which must be attacked and controlled, exactly as antibiotics attack bacteria. In this attitude, one can also see the organic link between contraception and abortion. If fertility can be mis-represented as an infection to be attacked, so too can new life. In either case, a defining element of woman's identity—her potential for bearing new life—is recast as a weakness requiring vigilant distrust and "treatment." Woman becomes the object of the tools she relies on to ensure her own liberation and defense, while man takes no share of the burden. Once again, Paul VI was right.*

8. *From the Holy Father's final point, much more has flowed: In vitro fertilization, cloning, genetic manipulation and embryo experimentation are all descendants of contraceptive technology. In fact, we have drastically and naively underestimated the effects of technology not only on external society, but on our own interior human identity. As author Neil Postman has observed, technological change is not additive but ecological. A significant new technology does not "add" something to a society; it changes everything—just as a drop of red dye does not remain discrete in a glass of water, but colors and changes every single molecule of the liquid. Contraceptive technology, precisely because of its impact on sexual intimacy, has subverted our understanding of the*

purpose of sexuality, fertility and marriage itself. It has detached them from the natural organic identity of the human person and disrupted the ecology of human relationships. It has scrambled our vocabulary of love, just as pride scrambled the vocabulary of Babel.

When we knock out the foundation stone, the unitive and procreative purpose of sex, from the basic unit of society, which is the family, society comes tumbling down. Newspaper headlines boast that the jobless rate is the lowest in 30 years. Yes, when 40 million people are missing due to abortion the jobless rate should be down. What the newspapers aren't saying is there is a serious shortage of employees available along with the shortage of vocations within the Church. Businesses are scrambling to find immigrants to fill positions. Global Depopulation is a reality. The contraceptive mentality is destroying countries while killing true progress. We are living in a dying world. According to Fr. Paul Marx, O.S.B., 79 countries are below replacement level. That means that within a few generations these countries will cease to exist. These countries include Italy, Spain, Germany, Austria, Japan, Belgium, France, Canada, Thailand, Russia, and yes, the U.S. He points out that our *relatively "high" birthrate right now is because of the more than one million mostly Catholic immigrants, such as Hispanics, Vietnamese, and Filipinos, who still have high birthrates as a group. If it weren't for them, we'd be way below replacement level.*[33]

Peter Peterson, chairman of the Federal Reserve Bank of New York, believes that in Japan alone there will be a loss of 25 percent of workers leaving the government to contend with a large retired population. How to handle the financial debacle created by "zero population" in the world? He proposes to raise taxes *20-40 percent over current levels* to pay for social security. Next he proposes that people will have to work longer hours for more years while at the same time being financially responsible for their own retirement funds. His third proposal is for the government to encourage citizens to have more children. Finally, labor will have

---

[33] *HLI* March 20, 1998 Newsletter.

to be imported from third world countries.[34] Contraception and abortion are even destroying our economy.

If we are open to life, God will generously bless our families and the Church with holy men and women who will transform our world. In addressing the problem of contraceptive mentality, John Paul II in his February 6, 2000 Angelus Message reminds us: *Every child is an immense gift: for parents, for the family, for the Church and for society. The worrisome demographic decline registered in recent years cannot but be a motive for attentive reflection...But above all it is up to married couples to re-establish a culture of love and life, **rediscovering the mission of parenthood assumed on their wedding day.***

Pope John Paul II, speaking to students at the Catholic University in Washington, D.C., in 1979, emphasized that: *Materialistic concerns and one-sided values are never sufficient to fill the heart and mind of a human person. A life reduced to the sole dimension of possessions, of consumer goods, of temporal concerns, will never let you discover and enjoy the full richness of humanity. It is only in God—in Jesus, God made man—that you will fully understand what you are.*

Cardinal Newman made a similar point when buttonholed by a man who wanted to boast about his financial success. After listening to him for a while, the Cardinal took out a piece of paper and wrote the word "God" on it. He asked the man if he could read it. *Sure, it says God,* the man replied. The Cardinal then took out a silver half dollar and put it over the word God. *Now can you read it?* No, the man replied, the *money's in the way.*

Since sanctity is our main concern, before leaving this section let's consider how the moral teachings of the Church influenced the life of Gianna Beretta Molla. Gianna, born October 4, 1922, in Milan, Italy, was the tenth of thirteen children. As a teen she was active in the St. Vincent de Paul Society and Catholic Action. At fifteen she wrote, *I promise You, Jesus, to submit myself to all that You permit to happen to me. Let me only know Your*

---

[34] Mithre J. Sancrasagra, "As People Live Longer, World's Economies Feel The Strain."

Will. She died fulfilling her promise.

Following in her brother's steps, she became a pediatrician. She married Pietro Molla, a young engineer whom she met in Catholic Action, September 24, 1955. They were blessed with three children born in 1956, 1957, and 1959. Then Gianna suffered two miscarriages. In 1961 Gianna became pregnant again but during this pregnancy she developed a uterine tumor that endangered her life and that of her baby.

Author Tim Drake in his article "She Gave Her Life That Her Child Might Live" explains that *Gianna and Pietro were faced with three choices: removing the tumor and terminating the pregnancy and all hope for future pregnancies; removing the tumor and terminating the pregnancy, but leaving open the possibility for future pregnancies; or removing the tumor in such a way that it would not interrupt the pregnancy, but would put Gianna's life in grave danger.*

Pietro recalls that Gianna chose the third solution. "She did it through charity, maternal responsibility, and the great respect she had for the child in her womb." The tumor was removed September 6, 1961. During this time Gianna intensified her prayers: *Yes, I have prayed so much in these days. With faith and hope I have entrusted myself to the Lord...I trust in God, yes, but now it is up to me to fulfill my duty as a mother. I renew to the Lord the offer of my life. I am ready for everything, to save my baby.* She entered the hospital on Good Friday telling Pietro, *If you must choose between me and the baby, no hesitation: choose—I demand it— the baby.* Her daughter, Gianna Emanuela was safely born on Holy Saturday, April 21, 1962 but Gianna died of septic peritonitis seven days later. She was 39 years old.

John Paul II beatified Gianna on Mother's Day in 1994. Present were her husband, siblings, and her children including Gianna Emmanuela, now a physician. The Holy Father extolled Blessed Gianna as a model for mothers calling her, *A woman of exceptional love, an outstanding wife and mother, she gave witness in her daily life to the demanding values of the Gospel. By holding up this woman as an exemplar of Christian perfection, we would like to extol all those high-spirited mothers of families who give themselves completely to their family, who suffer in giving birth, who are prepared for every labor and every kind of sacrifice, so that the best they have can be given to others.* [35]

Some Other Considerations

Archbishop Chaput addressed some other topics that are equally important for us to consider:

16...*Whether to prevent a pregnancy or achieve one, all techniques which separate the unitive and procreative dimensions of marriage are always wrong. Procreative techniques which turn embryos into objects and mechanically substitute for the loving embrace of husband and wife violate human dignity and treat life as a product. No matter how positive their intentions, these techniques advance the dangerous tendency to reduce human life to material which can be manipulated.*

Archbishop Chaput is addressing fertility treatments and techniques that include in vitro fertilization, surrogate motherhood, the harvesting of sperm through masturbation, purchasing of sperm or fertilized eggs, and cloning. As many as 100,000 human embryos are frozen—and largely forgotten—in fertility clinics across the United States when parents are finally successful in having a child but are unwilling to give birth to their other fertilized eggs.[36] In Scotland, Mrs. Morag Riva, a surrogate mother, has carried seven babies for other women. According to the ***Daily Record***[37] Mrs. Riva views surrogacy as a "business-transaction." She uses the 40,000-pound payments to fund family vacations.

The executive director of the American Bioethics Advisory Commission of the American Life League, Father Joseph C. Howard, Jr., explains *Surrogate parenting first involves in vitro fertilization, which is gravely immoral. In vitro fertilization combines sperm with eggs in a glass dish which results in a living human embryo—a living human person. Such human embryos*

---

[35] Tim Drake, "She Gave Her Life That Her Child Might Live," *Celebrate Life* of the American Life League (Jan.-Feb. 2000) pp18-20.

[36] Zenit, March 11, 2001.

[37] Feb. 7, 2000.

are transferred to the uterus of the mother or some other "surrogate" woman who agrees to carry the child in her womb for nine months. Other human embryos are then frozen for later use, set aside for research and/or experimentation or destroyed.

In vitro fertilization is unethical because it generates embryonic children—outside of the bonds of marriage—in a glass dish. This renders the new human person an "object" or "commodity" who is easily exploited or, in fact, destroyed during the process. It is always unethical to treat any human person from fertilization onward as a "means" to an "end." [This is why Deby Schlapprizzi, noted in Chapter 1, fought the American Heart Association's decision to approve and help fund embryonic stem cell research.]

Surrogate motherhood is likewise gravely unethical. This involves a woman who enters a contractual agreement to carry a child generated by in vitro fertilization in her womb for nine months in exchange for money. This amounts to nothing less than the buying, selling and killing of embryonic children. This is slavery. It offends the child's dignity and right to be conceived, carried in the mother's womb, and brought up in the world of his own parents. To the detriment of families, it sets up a division between the physical, psychological and moral elements that constitute those families...

Both procedures are objectively immoral. Both are contrary to the unity of marriage and to the dignity of the procreation of human persons. Both have resulted in the deaths of tens of thousands of embryonic human persons. We must work together to ensure they are prohibited by civil law.[38]

There are morally approved medical procedures for those who experience infertility. Contact the Couple-to-Couple League for help in regard to infertility or Natural Family Planning.[39]

Archbishop Chaput continues:

18...I especially encourage couples to examine their own consciences regarding contraception, and I ask them to remember

---

[38] Fr. Joseph C. Howard, Jr., "In vitro fertilization and surrogate motherhood," *Celebrate Life,* May-June, 2001, p. 13.

[39] (513)471-2000.

that "conscience" is much more than a matter of personal preference. It requires us to search out and understand Church teaching, and to honestly strive to conform our hearts to it. I urge them to seek sacramental Reconciliation for the times they may have fallen into contraception...But do not lose heart. Each of us is a sinner. Each of us is loved by God. No matter how often we fail, God will deliver us if we repent and ask for the grace to do His will.

21. Two final points. First, the issue of contraception is not peripheral, but central and serious in a Catholic's walk with God. If knowingly and freely engaged in, contraception is a grave sin, because it distorts the essence of marriage: the self-giving love which, by its very nature, is life-giving. It breaks apart what God created to be whole: the person-uniting meaning of sex (love) and the life-giving meaning of sex (procreation). Quite apart from its cost to individual marriages, contraception has also inflicted massive damage on society at large: initially by driving a wedge between love and the procreation of children; and then between sex (i.e. recreational sex without permanent commitment) and love...

22...Paul VI told the truth about married love. In doing it, he triggered a struggle within the Church which continues to mark American Catholic life even today. Selective dissent from **Humanae Vitae** *soon fueled broad dissent from Church authority and attacks on the credibility of the Church herself. The irony is that the people who dismissed Church teaching in the 1960s soon discovered that they had subverted their own ability to pass anything along to their children. The result is that the Church now must evangelize a world of their children's children— adolescents and young adults raised in moral confusion, often unaware of their own moral heritage, who hunger for meaning, community, and love with real substance...May the Lord grant us the wisdom to recognize the great treasure which resides in our teaching about married love and human sexuality, the faith, joy and perseverance to live it in our own families—and the courage* *which Paul VI possessed to preach it anew.*

The Question Of Divorce

"...[I]f someone were to put limits on what God asks of him, he would limit his union with Christ; hardly would he identify himself with Jesus..."   Fr. Francis Fernandez

Remember those wedding vows "for better and for worse"? When we married we promised our spouse and God that we were committing ourselves for life—no matter what. We pledged to love our spouse despite his/her failings, flaws or trying disposition. Yet, when things begin getting a little tough, many spouses flee rather than digging in their heels to exercise true love. The Church was wise in putting in our vows the word "worse." It's easy to love someone when they are "better" but when they get "worse"...that's when we have to practice heroic virtue. As I was working on this book a friend called very upset, *Please pray that my daughter divorces her husband!* As I tried to talk her through her daughter's situation pointing out that marriage is forever, my friend became angrier with me saying, *Even my aunt, a religious, said she should dump the fellow.* Our western culture has become a "throw-away" society from possessions to people. H. Daniel-Rops notes that *When a revolutionary doctrine penetrates an existing society, it forces the latter to model itself largely upon it; so much so that it may finish by permeating it entirely.*[40]   The secular ideal of personal happiness at any cost has permeated our culture and is destroying the basic unit of society, the family. What is interesting is that this is not so in many non-Christian societies. The family is still protected by government and extended family. Divorce is almost unheard of in Moslem countries. If a couple has marital problems, the parents of both, if alive, come to live with the couple until the problems are resolved. Likewise, in Hindu India both sets of parents work with the couple to keep the marriage intact. The Indian film industry produces movies that extol the virtues and

---

[40] H. Daniel-Rops, *The Church of Apostles and Martyrs* (NY: E. P. Dutton & Co.Inc., 1960) p. 359.

joys of married life. These films promote fidelity and the importance of the family. According to our newly married Indian neighbors, the influence of U.S. movies is introducing the idea of divorce into India.

Fr. Gerrard points out: *The mere procreation of children could not possibly be the end of matrimony; for this could be done without the bond, without the unity, without the perpetuity, without the love. Manifestly, then, the chief reason for the institution of matrimony was the welfare of the offspring, not merely the existence of the offspring, but its growth and development, the promotion of all its interests. Therefore it was that God so made man and woman that they should love each other, that they should foster that love and concentrate it on each other by excluding all other love of the same kind, that they should make it so strong and lasting that only death should be able to bring about a breach of its union.*

All of this points to the fact that the marriage bond is a law of nature. It is a mutual agreement by which a man and a woman give themselves to each other until death, and this chiefly for the sake of the highest interest of the children which shall be born to them...

Forbidding divorce and insisting on the essential unity and indissolubility of the marriage tie, Christ raised it to the dignity of a Sacrament. Thus it became a more perfect figure of the Incarnation and the Church...

The union between Christ and His Church consists of sanctifying grace. It consists further of a continual flow of all those graces which are needful for attaining the Church's end, namely, the salvation of all the souls for whom the Church was instituted. If, therefore, the marriage bond is like the bond between Christ and His Church, it must be the means by which graces sanctifying the marriage state are conferred. A Sacrament of the new law is a sacred sign instituted by Christ to signify and to confer grace..."What, therefore God hath joined together let no man put asunder."[41]

---

[41] *Marriage and Parenthood, The Catholic Ideal, Op. Cit.,* p. 11.

Each married couple goes through rough patches when they are tempted to divorce and move on. But because of our covenant vows, it can only be a temptation, never a reality. It's these difficult stages in our marriage which increase our spiritual depth, but only if we turn to God for help. It's these stressful times that force us to develop the various virtues that we all need to grow holy. To flee is the animal instinct but we are more than animals. We are made in the image and likeness of God. We have a will, an intellect, and an eternal soul. God gives the graces to sustain us through every rough patch. We must move our wills to accept these graces, and then use our intellect to put them into effect. But if God is left out of our marriage, life will not work out well for us no matter how hard we try. A case in point is Ellen Fein, the best selling co-author of the series on **The Rules.** This three book series promises women that they can avoid a "messy divorce" if they follow **The Rules.** *Instead, you will have one of those made-in-heaven marriages. A **Rules** marriage is forever,* the two authors proclaimed.[42] Unfortunately, right before the third book, **Rules III, Time-Tested Secrets for Making Your Marriage Work** hit the bookstores, Ellen Fein filed for divorce thus ending her marriage of sixteen years.

For your faithfulness, you will find that your love for your spouse has deepened once the difficult period passes. In addition, through the process of carrying the cross, you have grown spiritually closer to God. You are advancing along the path of sanctity. It's all part of the vocation of marriage.

Cardinal Alfonso Lopez Trujillo, President of the Pontifical Council for the Family, in an interview with **Alfa y Omega** Magazine explained: *The life of a child requires the gift of a stable home and today children are great victims in this respect. What is at stake, no more and no less, is the harmonious and integral development of the child who has the right to a real home.* In a divorce situation, the child is torn between two parents, two homes. The child has no permanent roots. Children are emotionally and psychologically damaged by divorce.

---

[42] Devon Spurgeon, "Author's Divorce Pits Her 'Rules' Against Reality," **The Wall Street Journal,** March 23, 2001.

Fr. John Hardon, S.J. explains the issue of indissolubility: *Three conditions, therefore, make a Christian marriage absolutely indissoluble, namely: when both spouses have been validly baptized before they marry; their marital contract was valid because they made it with sufficient understanding of what Christian marriage means and freely chose to marry; and their union was then consummated.*

No single feature of Christian wedlock has been more severely tested than its indissolubility. This has been the single principal cause for persons leaving the Catholic Church, for the separation of whole nations from Catholic unity [England], and for the intrusion of State authority in presuming to grant divorces with the right to remarry for baptized Christians.

Certainly the grace of God is available to preserve a Christian marriage. But this grace requires cooperation on our part. Married people have a free will. There is no more basic use they can make of this freedom than to use the supernatural life and strength they receive from prayer and the sacraments.[43]

John Paul II speaks forcibly on this same issue. In a meeting with officials of the Roman Rota Court, which rules on requests for marriage annulments, he stressed the indissolubility of marriage: *Being faithful to Christ, the Church cannot but repeat with firmness the joyful news of the definitive character of conjugal love...to all those who in our day consider it difficult or even impossible to be united to a person for the whole of life and to those who are drawn by a culture that rejects matrimonial indissolubility and laughs openly at spouses' commitment to fidelity.*

The Pope acknowledged that the Church has the authority to annul a marriage, which in truth never existed. He then emphasized that not even he, the pope, could annul a valid marriage that is consummated: *To hold otherwise would imply that there is no marriage that is absolutely indissoluble, which would be contrary to the sense in which the Church has taught and continues to teach the indissolubility of the marriage*

---

[43] *The Catholic Family In The Modern World, Op. Cit.,* p.51.

bond...Moreover, this is a doctrine confirmed by centuries of practice in the Church, maintained with complete fidelity and heroism even in face of heavy pressures by the powerful of this world.[44]

Here are some practical tips from Fr. Hardon, S.J. on how to avoid divorce:

1...[M]arried people must be prayerful people if they want their marriage to last.

2. A daily examination of conscience is a valuable asset for stabilizing Christian marriage...In order for married people to check themselves on their duties as husband and wife, father and mother. Why? Because marriages become unstable through uncorrected failings in the moral order. Along with an honest self-assessment each evening there should be at least a short act of contrition and resolution to avoid the failing in kindness or thoughtfulness, and to be more patient, more prudent, less lazy, less talkative and less self-seeking the next day....

3. ...[S]pouses and parents should develop a certain regularity [set routine] in their lives. Regularity produces stability. Irregularity tends to instability...

4...A stable marriage does not merely "happen." It is the result of prudent foresight, anticipating days, weeks, and even months ahead. This may mean that the spouses (and parents) will have to change some of their cherished habits, especially those which irritate their married partner or prevent them from being examples of stability to their families.

5. Married people should periodically examine their lifestyle. Are they living beyond their means? Are they working wives or mothers? Is this necessary?

6. A stable marriage has to be worked at...Husbands and wives should each know what the other most needs. It is the evidence of generous love... Nothing can substitute for this constancy of selfless love. However, it must be a love that is shown not only in words or

---

[44] ZENIT News Agency, Jan. 21, 2000, pp. 1-2.

emotions. It must be proved in deeds. Husband and wife live in such close intimacy that no pretense is even possible. Nothing but true Christ-like charity is the foundation for marital stability.[45]

Other tips include avoiding the companionship of couples or individuals who lack Christian morals. It's prudent to avoid any looks, words, or actions that could lead to infidelity. Instead, associate with couples committed to their marriages. Remember we tend to imitate those we associate with. In business situations or at social occasions, keep the hugs, kisses, dances and affectionate pats solely for one's spouse. *A violation of the sanctity of marriage then by either party is a double violation of God's law, a violation of chastity, and a violation of justice.*[46]

Added benefits of perseverance in married life are that you will live longer, better and happier. **USA WEEKEND** did a poll asking "Who is happiest?" Power, wealth and fame didn't even make the cut. The poll showed that *good health, strong faith and love are more important than material wealth or fame.* The happiest people are the married regardless of income or age. *"It positively influences your state of mind if you have strong social support," says L. Stephen Coles..."And marriage is the maximum level of social intimacy." Indeed, studies show marriage increases longevity...People whose parents divorced are not as happy as those from intact families.*

Another finding was that *religious faith is the single most important factor in personal happiness, after health.* The article notes, *religion provides a sense of purpose, experts say, and a social structure for healthful living.*

Duke University research found that those who attend religious services at least once a week have healthier immune systems. Spirituality gives them mental well-being too. "They have a better network to draw from for emotional support and health care."[47]

---

[45] *The Catholic Family In The Modern World, Op. Cit.,* pp. 53-54.

[46] *Marriage and Parenthood, The Catholic Ideal, Op. Cit.,* p. 21.

[47] Anne Lewis Black and Dennis McCafferty, "The Age of Contentment." *USA WEEKEND,* July 3-5, 1998, pp. 4-6.

Don't believe the folktale that it's better to divorce than stay in a bad marriage. The damage to the spouses and children from divorce is greater than the trauma of living in an unhappy marriage situation. In addition, Dr. Waite, a sociologist from the University of Chicago, found in her survey that *85 percent of couples who rated their marriages as miserable—but stayed married—were happy again five years later. Yes, you can fall out of love. But, amazing as it sounds, "healthy couples are teaching us you can also fall out of hate."*[48]

One such couple is David and Teresa Gorsage of Indianapolis, Indiana. David, a Baptist, and Teresa, a fallen away Catholic, married in 1987. Teresa was 26 and David was 27. Residing in California, the Gorsages were living in the fast lane the first two years of their marriage. Then their lives fell apart. David lost his job and securities license, the IRS garnished a month's worth of Teresa's salary, and their first child, Alexandra was born with severe neurological problems.

In the hopes of putting their lives back together again, Teresa transferred back with her company to Indianapolis to be near family. Pressures mounted. Unable to sell their home in California, they had to make house payments as well as pay rent in Indianapolis. To make matters worse, Teresa had to continue to work fulltime to keep their medical insurance coverage since their daughter had a pre-existing condition.

With David looking for a job, Teresa had to hire help to care for their child. Torn by her desire to care for her daughter and the necessity to work, anger and resentment toward David was building. Pressures continued to mount. The equity from their home in California went to pay back taxes. Struggling to deal with the almost insurmountable problems, Teresa began to think that David was simply irresponsible. She was unaware that David was dealing with the consequences of depression and the lack of self-esteem due to his job loss. *I knew the job-hunting procedure but seemed paralyzed by depression and low self-esteem.*

Teresa began feeling guilty about being a lapsed Catholic.

---

[48] Sue Ellen Browder, "The Power of Marriage," *Women's Day,* 6/1/99 p.85-86.

Raised in a family of *"Sunday Catholics,"* she confessed, *we never discussed our faith outside of Mass.* Finally three issues brought her back to the Church: her children, the crisis in her life and the fact that her marriage was falling apart. Desperate for help, she went one night to her parish church to pray but it was locked. Unable to pray in church she drove around the I465 bypass for several hours since she had no other place to go. *This became my prayer routine. I would just drive, pray and think. I was reluctant to let my family or friends know about my marital problems and financial problems.*

Teresa began to attend Mass on Sunday. Despite their problems David attended with her, although he was still a Baptist. At the height of their troubles David began attending RCIA classes with the intention of converting to Catholicism. As the cares of day-to-day living intensified, Teresa gave David an ultimatum: *Get a job or get out. You have one month.*

At the end of the month, when he had not attempted to find a job Teresa threw him out. *I told him that he had to grow-up and become responsible. I would no longer fix his messes. David did not think I was serious.* Pregnant with their second child, she tried to file for divorce but Indiana state law prohibits a divorce during pregnancy.

Shocked by her own actions, Teresa sought help from her pastor. *Thus began weeks of marriage counseling. We both agreed that we loved each other and wanted our marriage to work out.* After a month of separation, David moved back in. Alexandra, age three, due to her illness, could barely crawl. She was incontinent, nonverbal and bottled-fed until age five.

Just before Gregory their second child was born David landed a sales position. Things looked like they were on an upswing when the baby was born six weeks premature through an emergency c-section. In the midst of this crisis, David had no choice but to leave for three weeks of training out East leaving Teresa to cope with a baby in critical condition, their multi-handicapped daughter and the effects of a c-section. David was still out East when Teresa brought little Gregory home from the hospital. With the baby on a heart apnea monitor and caffeine to stimulate his heartbeat, the baby seldom slept. Teresa found herself alone trying to deal with the serious health problems of two children, fighting sleep deprivation and working fulltime.

On their fifth anniversary, in February, the Gorsages reached such a crisis point that they separated again. This time Teresa changed the locks. In one last effort to save their marriage they again returned to their elderly pastor who after talking with them for about twenty minutes said, *I have never seen two people so angry with each other. I don't see hope in this relationship.* By June they were divorced although David did not want the divorce. He recalls, *I thought it was the only option.*

Although David immediately moved to Fort Wayne, Indiana, he kept coming back on the weekends to attend Mass, the RCIA classes, and the Christ Renews His Parish formation series. His actions irritated Teresa. *It seemed like hypocrisy on his part.* When he requested permission to join the Church, the pastor deferred it until David could get his life more in order.

As a result of the separation and divorce, Alexandra, now three, developed a severe sleep disorder. She missed her father whom she loved dearly. *She would wake up during the night waiting for him to come home.* To soothe the child, Teresa would rock Alex, showing her pictures of her father while telling the little girl how much her daddy loved her. This despite her own anger and hurt. *My daughter didn't need to know his shortcomings. I always hoped that it was possible that he could turn his life around. I prayed for him even though I thought he was a jerk. At the same time he was praying for me but I didn't know it at the time.*

Although suffering from depression, David continued selling instruments to hospitals. To economize he parked in the church parking lot across the street from one of the hospitals. Coming out late one night when it was dark, he began getting into his car when he noticed an illuminated awning over one of the doors of the church. Curious, he got out of his car and went in. It was St. Jude's Eucharist Adoration chapel. He went to the front of the chapel then sat down. Immediately the question that Christ asked His disciples hit him, **Who do you say I am** (*Matt.* 16:16). Instantly David knew he was in the presence of God. Echoing the words of St. Peter, he told Our Lord, **You are the Christ, the Son of the living God** (*Matt.* 16:17). For the next three hours he prayed from his heart. *It was at this time that I experienced mercy, compassion, relief and an energizing hope for my future. This was the moment that I began to say "yes" to God, to trust in Him. At the same time God was working to create a new direction in my life, to build my self-confidence.* This was the beginning of David's transformation. As he rose to leave, he found a pamphlet on the Chaplet of Divine Mercy in the pew.

Over the coming summer months he would attempt to pray daily at the chapel teaching himself the Chaplet and the rosary. Why? David points out that *although many Catholics are familiar with Eucharistic Chapels where Christ is exposed, it is important to realize that it is not just a chapel. It is a furnace of transformation where Christ is truly present. The same Christ that kings traveled hundreds of miles to witness His birth...the same Christ that raised Lazarus from the dead...the same Christ that crowds pushed in to catch a glimpse of...The same Christ that the sick woman reached out to touch His tassel so she could be healed. When she did so Jesus said,* **"Who touched me?...Someone touched Me; for I perceived that [healing] power had gone forth from me** (*Lk.*8:45-46). *And the woman who suffered from a bleeding condition for years was healed. This is the same Christ that touched my heart and began the healing process of my sin. When we kneel before the Blessed Sacrament we are thinking who we are but He tells us who we really are. He loves us so much that He wants to transform us. Because of this transformation I have learned to love my wife in a way I never knew existed.*

During my prayer time before the Holy Eucharist, despite the fact that I had broken every commandment, God made me realize that I had to get my marriage back in order. In an attempt to reconcile, David called Teresa wanting to talk to her but she would only talk about the children, not herself or their relationship. As his spiritual growth continued, David enlisted friends to intercede with Teresa but she was closed to their attempts.

Then one night when David called to talk about their relationship, instead of the usual rebuff Teresa was suddenly overcome by a feeling of peace and calm. *I told him that I would listen. He talked for two to three hours apologizing for everything he had done. He seemed to have changed. He asked if he could come over the next weekend to talk.. I told him he could come over but after the kids were in bed and not in the house. I did not want the children to see us together and have false expectations. So we talked outside on the patio. This time our conversation was deeper than at any time in our marriage. As we talked I thought, this is how marriage should be. We began dating again.*

By September I realized that we could make it as a married couple. Our pastor was somewhat skeptical of David's conversion and advised me to be cautious. We were remarried the following June. This time we made a commitment that this was forever.

Although I went to Sunday Mass, I really did not comprehend the Real Presence. David, the convert, was the catalyst for me to get to know my faith and fall in love with Jesus.

Through this experience I learned that without Christ we could not have a marriage relationship. The first year back together wasn't easy. Our old ways of being had to change. David had to learn how to become the head of the household and I had to become the heart. Teresa had to struggle to let go of controlling situations while David had to learn to take on the responsibilities of a husband and father.

It took two years before we were able to work through our issues and feel comfortable in our new roles. There's a healing process that takes time...that building of trust. If we didn't go through what we did, we wouldn't have the depth and richness of our marriage that we were suppose to have. I read a book entitled **How to Change Your Husband***. It's an excellent book but it actually explains how one has to really change oneself. I learned that how I act or react has an effect on my spouse. I could only change David by changing myself.*

Teresa learned that David and a friend were instrumental in

organizing and beginning a perpetual adoration chapel at St. Louis De Montfort Church. In time Teresa became the overall coordinator of the adorers at the Adoration Chapel. *Now people who have problems like we had have a place to go for help.* She gave up her job that paid twice what David was earning and became a stay-at-home mom. In addition to home schooling her children she coordinates the yearly Catholic Indiana Home Schooling Conference.

The impact of the marital struggle of the Gorsages has also positively impacted Teresa's family. *The crisis in our family has had a"trickle down effect" for the good. Before our [marital crisis] family members were lukewarm Catholics. Just by the example of living our faith with all its struggles has brought all my family members to a deeper faith.*

David, now a convert to the faith, is a successful vice president of a business training and development company as well as the founder of Civitas Dei, an organization for Catholic professionals. But his most important role is as the father of seven beautiful children. Should you have the pleasure of meeting the Gorsages you would never imagine their marriage had such a rocky beginning. They are the most delightful, devout, and devoted young couple. So you see, if one cooperates with the grace of God anything is possible!

Just in case you are tempted to think the Gorsages' marriage history is unique and could never be repeated, let me share with you a similar story, but from a non-Catholic perspective. To better understand this situation, let's refer to **Dominus Iesus** written by John Paul II, June 16, 2000. In this beautiful document the Pope explains, *The Church...has...an indispensable relationship with the salvation of every human being. For those who are not formally and visibly members of the Church "salvation in Christ is accessible by virtue of a grace, which, while having a mysterious relationship to the Church, does not make them formally part of the Church, but enlightens them in a way which is accommodated to their spiritual and material situation. This grace comes from Christ; it is the result of His sacrifice and is communicated by the Holy Spirit"; it has a relationship with the Church, which* *"according to the plan of the Father, has her origin in the mission of the Son and the Holy Spirit'* (Art. 79-82). Such is the case of Lorie and Dick.

Waiting for a doctor, I began chatting with his nurse. In the course of our conversation she told me about her three children. When asked how long she has been married, she proudly revealed *sixteen years.* Then her face clouded, *it hasn't all been smooth sailing. We've had our rocky moments.*

Lorie and Dick met racing cars out West. They married and moved to the Midwest. After their three children were born, Lorie felt that *something was missing from our lives. As I searched, I realized that "something" was God. So I joined a [Protestant] church. Although the children and I would go to church each Sunday, Dick always had an excuse why he couldn't accompany us. One week it was because he had to cut the grass, the next because he had to trim tree branches, etc. But each time he made an excuse to skip church, his Sunday did not go well. The lawnmower or saw would breakdown and he would spend the whole day trying to repair it.*

Dick, influenced by his fellow employees, began partying at night and on weekends while Lorie stayed home with the children. Tension mounted escalating into heated arguments. Something was wrong with her husband but Lorie did not know what. The stressful atmosphere in their home began to affect their four-year-old, Christopher, who began developing serious behavior problems. Lorie took Christopher first to a counselor, then to a psychologist who wanted to put him on medication, and finally to a homeopathic doctor who told her, *your son feels frightened and insecure. He's not sure what is going to happen to him and his family.*

As Lorie and her children were driving home from church on Christmas Day three years ago, she decided to confront her husband. *Something was wrong in our marriage and I had to know what it was.* When Lorie insisted that Dick tell her what was wrong, he broke down and confessed that he had been having an affair for the past three years with a fellow employee who was also bisexual. Lorie, heartbroken, agreed to give Dick another chance *only if Christ became the head of our household and my husband learned to become the head under Christ. We talked out our marital problems for a week. Besides agreeing to work on his spiritual life, he also promised to work on the other issues that concerned me. He explained that in the past he could not bring himself to go to church with me because he felt so guilty. He found it hard to even look at himself in the mirror. Now that everything was out in the open, he could ask my forgiveness and God's.*

Dick began going to church with Lorie, became involved in church activities and both were baptized eleven months later. *But that does not mean that everything was resolved immediately. It took time, about two years, for both of us to change and for me to begin to trust him again. This past year we have been the happiest we have ever been. Since spring my son is finally emotionally healed and no longer disruptive in school.*

Lorie concluded her story by saying, *Dick thinks that maybe we had to go through this so that we can help other couples in similar situations stay together. We are a living example that God can bring good out of evil. I can't believe I'm telling you this. I haven't told anyone our story.* Apparently God wanted Lorie to share her experience with you.

Remember, in God's plan for each of us there is a reason for everything that happens or occurs. It's usually only in retrospect that we understand the lessons God was teaching us.

The only way to be happy in love and marriage is to steadily grow in love of God. To grow in love of God, our faith needs to be continually growing and deepening. We can never slack off on "our pilgrimage to Our Father's house." The forces of the world, the flesh and the devil are like a terribly strong river current. This current threatens to destroy us through immorality, pornography, infidelity, divorce, adultery, abortion, and contraception. In striving for holiness we have to fight against the current like a salmon does trying to go upstream. If we stop, even for a minute, the current pushes us back into the world of decadence and misery. If we do not battle with consistency against the strong current we will be swept away from God and happiness forever. That is why our vocation to marriage needs a vibrant, growing, applied faith.

 *Additional Helps*

To learn more about marriage read:

✓ **Covenanted Happiness** by Fr. Cormac Burke (Ignatius Press)

✓ **Marriage Is Love Forever** by Fr. James Socias (Scepter Publishers)

✓ **Marriage, A Path To Sanctity** by Javier Abad and Eugenio Fenoy (Scepter Publishers)

✓ **About Marriage** by Fr. James Socias (Scepter Publishers)

✓ Listen to Marie Bellet's ballads on marriage, *What I Wanted To Say* Elm Street Records (615-353-7186).

✓ Read **Until Death Do Us Part** by Fr. Robert J. Fox and Fr. Charles Mangan of the Family Apostolate in Alexandria, South Dakota

✓ Listen to "Contraception, Why Not?" an audiotape by Janet E. Smith, Ph. D. One More Soul (1-800-307-7685).

✓ Listen to "John Paul II's Theology of the Body: The Foundation of the Culture of Life" an audiotape by Christopher West. Our Father's Will Communications (719-494-0566).

✓ Listen to the audiotape set by Drs. John & Lyn Billings, "Natural Family Planning," as well as *Humanae Vitae* by Pope Paul VI; "Selections from *Familiaris Consortio*" by John Paul II; "Life-Giving Love," by Bishop John Myers; "Humanae Vitae vs. The Contraceptive Mentality," by Bishop R. Kaffer; "Conjugal Love," by Dr. Daniel Hauser; "Human, Total, Fruitful, and Faithful Love," by Dr. Hauser, Steve & Rosemarie Rudolph, and Steve & Susan Aumann, available from R.B. Media, Inc.

✓ For more information on Natural Family Planning contact the Couple to Couple League (513) 471-2000 or www.ccli.org

✓ Read **Breast Cancer, Its Link to Abortion and the Birth Control Pill** by Chris Kahlenborn, MD, (One More Soul, 616 Five Oaks Avenue, Dayton, OH 45406).

✓ If you are having marital problems contact Retrouvaille at (800) 470-2230. They have a great success rate in healing marriages as well as reconciling divorced couples.

Chapter 3

What's So Important About Virtues?

"When we speak of virtues...we should always have before our eyes real men, concrete individuals. Virtue is not abstract, disconnected from ordinary life. On the contrary, it is deeply rooted in life itself; it springs from life and forms it. Virtue affects man's life, actions and behavior. One can deduce that in all these reflections, we are speaking not so much about virtue as about an individual who lives and acts 'virtuously': we are referring to a person who is prudent, just, and brave."

John Paul II[1]

After wrestling control of the crumbling, pagan Roman Empire from his rival, Constantine became the first Christian Emperor. Immediately he mandated that his government be based on virtue and loyalty. Constantine wisely understood that without virtue, his government would have no permanent foundation. He even insisted that his nobles and his guard *practice chastity when carrying out their court duties.*[2] This

---

[1] John Paul II, Allocution, November 22, 1978.
[2] *The Church of Apostles and Martyrs, Op. Cit.*, p.441.

was mandated even before his baptism as a Christian.

John Adams, one of the Founding Fathers of the U.S. and the second President of the United States, was known for his love of virtue and virtuous people. He described his father in his diary as *the honestest man. In wisdom, piety, benevolence and charity in proportion to his education and sphere of life, I have never known his superior.* He called President George Washington a *virtuous man.* Samuel Adams, another Founding Father and a cousin, he labeled as being of *steadfast integrity* as well as having a *universal good character.*

But virtues were to be lived, not just admired in others. In a letter to his wife, Abigail, he counseled her to teach their children virtues: *Let frugality and industry be our virtues. Fire them [our children] with ambition to be useful.* He himself was labeled as honest, a man of integrity, a man who lived chastely. He lived the virtues of friendship, patience, optimism, cheerfulness, industriousness, self-control, temperance and fortitude well. In fact, when the English governor of Massachusetts offered Adams a high government position guaranteed to bring him wealth and prestige he turned it down out of principle. Although ambitious, Adams no longer believed that England had the right to rule the Colonies so he refused to be part of their government. Daily he worked to *conquer my natural pride and conceit,* which he felt was his main defect, along with his shyness. John Adams believed that *[t]he preservation of liberty depends upon the intellectual and moral character of the people.*[3] Like Constantine, Adams firmly believed *happiness derived from virtue[.] [T]hat form of government with virtue as its foundation was more likely than any other to promote the general happiness.*[4] This answers the question *Does character count?* Yes, very much so.

His wife, Abigail, also knew the value of virtuous people. She wrote to her husband, *You tell me of degrees of perfection to which human nature is capable of arriving and I believe it, but at*

---

[3] David McCullough, *John Adams* (NY:Simon & Schuster, 2001) p. 71. All quotes attributed to John Adams are from this book.

[4] *Ibid.,* p. 102.

the same time lament that our admiration should arise from the scarcity of the instances.[5] She had been taught by her parents to only talk about topics, not about people. If she did talk about people she was only to say *handsome things.*

On his way to the Continental Congress, Adams wrote to Abigail, *God Almighty grant us wisdom and virtue sufficient for the high trust that is devolved upon us.*[6] When working on the structure for the new government he insisted that the judiciary branch be filled with men of *exemplary morals.*

Thomas Jefferson, the author of the U.S. Declaration of Independence, was not only a brilliant man but was likewise a virtuous man despite attempts to blacken his name.[7] Jefferson was known for his courtesy, politeness, and self-control. To a grandchild he explained, *when I hear another express an opinion which is not mine, I say to myself, he has a right to his opinion, as I to mine.* At another time he counseled, *Be a listener only, keep within yourself, and endeavor to establish with yourself the habit of silence, especially in politics.*[8]

In addition to other virtues, former President Ronald Reagan was taught optimism and cheerfulness by his mother. *She showed him the importance of never letting real-life problems destroy his ideals. Rather, the ideal supplies a standard of hope and of measurement to which he should always aspire.*[9] He was also taught not to complain. No one ever knew when he felt sick or was sick.

The virtues we have described above are the natural virtues. St. Anthony of Padua links the natural and supernatural virtues: *The man who is filled with the Holy Spirit speaks in different*

---

[5] *Ibid.,* p. 101.

[6] *Ibid.,* p. 25.

[7] Robert F. Turner, "The Truth About Jefferson," *The Wall Street Journal*, July 3, 2001.

[8] *John Adams, Op.Cit.,* p. 113.

[9] Dinesh D'Souza, *Ronald Reagan, How An Ordinary Man Became an Extraordinary Leader* (New York: Simon & Schuster, 1997) p.39

languages. These different languages are different ways of witnessing to Christ, such as humility, poverty, patience and obedience; we speak in those languages when we reveal in ourselves these virtues to others. Actions speak louder than words; let your words teach and your actions speak. We are full of words but empty of actions, and therefore, are cursed by the Lord, since He Himself cursed the fig tree when He found no fruit but only leaves.[10]

Happiness depends on sanctity, which in turn is dependent upon our spiritual maturity. Spiritual maturity is achieved by:

✓ Acquiring God's grace;
✓ Growth in the theological and moral virtues (faith, hope, charity, prudence, justice, fortitude, and temperance), which are infused at Baptism and Confirmation;
✓ Corresponding to the gifts of the Holy Spirit (wisdom, understanding, counsel, fortitude, knowledge, piety and fear of the Lord);
✓ Developing human maturity through the acquisition of human (natural) virtues.

What happens if we lack virtues? We fall into vices, which are sins. What happens when we sin? *Since by sinning man refuses to submit to God, his internal balance is also destroyed and it is precisely within himself that contradictions and conflicts arise. Wounded in this way, man almost inevitably causes damage to the fabric of his relationship with others and with the created world.*[11]

The more virtues we acquire through the repetition of good habits the less damage we cause to all our relationships, especially our relationship with our spouse, children and extended family. As Fr. Peter Cameron, O.P., writes in the August, 2001 *Magnifcat: The virtues transform our psychological capacities and shape our character. Virtue overcomes what is incomplete and unfinished in us...and in the process, virtue displaces our otherwise tyrannical inclination to sin.* Virtuous people are happy, joyful people who

---

[10] Sermon I, 225.

[11] John Paul II, *Reconciliation and Penance* (Boston: St. Paul Books & Media, 1984) p. 35.

establish happy marriages that in turn produce happy children. Praying for virtues or wishing for them does not make them suddenly appear in our actions or lives. Human virtues are acquired in the same way one acquires any skill—by constant practice. For instance, to develop the virtue of fortitude (the strength to carry on despite difficulties) one must seek out the means to exercise this virtue. A timid person may fear speaking up in defense of the Church at a cocktail party, or to confront his child's teacher who is teaching doctrines contrary to the Magisterium. Should that person overcome his fear by forcing himself to speak out, there is some growth in the virtue of fortitude. On the other hand, if this same person is asked to give a talk or make a difficult phone call but refuses, out of fear, the virtue of fortitude is diminished. Furthermore, our timid person was given the opportunity by God to grow in the virtue but he refused.

Growth in all the virtues must be steady, consistent and ongoing. We cannot say we possess a certain virtue until we continuously act in a virtuous manner in that area. The graces we receive through our prayers and the reception of the sacraments give us the spiritual strength to go "against the grain," to practice the virtues. We also have the obligation to seek out situations or permit ourselves to accept circumstances that will stretch us in the practice of the virtues.

In *The Spiritual Combat,* written in 1589, Father Lawrence Scupoli explains how to develop the virtues: *Every duty must be performed with the greatest fervor and exactness, and you must on all occasions be habituated to the practice of every virtue. Embrace, therefore, any opportunity to advance towards perfection and sanctity, especially such as are difficult; for such efforts are most effective in forming virtuous habits in the souls within a short time. And love those who furnish you with such opportunities.*[12]

It cannot be emphasized enough that virtues, like muscles, must be continuously exercised or they are lost. Fr. Scupoli insists: *The moment we cease performing acts of virtue, our inclinations,*

---

[12] Rev. Lawrence Scupoli, *The Spiritual Combat* (NY:Paulist Press, 1978) p.105.

naturally prone to ease and pleasures of the senses, raise in us disordered appetites which overthrow or at least weaken our virtuous habits. This is to say nothing of the loss, through such neglect, of countless graces which we might have merited by a constant application to our spiritual advancement.[13]

Be vigilant, therefore, that you overlook no opportunity of acquiring a virtue, and sedulously guard yourself against the common fault of avoiding what is contrary to the inordinate affections of our nature, since it is by combating them that we rise to heroic virtue.

Rather, accustom yourself to the person you find most disagreeable, and to the task you find most irksome, for there is no other way of acquiring habitual patience.

If any employment, by its very nature, its author, or its contrariety to your inclinations, is the source of personal discomfort, be sure not to give it up on any of these accounts; show your courage, not only in cheerfully accepting the situation, but in persevering in it despite the vexations that arise and the satisfaction you would derive in quitting it.[14]

Briefly let's consider the three theological virtues: faith, hope and charity. **Faith** is the virtue that enables us ***to distinguish good from evil, and no longer to be like storm-tossed sailors, driven before the wind of each new doctrine that human subtlety, human skill in fabricating lies, may propound*** (*Eph*.4:14). Catholicism is a mystery taken on faith. With our finite minds we cannot humanly comprehend all the teachings of the Church. That is why God, in His goodness and mercy, infuses our souls with the virtue of faith. **Hope** is the virtue that keeps us free from fears, serene and firm in the midst of contradictions or obstacles. St. Paul tells us that **charity** (love), the source of all virtues, is the ***bond which makes us perfect*** (*Col*. 3:14). This virtue produces selflessness, truth, generosity, understanding, kindness, and flexibility.

---

[13] *Ibid.*, p.112.
[14] *Ibid.*, pp.114-115.

Next to consider are the four infused moral virtues—**prudence, justice, fortitude** and **temperance.** **Prudence** enables us to think or act in a Christ-like manner. *Brethren, do not be children in your thinking; be babes in evil, but in thinking be mature* (I Cor. 14:20.) *Forsake childishness, and live, and walk by the ways of prudence* (Prov. 9:6). **Justice** must govern our actions towards God and those we deal with. **Fortitude** gives us the ability to cope despite the fact that *in all things we suffer tribulation, but we are not distressed; we are sore pressed, but we are not destitute; we endure persecution, but we are not forsaken; we are cast down, but we do not perish; always bearing about in our body the dying of Jesus, so that the life also of Jesus may be made manifest in our bodily frame. For we, the living, are constantly being handed over to death for Jesus' sake, that the life also of Jesus may be made manifest in our mortal flesh* (2 Cor. 4:8-12). **Temperance** controls or modifies our senses and appetites.

The Unity Of Body And Soul

Possessing human virtues is necessary but Blessed Escrivá warns: *What a sorry state someone is in when he has marvelous human virtues but a total lack of supernatural outlook, because he will apply those virtues quite easily to his own selfish ends. Meditate upon this.*[15] Strangely, sanctity is fine for others...but not for us. Why? Is it because it may make us appear odd or different? Do we fear that our friends may avoid us? Or can it be we fear the effort? What a foolish attitude! *The supernatural order not only does not in the least destroy the natural order, but elevates the natural and perfects it, each offering mutual aid to the other and complementing it in a manner proportioned to its respective nature and dignity. [Man, elevated by grace, is] a soul united to a body in the unity of nature, in all his faculties, natural and supernatural.*[16]

---

[15] *Furrow, Op. Cit.,* #427.
[16] Pius XI, *Divini illius magistri,* December 31, 1929.

The graces of baptism build upon our human nature. God the Father told St. Catherine of Siena, and through her us: *your soul has been given such power that neither the devil or any other creature can steal it without the will's consent, for in holy baptism the will was armed with a knife that is love of virtue and hatred of sin...So you have this knife for your free will to use, while you have time to uproot the thorns of deadly sin and to plant the virtues...[Y]ou must first rouse yourself to heartfelt contrition, contempt for sin, and love for virtue. Otherwise you will not have done your part to be fit to be joined as branches to the vine that is My only-begotten Son...[When] joined and engrafted to this vine...you will produce much fruit, because you will share the vital sap of the vine.*[17]

Next, the graces of confirmation refine our human nature even more. With this wealth of graces we can lead a divine life. We can perform supernatural acts. When we are in the state of grace, St. Paul reminds us: ***...you are not in the flesh, you are in the Spirit, if the Spirit of God really dwells in you*** (Rom. 8:9). Yes, growing in holiness will affect your personality, actions, and priorities...but only for the better. Look how crowds surge around, vie to speak to people who radiate Christ. On the other hand *so many people...call themselves Christians because they have been baptized and have received other sacraments, but then prove to be disloyal and deceitful, insincere and proud, and...they fail to achieve anything. They are like shooting stars, lighting up the sky for an instant and then falling away to nothing...*[18] *Union with God, supernatural virtue, always brings with it the attractive practice of human virtues.*[19] Why settle for being mediocre when you can become a saint?

As we spiritually and emotionally mature, we become more objective. We view events in a realistic manner. We work within our limitations. We know what we have to do and how to go about doing it. There is a feeling of confidence and security, as well as, responsibility for our actions. We easily adapt to circumstances

---

[17] Suzanne Noffke, O.P., *Catherine of Siena, The Dialogue.*

[18] Blessed Josemaría Escrivá, *Friends Of God* (NY: Scepter, 1981) #75.

[19] *Furrow, Op. Cit.,* #566.

without being rigid or whiny. We know when to give in and when to stand firm. A mature person contributes to the common good. He is patient, docile, diligent, prompt, reflective, understanding, and balanced. The immature person is rigid, stubborn, foolish, insolent, irresponsible, insecure, arrogant, haughty, frivolous, and lacks commitment.

To reach spiritual maturity, besides personal effort, each of us needs guidance because *sin has diminished man, blocking his path to fulfillment*[20]. To be receptive to spiritual direction/guidance through a spiritual director or confessor, one must develop the virtue of humility. One husband, we know, thinks it's wonderful when his wife goes on retreat because *she is simply great when she comes home.* But he is unwilling to go on retreat himself because *he* may have to *change.* Proud people resist spiritual direction because they already think they are perfect. If this is our thinking, it's time to grow up spiritually. St. Paul stresses: ***When I was a child, I spoke like a child, I thought like a child, I reasoned like a child; when I became a man, I gave up childish ways*** (*I Cor.* 13:11). Sanctity is not for wimps. Christ points out: ***The kingdom of heaven has been enduring violent assault, and the violent have been seizing it by force*** (*Mt.* 11:12). Unless we are doing violence to our vices we will not achieve heaven.

While we have to give up childish ways to grow in spiritual maturity, we are spiritually children of God. Blessed Escrivá explains: *Spiritual childhood demands submission of the mind, which is harder than submission of the will. In order to subject our mind we need not only God's grace, but a continual exercise of our will as well, denying the intellect over and over again, just as it says "no" to the flesh. And so we have the paradox that whoever wants to follow this "little way" in order to become a child, needs to add strength and manliness to his will.*[21] St. Paul adds: ***But we exhort you, brethren, to do so more and more, to aspire to live quietly, to mind your own affairs, and to work with your hands, as we charged you*** (*1 Thess.* 4:10-11).

---

[20] Second Vatican Council, Pastoral Constitution *Gaudium et spes*, no. 13.

[21] *The Way, Op. Cit.,* #856

Human virtues can be acquired without supernatural grace, but why make something difficult even harder to do? Besides, without grace the human virtues are not rooted but in a state of continued flux depending on our emotional or spiritual highs or lows. Since we are composed of body and soul, God sanctifies us by two means—His grace and our human effort, both of which are complimentary. St. Augustine explains: *God, who created you without your help, will not save you without it.*[22] Vatican II documents urge us to *practice moral and social virtues and foster them in social living. Then, under the necessary help of divine grace, there will arise a generation of new men, the molders of a new humanity.*[23] Why? *A saint keeps watch over his country and obtains its salvation. His prayers and virtues are more powerful than all the armies in the world,* insists St. Peter Julian Eymard.[24] This is the will of God for you and your children. This will trigger the new evangelization that John Paul II desires.

Scripture is filled with points related to virtue. St. Paul stresses the importance of industriousness bluntly: *[I]f anyone man will not work, neither let him eat (1 Thess.* 4:10-11). Paul also teaches that one's labor should be used not only for financial support but also as a means to do charity: *You yourselves know that these hands of mine have provided for my needs and those of my companions. In all things I have shown you that by so toiling you ought to help the weak and remember the word of the Lord Jesus, that He Himself said, "It is more blessed to give than to receive"* (*Acts* 20:24-25).

Jesus criticizes bad manners when he tells Simon the Pharisee, *I came into your house; you gave me no water for my feet...You gave me no kiss...You did not anoint my head with oil...*(*Lk.* 7:44-66). Manners and refinement are important virtues. Christ expects us through virtuous living to adhere, not only to the letter of the law, but also the spirit: *But I say to you that everyone who is angry with his brother shall be liable to judgment...and whoever says, "You fool!" shall be liable*

---

[22] St. Augustine, *Sermon* 169.

[23] Second Vatican Council, Pastoral Constitution, *Gaudium et spes,* #30.

[24] *The Real Presence, Op. Cit.,* p.22.

to the fire of Gehenna. And you have heard that it was said..."you shall not commit adultery." But I say to you that anyone who so much as looks with lust at a woman has already committed adultery with her in his heart (Mt 5:21-28).

Christ expects us to be sincere in our speech: **But let your speech be, "yes, yes"; "No, no"; and whatever is beyond these comes from the evil one** (Matt. 5:37). He even educates His disciples in the principles of sound judgment when they ask him whose sin caused the man to be blind, his parents or himself? **Neither has this man sinned, nor his parents, but the works of God were to be made manifest in him** (Matt. 5:37).

The crowds talked about Christ, saying, **He has done all things well** (Mk. 7:37). As followers of Christ, the people we deal with should say the same thing about us. *We have to act in such a way that others will be able to say, when they meet us: this man is a Christian, because he does not hate, because he is willing to understand, because he is not a fanatic, because he is willing to make sacrifices, because he shows that he is a man of peace, because he knows how to love.*[25]

The Major Human Virtues

The four main human virtues are called cardinal virtues, which means, "hinge." All of the other virtues "hinge" on the development of these four. The cardinal virtues are **prudence, justice, fortitude** and **temperance.** There is so much to learn about each of these virtues but our discussion here will be limited to how they impact marriage and family life. These virtues will be further developed in *Raise Happy Children...Teach Them Virtues.* Under each cardinal virtue, I will also name some of the other virtues that "hinge" on to that specific cardinal virtue.

Prudence is the first cardinal virtue since it helps us to find truth. Without truth one cannot make prudent decisions so it is a critical virtue needed for marriage and raising children.

---

[25] Blessed Josemaria Escrivá, *Christ Is Passing By* (NY: Scepter, 1982) #122.

St. Augustine writes that *prudence is the science of what should be sought after and what should be avoided.*[26]   St. Thomas Aquinas adds: *The role of prudence is to imbue our conduct with right reason, which requires an upright will...Prudence is right reason applied to human conduct.*[27]

The Holy Father completes the definition: *The prudent man, eager for what is truly good, strives to measure everything, situations and actions, according to the standard of moral good.*

A widespread belief considers a person prudent if he knows how to go through life obtaining maximum profit for himself. But this is not the case: the prudent person orders his life according to the voice of an upright conscience and the demands of morality. Thus, prudence becomes the key for each one to carry out the task he has received from God: the perfecting of man himself.[28]

Three stages lead to a prudent decision:

✓ Knowledge—To make a decision one must clearly understand the objective reality of the issue along with the moral implications involved in the decision. We arrive at objective reality through study, reflection on our past experiences and the advice of prudent, well-formed advisors. **Do nothing without counsel, and then you need have no regrets (Sir. 32:24).**

✓ Judgment—Next we must make a practical judgment about the morality of our anticipated action and how we plan to carry it out.

✓ Action—Our will has to decide to carry out the action or refrain from the action promptly. (A prudent person does not hem and haw but acts after reflection.)

These three stages are part of the acquired virtue of prudence. In addition, Christians rely on grace to help them make prudent decisions. The infused virtue of prudence is able to build on the acquired virtue of prudence so that our decisions lead us toward holiness.

A truly prudent person is ever attentive to God's promptings

---

[26] St. Augustine, *De diversis quaestionibus* 83, q. 61.
[27] St. Thomas quinas, *S.Th.,* II-II, q. 47, a.4, a.8.
[28] John Paul II, Address, October 25, 1978.

and, by his vigilant listening, receives in his soul that promise and reality of salvation: **I glorify thee, Father, Lord of heaven and earth, for having hidden these things from the wise and prudent and revealed them to little ones** (*Matt.* 11:25).[29]

Prudent actions are not based on "feelings" but on a sound moral foundation built on the natural law. *[D]eep within his conscience man discovers a law which he has not laid upon himself but which he must obey. Its voice, ever calling him to love and to do what is good and to avoid evil, tells him inwardly at the right moment: do this, shun that.*[30] Unfortunately, our conscience may be poorly formed due to influences from our pagan culture, the weight of our own sinfulness or faulty moral education. *To be prudent the first step is to acknowledge our own limitations. This is the virtue of humility. We admit that in certain matters we cannot cover everything, that in so many cases we cannot take in all the circumstances that have to be weighed to make a fair judgment. So, we look for advice; but not from just anyone. We go to a person with the right qualities, to someone who wants to love God as sincerely as we do and who tries to follow Him faithfully. It is not enough to ask just anyone their opinion. We must go to a person who can give us sound and disinterested advice.*[31]

Seeking the counsel of a spiritually well-formed person should not be reserved for just major decisions but also in regard to books, magazines, newspapers, television, movies, plays and other forms of entertainment we wish to read or view. To attend plays or movies without checking them out is imprudent. Just as we would not drink poison because it will harm us, reading suggestive, immoral material or watching certain forms of entertainment can likewise harm us by destroying our morality and faith. Fr. John Hardon, S.J. asserted *what you memorize literally becomes part of your brain.* As you unconsciously memorize what you see, it sticks in your mind like glue subtly undermining your morals, at other times triggering temptations.

---

[29] *Friends Of God, Op. Cit.,* no. 87.

[30] *Gaudium et Spes, Op. Cit.,* no. 16.

[31] *Friends Of God, Op. Cit.,* no.86.

A component of the virtue of prudence is **consistency**. Our judgment cannot fluctuate according to our mood or circumstance. The fathers of Vatican II stressed that human maturity *is chiefly attested to by a certain stability of character, the ability to make carefully weighed decisions, and a sound judgment of events and people.*[32] But as Bl. Escrivá reminds us: *A person who does not choose, with complete freedom, an upright code of conduct, sooner or later ends up being manipulated by others. He will lead a lazy, parasitic existence, at the mercy of what others decide.*

The indecisive and irresolute person is like putty at the mercy of circumstances. Anyone and anything can mold him according to whim, especially his passions and the worst tendencies of his nature wounded by sin.

Other habits that are part of prudence are **caution** and **circumspection.** These help us to avoid rash decisions and to see the possible repercussions of our action. They help us to gather necessary facts before making a decision—as when a person looks both ways before crossing the street.

Truly prudent people are prepared to change their mind when considering an action. Stubbornness is a vice, not a virtue. *Prudence as a rule demands that we come to a suitable decision, and promptly. Though at times it is prudent to delay a decision until all the factors that should influence our judgment have been brought together, on other occasions it would be very imprudent not to begin to carry out immediately what we see needs to be done. This is especially true when the good of others is at stake...A person is prudent not because he never makes a mistake, but because he corrects his errors. He shows his prudence in preferring to miss the mark twenty times rather than give in to an easygoing "do-nothing" attitude. He won't rush into things foolishly or behave with absurd rashness. He will run the risk of his decisions. Fear of failure will not make him give up in his effort to do good. As we go through life we find ourselves coming across people who are objective and know how to weigh things, who don't get heated or try to tip the balance in their favor. Almost instinctively, we find*

---

[32] Second Vatican Council, Decree *Optatam Totius*, no. 11.

ourselves trusting such people, because, unassumingly and quietly,
they always act in a good and upright manner.[33]

The Holy Father also speaks of the importance of prudence:
Am I prudent? Do I live consistently and responsibly? Is my life
in service of authentic good? Does it further the salvation that
Christ and His Church want for us? If today a student, a son or
daughter, is listening to me, consider for a moment your
schoolwork, classes, interests, pastimes, friendships. If a father
or a mother is listening, consider your commitments as a spouse
and parent. If a politician or statesman is listening, consider your
duties and responsibilities. Do you seek the true good of society, of
your country, and all humanity? Or only partial or sectarian
interests? If a journalist is listening, or anyone who influences
public opinion, reflect on the value and aim of your influence.[34]

As you can see, our will must be directed by prudent judgments.
But we must avoid the **prudence of the flesh** that St. Paul
condemns (**Rom.** 8:6). This vice puts off good actions and deeds
out of fear or laziness. We may not want to upset our spouse,
child, relative or friend. A common example I run into a lot is
fear of suggesting that dying family members be anointed. Rather
than giving the person on his deathbed all the spiritual helps
available, the dying are left without spiritual consolation because
no one wants to *hurt somebody's feelings* or frighten the person.
Fallen away Catholics are left in error because we *don't want to*
offend them by encouraging them to come back to the Church.
This is when prudence wedded to fortitude (courage) is needed.

Many times prudence means we must be daring. *"Tomorrow!"*
Sometimes it is prudence; many times it is the adverb of the
defeated.[35] *There is a false kind of prudence (cunning would be a*
better name for it) at the service of the selfishness and expert in
using the best means to achieve warped ends. Here cleverness and
perspicacity only serve to worsen one's dispositions and to bring
upon oneself the reproach St. Augustine said in one of his sermons:

---

[33] *Friends Of God, Op. Cit.* no.86, no.88.

[34] John Paul II, Address, October 25, 1978.

[35] *The Way, Op. Cit.,* no. 251.

*"Are you trying to bend the heart of God, which is always upright, so that it may fall in with your own perversity?" (**Enarr**. in Ps 63:18) This is the false prudence of the person who thinks his own efforts are quite sufficient to save him. **"Do not seek to consider yourselves prudent,"** (**Rom**. 12:16) says St. Paul, **"for it is written, I will destroy the wisdom of the wise and the prudence of the prudent** (1 Cor 1:19)."*[36]

Consider this example of prudence exhibited by St. John Vianney's mother. French priests were compelled by the civil constitution of 1791 to take a schismatic oath. The parish priest of Dardilly, the town in which the Vianneys lived, out of fear took the oath. A visiting relative was shocked to see the Vianneys still attending Mass at their parish. *"What are you doing?" she exclaimed, "all good priests have refused the oath, and in consequence are being hunted and persecuted and driven into exile. Happily at Ecully we still have some good priests. It is to these you must go. By taking the oath your new parish priest has separated himself from the Catholic Church; he is not your true shepherd and you cannot make yourselves his abettors."*

This staggering revelation drove Mms. Vianney almost frantic. She did not hesitate to speak to the unfortunate priest, reproaching him with having severed himself from the true Church. When she reminded him of the saying of the Gospel that the branch that is cut off from the vine shall be cast into the fire, the priest owned to the truth of her words: "True, madam, the vine is better than the branch."[37] The Vianneys attended Mass elsewhere.

How is prudence lived in marriage? One of the goals of marriage is to help our spouse and children win eternity with God. The Holy Spirit tells us: *To him who conquers I will grant to eat of the tree of life, which is in the paradise of God (Rev.2:7).* To conquer means to eradicate our defects and failings. If we lack prudence, there is a tendency to cover-up the defects of self, spouse and children. Why? If one knows the truth, one must react, which in turn will cause suffering. People do not like to

---

[36] *Friends Of God*, no. 85.

[37] Abbe Francis Trochu, *The Cure D'Ars*, (Rockford: Tan Books and Publishers, Inc.1977) p. 12.

suffer. Laziness, which we talked about before, is also involved in not wanting to do some good or to learn the truth.

Prudence also prevents one from making rash judgments or holding certain prejudices toward our spouse such as thinking the wife is not an intellectual or the husband lacks religious faith. When one possesses prudence, rather than labeling one's spouse, one will help the other to develop talents and abilities.

Prudence is also active in intuition. What is happening in regard to a particular situation within our marriage? Within our family? How can the situation be resolved? For example, there may be a concern that our marriage is not deepening. A prudent study of the problem on how to improve the marriage relationship may be to join a marriage enrichment course or read and discuss books on the topic of marriage.

Wisdom of the heart guides and governs many other virtues. Through prudence, a man learns to be daring without being rash. He will not make excuses (based on hidden motives of indolence) to avoid the effort involved in living wholeheartedly according to God's plans. The temperance of the prudent man is not insensitive or misanthropic; his justice is not harsh nor is his patience servile... **"The prudent heart shall possess knowledge"** (Prov. 18:15) *the knowledge of God's love, the definitive knowledge, the knowledge that can save us, that brings to all men peace and understanding and, to each soul, eternal life.*[38]

Justice

The second cardinal virtue, **justice**, is defined as giving each person his fair due...beginning with God. To be just is to render to God His due, which is reverence and piety. *By prayer...man gives God the greatest glory possible. Prayer is man's greatest virtue. All virtues are comprised in it, for all the virtues are a preparation for it and a part of it. Faith believes, hope prays, and charity begs in order to give to others; humility of heart forms the prayer, confidence speaks it, and perseverance triumphs over God*

---

[38] *Friends Of God,* no. 87, no. 88.

Himself, contends St. Peter Eymard.[39]

St. Paul reminds us of man's failing in this regard: ***...although they knew God, they did not honor Him as God or give thanks to Him, but they became futile in their thinking and their senseless minds were darkened*** (**Rom.** 1:20). *[T]hose who willfully try to drive God from their heart and avoid all questions about religion, not following the biddings of their conscience, are not free from blame*[40] since it is natural for man to acknowledge his Creator.

The virtue of **religion**, which is not only to be practiced by Christians, is the virtue that leads us to acknowledge our dependence on God and to worship Him. *[T]he worse and most ungrateful injustice is to deny our Creator and Redeemer the recognition of the abundant and wonderful gifts He has given us. If you are really striving to be just, you will often reflect on your utter dependence upon God.*[41] When we ignore our obligations towards God the effect impacts all other aspects of justice. *[W]hen [man] fails to acknowledge his dependence on God...he inevitably ends up going astray. His heart claims to be the sole measure of reality...[H]is will no longer recognizes the law inscribed in his heart by his Creator* (**Rom.** 7:23), *and he ceases to pursue the good. Seeing himself as the final arbiter of both truth and error, he imagines these to be equally elusive, and thus deceives himself. In this way, the spiritual dimension of reality fades from his experience, and as a result, his ability to discern what is mystery as well.*[42]

To live justice towards God means to give Him priority in our hierarchy of goals. What He wills for our lives comes first—be it frequent confession, Sunday Mass, a retreat, daily Mass, daily mental prayer, adoration, or other opportunities to grow closer to Him. This also pertains to our children. If we allow sports or the hobbies of our children to come before their obligations toward

---

[39] *The Real Presence,* Op. Cit., p.13

[40] Vatican II, *Gaudium et spes*, no. 19.

[41] *Friends Of God*, no. 167.

[42] John Paul II, Address, October 26, 1983.

God, it is a sin against justice. Likewise, if we compromise with error in regard to religious matters, we sin against justice. The saints made their contemporaries uncomfortable by their uncompromising loyalty to God...and so must we.

Also linked to justice is the virtue of **piety**, which refers to the honor we owe to our parents and lawful authority. *You that are younger be subject to the elders* (*1 Pet.* 5:5).

Patriotism is part of the virtue piety. *Love your own country: it is a Christian virtue to be patriotic. But if patriotism becomes nationalism, which leads you to look at other people, at other countries, with indifference, with scorn, without Christian charity and justice, then it is a sin.*[43] Patriotism is so important to God that He sent St. Joan of Arc, a seventeen-year-old peasant girl, to save France. Her country's enemies killed her.

Justice means to render good toward others. In fact, the depth of our love of God is measured by the quality of our justice towards others. To live this virtue one cannot be a loner or anti-social. To live the virtue of justice well, we have to practice the virtues of **charity**, **truthfulness**, **honesty**, **naturalness**, **sincerity**, **loyalty**, **gratitude**, **optimism**, and **love for freedom**.

Isaiah bluntly reminds us: *When you spread forth your hands, I will hide my eyes from you; even though you make many prayers, I will not listen; your hands are full of blood. Wash yourselves; make yourselves clean; remove the evil of your doings from before My eyes; cease to do evil, learn to do good; seek justice, correct oppression; defend the fatherless, plead for the widow* (*Is.* 1:15-17). St. James is equally sharp: *Your riches have rotted and your garments are moth-eaten. Your gold and silver have rusted...Behold, the wages of the laborers who mowed your fields, which you kept back by fraud, cry out; and the cries of the harvesters have reached the ears of the Lord of hosts* (*Jas.*5:2-4). Vatican II insisted that as Christians we must not only foster justice in the world but also live it. *[We] should also hold in high esteem the*

---

[43] *Furrow, Op. Cit.,* no. 315.

virtues related to social behavior such as honesty and a sense of justice.[44]

St. Thomas Aquinas, understanding human nature so well, observed: *It is not enough to wish to observe justice for the time being in some particular affair; indeed scarcely anybody could be found who wills to act unjustly in every case. What is required, however, is that a man has the will to preserve justice permanently and in all cases.*[45] St. Thomas More comes to mind as a perfect example of constancy in the virtue of justice. He gave his life to live it perfectly.

There are four types of justice: **commutative justice, distributive justice, social/legal justice,** and **penal justice. Commutative justice** obliges us to be fair in transactions and contracts in addition to all of our daily dealings with people at work, in society, and within the family. Employers are obliged to pay a fair wage and treat employees with dignity. They are to provide them with the help they need to discharge their job. In justice, employees must give a full day's work for a full day's pay. The virtue of **industriousness** is part of justice. Taking supplies for personal use from work without permission is unjust. Students are obligated by justice to work hard, study, and successfully complete the course work paid for by the sacrifices of their parents and the citizens of the state. Students tend to forget that their public education is mostly funded by the taxes of complete strangers. They are obligated to give back, in some way, what they have received. By taking one's course work seriously a person can better serve his family, Church, state, and country in the future.

Attached to commutative justice are the virtues of **sincerity** or **veracity**, which means truthfulness in all we do and say. Misleading people or telling lies, even if they are "white lies" is wrong. St. Thomas reminds us that *men live in society, which*

---

[44] Second Vatican Council, Decr. *Apostolicam actuositatem,* no. 4; cf. Decr. *Presbyterorum ordinis,* no. 3; Decr. *Optatem totius,* no. 11.

[45] St. Thomas, *S. Th.* II-II, p. 58, a. 1-3.

would not be possible if they did not speak the truth to one another.[46] Sincerity and truthfulness are part of the foundation for marriage. A marriage built on the lies of one or both spouses will soon collapse. *I cannot believe in your truthfulness if you feel no uneasiness—a disagreeable uneasiness too—when you countenance the smallest and most harmless lie. It is far from being small or harmless for it is an offense against God.*[47]

When we hurt another in any way, justice requires that we say, *"I'm sorry!"* Have the humility to admit that you were wrong, that you erred. The stronger one's pride, the harder it is to say *I'm sorry.* If the words are too difficult to say, write them in a note to the injured party. If it's your spouse, pin the note on his or her pillow, or simply hand your spouse the note. If you injured or hurt a friend or other family member but lack the courage to call and apologize, send a card with a personal note saying that you are sorry.

Friendship also plays a part in the virtue of justice. To cultivate friends requires the virtues of **loyalty**, **humility**, **generosity**, **politeness**, **kindness**, **spirit of service**, **thoughtfulness,** and **cheerfulness**. It is a giving of oneself in a disinterested manner to another. It is also a way to practice charity. Unfortunately the difference between a "friend" and "an acquaintance" has become blurred. A friendship is based on affection based on getting to know one another. It leads each person to share himself or herself with the other. A friend is one in whom we confide our joys and sorrows; someone we can call on for advice or in time of need. An acquaintance is simply someone we know. Friendship means availability, sacrifice, and love. Without sacrifice there can be no friendship. Cheerfulness is important in all relationships but especially in regard to friendship. Remember, *true virtue is not sad or disagreeable, but pleasantly cheerful.*[48] It wearies the soul to have to continually work to lift another's spirits. Our best friend should be our spouse.

---

[46] St. Thomas, *In duo praecepta caritatis et in decem praecepta decalogi.*

[47] *Furrow, Op. Cit.,* no. 577.

[48] *The Way, Op. Cit., no. 657.*

Generosity is also part of the virtue of justice. *Mine, mine, mine, is the way many people think and talk and act. How unpleasant an attitude this is...It is pride that constantly makes people think: mine, mine, mine. It is a vice that makes men sterile and fruitless. It destroys their keenness to work for God and leads them to waste their time. As for you, don't lose your effectiveness; instead, trample on your selfishness. You think your life is for yourself? Your life is for God, for the good of all men, through your love for our Lord. Dig up that buried talent! Make it yield.*[49]

Generosity was practiced by all the saints and by most of the parents of saints. The grandfather of St. John Vianney, Pierre Vianney, was known for his charity toward the poor. Each evening beggars gathered at his home for their evening meal, for clothing and a place to sleep. Among them one night was St. Benoit Labre. St. John's parents continued this custom. His father would send Jean-Marie to take firewood to the poor. *One night Providence sent the Vianneys as many as twenty such guests. "There is not enough broth for all," the farmer's wife...said to her husband. "Very well, I will go without," was the good man's reply.*[50]

Bl. Escrivá insists: *A Christian cannot be content with a job that only allows him to earn enough for himself and his family. He will be big-hearted enough to give others a helping hand both out of charity and as a matter of justice...How much does it cost you—also in financial terms—to be Christians?*[51]

The virtue of **gratitude** likewise plays a role in the virtue of justice. Recall how Jesus questions the sole leper who returned to give Him thanks: **Were not ten cleansed? Where are the other nine?** (*Lk.* 17:17) He was wounded by the ingratitude of the nine He saved from a terrible illness. It is an offense against the virtue of justice to be ungrateful toward God and anyone else who does something for us. St. Thomas insists: *The natural order itself requires that whoever has received a favor respond with gratitude to his beneficiary.*[52]

---

[49] *Friends Of God,* no. 47.

[50] *The Cure D'Ars, Op. Cit.,* p.20.

[51] *Friends Of God,* no. 126.

[52] St. Thomas Aquinas, *S. Th., II-II, q. 106, a.3.*

The virtues of **loyalty** and **fidelity** round out justice. These virtues move our will so that we keep our commitments despite the difficulties encountered or the sacrifices required. These virtues keep us faithful to our convictions, duties, spouse, family, and organizations to which we are dedicated. St. Thomas says that *the virtue of fidelity consists in fulfilling what one has promised.*[53] St. Joan of Arc, nineteen years of age at the time of her 114-day trial, was consumed with panic by the threats of her inquisitors. Not only did the clerics refuse her the sacraments, but they also threatened her with death and excommunication unless she denied the heavenly Voices guiding her to save France. Physically weakened by sickness and the rigors of imprisonment, Joan signed a statement denying supernatural intervention in her life. After being condemned to life imprisonment, Joan recanted her denial although it meant her certain death saying, *"my Voices, which I have heard since Thursday, told me that God had pitied me for the treason to which I consented in St. Ouen; they told [me] that in saving my life I was damning myself…If I were to say that God has not sent me, I should be damning myself, for it is true that God did send me. My Voices have told me, since Thursday, that I did very wrong in doing that which I did, and that I must confess that I did wrong. What I declared on Thursday was done through fear of the fire. Whatever I was made to deny at St. Ouen, I never did anything against God or the Faith; I did not understand what was in the formula of abjuration."*[54] St. Rutilius, who lived in the third century, ran from town to town trying to excape the Roman persecution. He even used bribes to save his life. When finally captured and tortured, he died with courage, loyal to his God. This same steadfast fidelity is what God expects from us.

Fidelity keeps spouses together when marriage becomes difficult. Fidelity helps an employee to meet his deadline. Fidelity keeps a soldier or sailor at his post in moments of danger. Fidelity makes a friend put aside his concerns to help another. *A husband, a soldier, an administrator, who faithfully fulfills at each moment, in each new circumstance of his life, the duties of love and justice*

---

[53] St. Thomas, *S. Th.* II-II, q. 110, a 3.
[54] Mary Purcell, *The Halo On The Sword* (Maryland: The Newman Press, 1952) p. 279.

which he once took on, will always be just that much better a husband, soldier or administrator. It is difficult to apply a principle to the changing realities of the contingent world. But it is the best defense against aging of the spirit, hardening of the heart and stiffening of the mind.[55]

St. Augustine adds: *Give what you demand of others. Fidelity is owed to you, and you owe others fidelity. The husband owes fidelity to his wife; the wife to her husband; both to God. You, who have promised continence, give what you have promised; for it would not have been demanded if you had not promised it. Guard against cheating in your business transactions. Guard against lying and perjury. Guard against idle words and wasteful expense. Do not do to others, to men or to God, whatever you do not wish to be done to you.*[56]

Fidelity moves our hearts to pray, to attend at least Sunday Mass, to give honor and praise to God. Loyalty makes God our first priority, not the pursuit of wealth or entertainment. *[I]t is not every kind of consistency and firmness of conduct based on subjective principles that makes true character but only constancy in following the eternal principles of justice...There cannot be full justice except in giving to God what is due to God.*[57] Fidelity and loyalty keep us anchored to the spouse of Christ, the Roman Catholic Church.

Distributive justice obliges those in authority to be equitable in dispersing benefits and positions of authority. In other words, they are not to abuse their office for political or monetary gain. ***Woe to those who decree iniquitous decrees*** *(Is.* 10:1). In family life this pertains to the finances. Husbands, who use their income on hobbies or gambling causing financial hardship for their families, sin against distributive justice. Treating one's spouse or family in a miserly manner or even in an excessively lavish manner causes offense.

Social justice urges each of us to work for the common good

---

[55] *Conversations With Msr. Escriva De Balaguer* (Dublin: Scepter Books, 1969) no. 1.

[56] St. Augustine, *Sermo 260.*

[57] Pius XI, Encyclical *Divini illius Magistri,* December 31, 1929, no. 82.

rather than waiting for someone else to take the lead. As citizens we have *the obligation of rendering to the state whatever material and personal services are required for the common good.*[58] This includes the moral duty to pay just taxes and obey just civil laws. Furthermore, the Second Vatican Council insists that *every citizen ought to be mindful of his right and his duty to promote the common good by using his vote.*[59] *[T]he Christian who wishes to live his faith in a political activity which he sees as a service, cannot support, without contradicting himself, political systems which radically or substantially go against his faith and his concept of man. He cannot adhere to the Marxist ideology, to its atheistic materialism, to its dialectic of violence and to the way it absorbs individual freedom in the collectivity, denying at the same time all transcendence to man and his personal and collective history. Nor can he adhere to a liberal ideology which believes it exalts individual freedom by withdrawing it from every limitation, by stimulating it through exclusive seeking of interest and power, and by considering social solidarities as more or less automatic consequences of individual initiatives, not as an aim and major criterion of the value of the social organization.*[60]

The common good also necessitates the ability to live in dignity, the right to work and the right to rest; the right to marry and to form a home; the right to have the number of children God chooses to send to the couple; the right to educate the children in faith and morals; the right to live in freedom.

Penal justice strives to correct unjust acts, to avoid repetition and to correct disorder. Those who educate such as parents, teachers, law enforcement officers, and judges, practice this last form of justice. Permissive parents are deficient in penal justice. By allowing their children to "do their own thing" rather than obeying, the parents are harming the character of their children. In addition, such parents encourage disorder in the family and home. As these children mature, not only will they not be able to contribute to the common good, but they could become inmates of

[58] *Gaudium et spes, no. 30*

[59] *Ibid.,* no. 75.

[60] Paul VI, *Octogesima adveniens,* no. 26.

our prison system.

Justice is the balance of our rights and duties. St. John Chrysostom points out that *the measure and height of Christian perfection, its most concise definition, is to do good to others...Nothing brings us to imitate Christ more closely than to take care of our neighbors. You can fast, sleep on the hard floor, and even be prepared to die; but if you do not look out for your neighbor, you have accomplished nothing great. Whatever else you do, you are still far from the ideal.*[61]

The seventh commandment, **Thou shalt not steal**, corresponds to the virtue of justice. As such, when we sin against justice, not only must we be contrite, but we are obliged to repair the harm we have done as far as morally possible. If our son drives our car over someone's lawn, he has the obligation to pay to have the lawn repaired. If he is short on funds, we pay restitution for him then the son repays us. "Finders" are not keepers. We have the responsibility to return over-payments as well as to pay our just debts promptly. Justice demands that the mass media proclaim the truth.

Not stealing or damaging our neighbor's goods is only a fraction of the virtue of justice. We are not to steal or damage our neighbor's character, work, family, spouse, reputation, nor future. John Paul II insists that justice is violated by *every sin against the rights of the human person, beginning with the right to life and including the life of the unborn, or against a person's physical integrity. Likewise "social" is every sin against others' freedom, especially against the supreme freedom to believe in God and adore Him; "social" is every sin against the dignity and honor of one's neighbor.*[62]

If we are responsible for breaking up a relationship, we must work to repair it. If we damage a person's reputation, we have to work to repair the harm done. *One also has the right to the good name, respect, consideration, and reputation that he has earned. The more we know someone, the more his personality, character,*

---

[61] St. John Chrysostom, *In I Epistolam I ad Corinthios homiliae 25, 3.*

[62] John Paul II, *Reconciliatio et Paenitentia,* December 2, 1984, no. 16.

intellect and heart are unveiled to us. And so much the clearer does it become...what criteria we have to use to "measure" him and what it means to be just with him.[63] Therefore, gossip, negative criticism, uncharitable thoughts/words, and calumny are some of the vices opposed to the virtue of justice. *For a man's reputation is one of his most precious temporal possessions; he is prevented from doing many good deeds if it is damaged.*[64] St. Thomas contends further that damaging another's reputation *may be the occasion of homicide in so far as his words provide the occasion for somebody else hating or despising his neighbor.*[65]

St. Gregory of Nyssa adds: *the fear of God teaches the tongue to say what is appropriate, and not vain things; to know when and how much to speak, and to give a suitable answer; to speak with moderation, not impetuously or thoughtlessly.*[66]

Connected to the right to one's good name is the right to privacy. Living in a small city of 100,000 people it never ceases to amaze me how much complete strangers know about our personal business. One woman, who I just recently became acquainted with, told me that she knew all about me eight years before we met because people talk about the manner in which we raised our daughters. Bl. Escrivá reminds us that *this way of acting is not a thing of the past. It would be no trouble at all to point out present-day cases of aggressive curiosity, which pries morbidly into the private lives of others. A minimum of justice demands that, even when actual wrongdoing is suspected, an investigation of this sort be carried out with caution and moderation, lest mere possibility be converted into certainty. It is clear that an unhealthy curiosity to perform autopsies on actions that are not illicit but positively good should be ranked under the heading of perversion.*

Faced with traders in suspicion who prey on the privacy of others we must defend the dignity of every person, his right to peace. All

---

[63] John Paul II, Address, November 8, 1978

[64] St. Thomas, *S.Th. II-II, q. 73, a. 2.*

[65] *S. Th.,* Op. Cit., q. 73, a. 3 and 2.

[66] St. Gregory of Nissa, *Homilia I de pauperibus amandis et benignitate complectendis.*

honest men, Christians or not, agree on the need for this defense, for a common value is at stake: the legitimate right to be oneself, to avoid ostentation, to keep within the family its joys, sorrows and difficulties. We are defending, no less, the right to do good without publicity, to help the disadvantaged out of pure love, without feeling obliged to publicize one's efforts to serve others, much less to bare the intimacy of one's soul to the indiscreet and the twisted gaze of persons who know nothing and want to know nothing of disinterested generosity, except to mock it mercilessly.[67]

The Christian virtue of justice is more ambitious. It enjoins us to prove ourselves thankful, friendly and generous. It encourages us to act as loyal and honorable friends, in hard times as well as good ones; to obey the law and to respect legitimate authority; to amend gladly when we realize we have erred in tackling a problem. Above all, if we are just, we will fulfill our professional, family and social commitments without fuss or display, working hard and exercising our rights, which are also duties.[68]

In what other ways does this virtue impact marriage and the family? Justice is the virtue of seeing the truth in others. Dr. David Isaacs, of the University of Navarra, maintains to live the virtue of justice each spouse has the obligation to be good for the common good of the family and society in general. Furthermore, in justice each person's virtue is needed for the others as an example. Surprisingly, justice is not needed in good marriages because the couple has such a deep love and practice of generosity that they are truly one flesh, completely united in justice. Justice is only needed within marriage when love is not lived, as it should be. The virtue of love (charity) helps one to practice the virtue of justice. Justice can assist love, lead to deeper love, when love is imperfect. The virtue of justice then assures certain rights such as the right to intimacy; the right to keep a private diary; the right to privacy when dressing, the right to one's religious beliefs and practices. A spouse has the right to conjugal relations; the right to be appreciated; the right to friends and the exchange of confidences with friends without disclosing

---

[67] *Christ Is Passing By*, no. 69.

[68] *Friends Of God, Op. Cit.,* nos. 168-169.

those confidences to one's spouse. Each spouse has the right to own private property exclusively; the right to food and clothing; the right to be encouraged to improve. I am failing my spouse if I do not help the other to improve. In keeping with justice, each spouse has the right to participate in the common good.

If one spouse dominates, forcing the other to follow, the marital relationship is stunted. Each spouse has the right to a good name. Avoid speaking negatively about your spouse in front of the children or to others. Saying *"Thank you"* is part of the virtue of justice. It is the right to gratitude. Speak the truth with simplicity. Be considerate towards others. Obedience, and just punishment (in disciplining children) are also part of practicing the virtue of justice.

Fortitude

The third cardinal virtue is **fortitude**. Fortitude plays a major role in developing all the other virtues. Without this virtue, we cannot persevere in our struggle to grow in any virtue. Fortitude is the ability to go against the grain for a greater good. This virtue strengthens the will to overcome the diversity of problems in life. Fortitude is that virtue that gives one the will to suffer for the good. The dictionary defines it as *strength of mind that enables a person to encounter danger or bear pain or adversity with courage.* In our vernacular we call it *grit, backbone, pluck,* or *guts.* Going deeper, we find that fortitude is *the virtue that represses fear in the midst of difficulties and danger so that we can follow right reason.*[69] In this sense fortitude is the mean between fear, which flees danger without a reasonable cause, and recklessness, which would lead us into danger without sufficient reason.

Fortitude *is the moral virtue that ensures firmness in difficulties and constancy in the pursuit of the good. It strengthens the resolve to resist temptations and to overcome obstacles in the moral life. The virtue of fortitude enables one to conquer fear, even fear of death, and to face trails and persecutions. It disposes one even to*

---

[69] Rev. Garrigou-LaGrange, *The Three Ages of the Interior Life*, p. 146.

renounce and sacrifice his life in defense of a just cause.[70]   As the **Catholic Catechism** explains, the highest act of fortitude is martyrdom. *From time to time I have wondered which kind of martyrdom is the greater: that of the person who receives death for the faith, at the hand of God's enemies; or the martyrdom of someone who spends his years working with no other purpose than that of serving the Church and souls, and who grows old smiling, all the while passing unnoticed. For me, the unspectacular martyrdom is more heroic. That is your way.*[71]

Let's take the virtue of fortitude apart. First of all, fortitude is the essential virtue needed for day-to-day living. Without this virtue we cannot persevere in our job, in our marriage, or in any other areas of responsibility. Without fortitude, our human development is stunted. Fortitude is the virtue of daring, courage, patience, perseverance, endurance and enterprise. It was their practice of this virtue that gave us American heroes such as George Washington, Patrick Henry, Thomas Jefferson, John Adams, John Paul Jones, Abraham Lincoln, brave military generals, and saints such as St. Maximilian Kolbe, St. Thomas More, St. John Fisher, St. Catherine of Siena, St. Joan of Arc, among others. Bl. Escrivá insists that we must acquire this virtue of heroes also: *As a child of God, with His grace in you, you have to be a strong person, a man or woman of desires and achievements. We are not hothouse plants. We live in the middle of the world, and we have to be able to face up to all the winds that blow, to the heat and the cold, to rain and storms, but always faithful to God and to his Church.*[72]

Fortitude is the virtue or good habit by which we strive for what is good, and keep trying to obtain it despite the obstacles, whether they are from inside of us or from outside influences. Fortitude keeps us on track when we would rather give up. Fortitude gives us the strength to fight our selfishness for a greater good than self. It is the virtue needed for self-sacrifice. Fortitude is the virtue that guides us to undertake arduous commitments despite

---

[70] *Catechism of the Catholic Church* #1808.

[71] Blessed Josemaria Escriva', *The Way Of The Cross* (NY: Scepter, 1982) Seventh Station, no. 4.

[72] Blessed Josemaria Escriva', *The Forge #792.*

the obstacles that may arise. It helps us to bear with adversity in standing up for a just cause. As mentioned before, it activates the virtues of **courage**, **daring**, **patience** and **perseverance**. Bl. Escrivá points out: *The person with fortitude is one who perseveres in doing what his conscience tells him he ought to do. He does not measure the value of a task exclusively by the benefit he receives from it, but rather by the service he renders to others. The strong man will at times suffer, but he stands firm; he may be driven to tears, but he will brush them aside. When difficulties come thick and fast, he does not bend.*[73]

The Holy Father especially stresses the importance of the virtue of fortitude in living a Christian life. *[T]he virtue of fortitude always requires overcoming human weakness, especially fear. For human nature fears danger, hardship and suffering. Therefore we need to look for courageous people not only on battlefields, but also in hospital corridors and at the bedside of the suffering. I want to pay tribute to all these unknown courageous people. To all those who have the courage to say "no" or "yes" when it is hard to do so. To those who give singular testimony of human dignity and deep humanity. Precisely because they are unknown, these persons deserve special tribute and gratitude.*[74]

Part of the virtue of fortitude is **magnanimity**. *The magnanimous person devotes all his strength, unstintingly, to what is worthwhile. As a result he is capable of giving himself. He is not content with merely giving. He gives his very self. He thus comes to understand that the greatest expression of magnanimity consists in giving oneself to God.*[75] A magnanimous person does not seek honor, praise, or flattery. Neither does the person boast nor have secret ambitions. Rather, the person is daring and persevering no matter how difficult the task entrusted to his care. St. Joan of Arc is a fitting example of this. She left her home, cut her beautiful hair and donned men's clothing to lead the army of France to victory. To protect her chastity, her Voices (the virgin martyres Sts. Margaret and Catherine as well as St. Michael

---

[73] *Friends Of God, Op. Cit.,* no. 77.
[74] John Paul II, Address, Novemember 15, 1978.
[75] *Friends Of God, Op. Cit., no. 80.*

the Archangel) commanded Joan to dress like a young boy. Captured by the Burgundians she was lodged in a fortress. When her Voices told her she was to be sold to the English, Joan panicked and leaped from the top of a sixty-foot tower. Regaining consciousness she confessed: *I did not fall. I leaped...I have sinned against the good God. Never before have I gone against the advice of my Voices; they told me not to jump but when they warned me that soon I am to be given into the hands of the English—I was afraid...I could not bear the thought and became terrified of what God has willed for me. I jumped off the tower.*[76] Despite her natural fear, Joan overcame her terror to save the national identity of France. That's why she is France's patron saint. Likewise, we are given the graces necessary to overcome our fears.

The virtue of **magnanimity**, linked to fortitude, includes the virtues of **generosity**, **benevolence**, **selflessness**, **altruism**, and **kindness**. A magnanimous person is not a rival to anyone, especially one's spouse. Nor is the magnanimous person envious or jealous—instead the person admires the virtues in others. Such a person acts in a calm manner not trying to do too much. The person restricts self to what had to be done then does it quietly. Such was the life of St. Bernadette. Obedient to the guidance of her pastor, she entered the convent. By doing so she gave up her identity, and the future marriage she planned with a young man of her village. Suffering silently from a debilitating disease, she was the object of contempt by a jealous nun. Yet, she accepted all insults with humble kindness and humility.

The virtue of **magnificence** or **liberality**, as part of the virtue of fortitude, moderates the love for material possessions. The person who possesses magnificence will use all the material means available to pursue a good. He is neither stingy nor mean.

Another virtue connected to fortitude is **patience**, a most difficult virtue! Patience helps us to handle the abundant setbacks, contradictions and sufferings of life. This virtue keeps us cheerful despite annoyances such as car trouble or a bout of the flu. It keeps us calm when the computer loses one's work;

---

[76] *The Halo On The Sword, Op. Cit.,* pp. 225-226.

when one is caught in a traffic jam; when the baby cries all night, or when none of our plans work out. We need this virtue to deal with our defects and those of others. Saint Paul lived patience heroically. Just consider how long he spent in prison for nothing! He encourages us by saying: *We rejoice in our sufferings, knowing that suffering produces endurance, and endurance produces character, and character produces hope, and hope does not disappoint us* (Rom 5:3-4).

Along with patience we need to develop the virtue of **perseverance**, which is the constancy in practicing virtue despite difficulties or duration of the hardship. If we have perseverance, we will not flutter from task to task but complete one before going on to the next. *To begin is for everyone, to persevere is for saints.*

May your perseverance not be the blind consequence of the first impulse, the effect of inertia; may it be a reflective perseverance.[77]

Virtues connected to perseverance include **constancy** and **tenacity**. These virtues help us to persevere despite failures, illness or moods. Spouses need fortitude and the connected virtues to be faithful in living their marriage vows. It is the lack of fortitude in spouses that leads to divorce.

Fortitude is especially critical for the age in which we are living. Its corresponding vice is fear. If we succumb to the fear of evil we see all around us, we will be too paralyzed to work to overcome it. Through osmosis evil will permeate our thinking. One example is when parents accept the fact that their married children use contraceptives. Another is the acceptance of remarriage outside the Church. Then there are the parents who accept the promiscuous conduct of their children whether it is live-ins or homosexual behavior. Without the acquisition of fortitude the evils of our culture will suck us in.

A "peaceful" family life might indicate a lack of fortitude. Dr. Isaacs points out consistent peace within the family means that the family is not striving for the good. To achieve good with our children and spouse, one has to insist on the good despite

---

[77] *The Way, Op. Cit.,* no. 983.

their reactions or objections. *How will the children and my spouse know something is important unless I insist?* asks Isaacs. *This takes fortitude.* Parental fortitude is lacking when the child decides which school to attend, how he will spend free time, and sets personal norms for behavior without parental guidance. Fortitude means that the parents direct the children's actions for the good of the children not vice versa. Peace at any cost injures the character of our children as well as our own personal and spiritual growth. All family members are called upon to improve on a natural level as well as on a supernatural level. In the book, ***The Three Ages of the Interior Life,*** we are told that *while fortitude is not the highest virtue, it is indispensable if we are striving to become saints. Christ tells us in Scripture that it is the violent that seize heaven.* To grow holy is personally costly. One must do violence to oneself to control pride, vanity, selfishness, and character defects. Just as we parents have to deal with the effects of original sin in our character, likewise we have to deal with the same defects in our children. To ignore their defects or faults is not only cowardly, it is spiritually deadly. Part of parenting is going toe-to-toe with the children. It's firmly saying "no" despite tantrums, sulking spells, or listening to a child tell us how much he dislikes us. At a dinner party, I watched as parents tried to get their four-year-old son to bed. It became such a struggle of the wills that finally the little boy threatened his parents with, *When you get old, I'm going to put you both into a nursing home!* That threat put him to bed.

To seek the good is to suffer. To raise children in an upright fashion will not only cause you to suffer but they will suffer as well. Our children are in the world but cannot be of the world. The struggle between good and evil is not a peaceful struggle. Christ tells us that He did not come to bring peace. ***I have come to bring a sword, not peace. For I have come to set a man at variance with his father, and a daughter with her mother, and a daughter-in-law with her mother-in-law; and a man's enemies will be those of his own household. He who loves father or mother more than Me is not worthy of Me; and he who loves son or daughter more than Me is***

*not worthy of Me. And he who does not take up his cross
and follow Me, is not worthy of Me. He who finds his life
will lose it, and he who loses his life for My sake, will find
it* (*Matt.* 10:34-39).

How do we acquire this virtue? Fortitude, as well as the other
virtues, is only acquired through ongoing repetition. It's doing
that chore you hate promptly and cheerfully. It's skipping the
second beer or doing something with the family instead of
watching a sporting event on TV. It's practicing the spiritual
and corporal works of mercy when you are tired or stressed out.
Or it could be taking your wife out for a date when you would
rather stay home. Maybe it's making a special dinner for your
husband when you are tired yourself. It can be going on a retreat
when you would rather skip it. Basically, it's doing a good that
you would rather not do.

Virtues are not acquired all at once but rather by degrees. For
example, each time we push ourselves to do something we dislike,
fear or dread, we grow a bit more in the virtue of fortitude but
we do not possess fortitude itself until we do what is good
consistently. Fortitude is the virtue of the great but the great did
not become great by one outstanding act. Greatness is developed
little by little. For example, when our faith is attacked or ridiculed,
which is commonplace today, what is your response? Do you
ignore the attack (which is the vice of cowardliness) or do you
stand up for the faith (the virtue of fortitude)? If you sometimes
stand up and at other times remain silent, you are not developing
the virtue but rather growing in vice because you know what you
should do but refrain from doing it out of fear, laziness, or human
respect. Do you speak out when family members leave the faith
or when they are living in serious sin despite the animosity it
may arouse?

Temperance

The last cardinal virtue is **temperance**. This is the virtue
that helps us to moderate the use of our senses through the
use of reason, which is illuminated by faith. Temperance is the
virtue that counters the prevailing attitude that *it's my body, I
can do with it what I want!*

Why is this virtue so important for us to cultivate and live? Once baptized, as long as we are in the state of grace we are temples of the Holy Spirit. God dwells within us. St. Paul notes: **All things are lawful for me but not all things are expedient [helpful]. All things are lawful for me but I will not be enslaved by anything. Food is meant for the stomach and the stomach for food...The body is not meant for immorality, but for the Lord, and the Lord for the body** (1 *Cor.*6:12-14).

Temperance is not repression but moderation. It fosters harmony between the spiritual and the material. It helps us to fully develop as a person. Bl. Escrivá notes: *I want to consider the rich rewards that temperance brings. I want to see men [and women] who are really men, and not slaves to cheap glitter, as worthless as the trinkets that magpies gather. A manly person knows how to do without the things that may harm his soul. And he also comes to realize that his sacrifice is more apparent than real. For living this way, with a spirit of sacrifice, means freeing oneself from many kinds of slavery and savoring instead, in the depths of one's heart, the fullness of God's love.*

Life then takes on again shades and tones which intemperance has tended to blur. We find ourselves able to care for the needs of others, to share what is ours with everyone, to devote our energies to great causes. Temperance makes the soul sober, modest, understanding. It fosters a natural sense of reserve which everyone finds attractive because it denotes intelligent self-control. Temperance does not imply narrowness, but greatness of soul. There is much more deprivation in the intemperate heart which abdicates from self-dominion only to become enslaved to the first caller who comes along ringing some pathetic, tinny cow bell.[78]

Temperance restrains our desire to possess material goods. Rather than purchasing the latest gadget, novelty or prestige item, we use the virtue of prudence to decide if the item is a "need" or a "want." If it is simply a want, we can live without it. On the other hand, is it truly a need or a thinly disguised want?

---

[78] *Friends Of God, Op. Cit.*, no. 84.

Christ tells us, *If you will be perfect, go, sell what you have, and give to the poor, and you shall have treasure in heaven; and come, follow me* (Matt.19:21-22). As parents, Christ is not asking us to give up everything because He expects us to care for our families. But He is asking us to be more careful in how we spend our money. The more we spend on ourselves, the less help we can give to others. Saint Augustine teaches that we are to use material goods *in accord with [our] needs and duties, with the moderation of one who makes use of them without overvaluing or being ensnared by them.*[79] *Seek what is sufficient, seek what is enough. Don't desire any more than that. The rest brings worry, not relief; it is bothersome, not uplifting.*[80]

The more we have the more we have to worry about it being stolen, repaired, protected, stored and moved. It was when my husband took a job two hundred miles away that I learned how chained we had become to our possessions. For thirteen months our family was separated because we could not sell our home in a Chicago suburb. If we moved, leaving our house vacant, our homeowners' insurance would not cover the house. In Springfield, we could not find temporary lodging that would take three children. It was a possession, our home, which not only kept us apart as a family but played havoc with our family life. That experience taught me several lessons: *Try to live in such a way that you can voluntarily deprive yourself of the comfort and ease you wouldn't approve of in the life of another man of God.*[81] *Be content with what is sufficient for leading a simple and temperate life.*[82]

If materialism is your struggle, ask St. Hyacintha for assistance. She joined a convent simply because her fiancé jilted her to marry her sister. In the convent she continued living a lavish lifestyle until she realized how sinful it was. Reluctantly she gave up her possessions but it was a lifetime struggle for her.

---

[79] St. Augustine, *De moribus Ecclesiae Catholicae* 1, no. 21.

[80] St. Augustine, *Sermo 65, no. 6.*

[81] *The Way, Op. Cit.,* no. 938.

[82] *Ibid.,* no. 631.

If we live temperance we need not become concerned when we do not have the financial resources to solve our needs. Jesus asks us to trust in God's help at such times: *[D]o not be anxious for your life, what you shall eat; nor yet for your body, what you shall put on. Is not the life a greater thing than the food, and the body than the clothing? Look at the birds of the air...your heavenly Father feeds them. Are not you of much more value than they? But which of you by being anxious about it can add to his stature a single cubit?* (*Matt.* 6:25-27).

Temperance also encompasses how we spend our time such as in watching TV, participating in sporting events, playing games, surfing the Internet, pursuing our hobbies and interests.

The virtue of temperance concerns eating and drinking. Let's face it, there seems to be a toss-up between promiscuity and gluttony as our national vice.

Jesus warns us: *Take heed...lest your hearts be weighed down with dissipation and drunkenness and cares of this life* (*Lk.* 21:34). St. Paul scorns those whose *god is their belly* (*Phil.* 3:19). St. Peter warns us: *Let the time that is past suffice for doing what the Gentiles like to do, living in licentiousness, passions, drunkenness, revels, carousing, and lawless idolatry* (*1 Pet.* 4:3). If we cannot control the amount of food and alcohol that we consume we cannot be virtuous people...we cannot be saints. Besides, *Gluttony is the forerunner of impurity.*[83] Why? Because if one is unable to control his appetite for food, how can he control his sexual appetite?

After the age of thirty-five our metabolism slows down by one percent a year so expanding waistlines are part of the natural aging process. To keep trim we either have to cut our food intake by one percent a year or increase our exercise. But the aging process is not the only reason that people are exploding into gargantuan sizes. It's rare to see people without food or drink in their mouths or hands. The National Institute of Diabetes, Digestive and Kidney Diseases claims that 58 million Americans

---

[83] *The Way, Op. Cit.,* no. 126.

are overweight. The World Health Organization claims that *more than half of the U.S. adults are overweight, and 22% are obese...Although genetic factors can influence a person's susceptibility to obesity, they do not explain the current epidemic...What has changed is how we eat and how much we eat...Portion sizes of restaurant meals, take-out foods, and snacks have increased, in some cases by more than 100%.*[84] When we overeat we are being gluttonous.

Suzanne Fowler, founder of *The Light Weigh* a Catholic diet program, insists that if people stop eating when they feel full they will lose weight. She suggests eating only half a serving, the amount which can fit into a mug or an equivalent portion that is about the size of your clenched fist. *Your stomach when shrunken down is the size of your fist. Think of this when you are taking your portion and when you are eating.* Tempted to eat when you are really not hungry? Fowler suggests saying the rosary or other prayers, reading the Bible, and using holy water.[85]

Suzanne's theory is supported by Bl. Escrivá: *You generally eat more than you need. And that fullness, which often causes you physical heaviness and discomfort, benumbs your mind and renders you unfit to savor supernatural treasures.*[86] We overeat because we are nervous, bored, or use food to comfort us when unhappy or depressed. Instead, we need to turn to God for help.

One day a young mother was having difficulty doing her mental prayer because her little boy kept interrupting her. Finally, she sat him down and said, *I'm going to read from this book called **The Way**. Let's just think about the points I read but not talk.* The little boy was quiet until she read point # 681: *The day you rise from the table without having made some small mortification you've eaten like a pagan.* Turning to his mother, the little boy confessed, *I've eaten like a pagan all my life!*

---

[84] *Harvard Women's Health Watch*, Vol. VII, #12, August 2000, p. 1.

[85] Suzanne Fowler, *The Light Weigh*, 4701 College Blvd.,Suite 102, Leawood, Kansas 66211

[86] *The Way, Op. Cit.*, no. 682.

To develop the virtue of temperance in regard to food and drink begin by mortifying yourself at each meal. Take smaller portions or leave a little something on your plate. Avoid snacking between meals except for an after school snack for the kids. Besides food, limit alcoholic and soft drinks. Coffee and tea should be used in moderation. Drink water instead.

If alcoholism is a problem, turn to Bl. Matt Talbot, a former drunk, for help. Terribly humiliated by his wretched condition, he suddenly decided that with the help of God he could abstain from alcohol for that one day. From that day on, each day until he died he had to consciously fight the temptation to take a drink. His struggle made him a saint.

Is drug abuse a problem? Again seek the intercession of Blessed Matt Talbot. Be cautious in the use of sleeping pills and other addictive medications.

Humility is part of temperance. Each spouse is called to temper the desire to dominate the other spouse. Developing the virtue of **meekness** diminishes uncontrollable anger. St. Francis de Sales worked for three years to control his temper. Ask him for guidance.

The desire for excessive knowledge, which is basically curiosity, is tempered by the virtue of **study**. St. Jerome was guilty of this vice until he experienced a terrifying spiritual dream. Ask St. Jerome for help in this area.

Another aspect of temperance is good manners—care and respect for our dignity and the dignity of others. How do we live **courtesy** towards others, especially when we are behind the wheel of our car? How do we treat people who work for us, wait on us, and phone us? Are we cheerful and kind, or brusque and rude in conduct and speech?

Temperance is reflected in our appearance, dress, and how we express joy or sorrow. Do we talk too much? Do we show off or boast? Are we prying and nosey? All are lacks of temperance. Can we interrupt a task we are doing cheerfully or are we workaholics? The latter is a vice.

How do we live Sunday? In *Dies Domini,* John Paul II asked us to keep Sunday holy. Do we practice temperance by refraining from shopping and doing work on Sunday?

Temperance is basically a question of regulating our instinct. Despite what we are told in popular journals, the body does not need sex. The virtue of **chastity** regulates the sex act as well as the words we use and the actions we take. *Temperance is self-mastery. Not everything we experience in our bodies and souls should be given free rein. Nor ought we to do everything we can do. It is easier to let ourselves be carried away by so-called natural impulses; but this road ends up in sadness and isolation in our own misery.*[87]

Struggling with chastity? Pray to St. Maria Goretti or St. Margaret of Cortona. A neighbor boy murdered Maria when she refused his advances. Margaret, at the age of 17, became the mistress of a young nobleman. For nine years she lived in sin with him until he was killed. When Margaret found his decomposed body, it was covered with maggots. It was with shock that she realized that her soul looked like his putrid body. Converted, she threw herself into arduous penances. When her confessor protested she insisted: *Father, do not ask me to come to terms with this body of mine, for I cannot risk such a compromise. Between me and my body there must always be a struggle until death.*[88] This is the same struggle we have to wage, particularly in our culture that exalts the sins of the flesh.

If we begin to slip in regard to holy purity, our faith could be the next victim because we would be tempted to ignore the teachings of the Church to justify our actions or passions.

Despite what the media and contemporary society want us to believe, sex does not rank first in life. *First comes spiritual ideas, with each person choosing his own. Next, a whole series of matters that normally concern ordinary men and women: their father and mother, home, children, and so on. After that, one's job or*

---

[87] *Friends Of God ,Op. Cit.,* no. 84.
[88] *Walk With The Wise, Op. Cit.,* p. 74.

profession. Only then, in fourth or fifth place, does the sexual instinct come in.[89] *[C]hastity is not merely continence, but a decisive affirmation on the part of the will in love. It is a virtue that keeps love young in any state of life. There is a kind of chastity that is proper to those who begin to feel the awakening of physical maturity, and a kind of chastity that corresponds to those who are preparing for marriage; there is a chastity for those whom God calls to celibacy, and a chastity for those who have been chosen by him to live in the married state.*[90] Likewise, *If we only think of food, drink and sex,* David Isaacs asks, *how can we improve?*

Virtues And Defects In Marriage

As a couple, it is important to grow together in the virtues, especially the virtues of charity (love), flexibility, cheerfulness, kindness, thoughtfulness, humility and generosity. Without each spouse actively trying to acquire virtues it is difficult to develop a strong, happy marriage relationship. Charity/love is crucial to happy marriages and happy families. The love found in charity is not the qualifying "love" which is so common in our culture, i.e. "I love you *if...*" *The supernatural charity that Christ expects of His followers is to be reflected in their selfless love as members of the Christian family. The adjective "selfless" is part of our faith,* according to Fr. Hardon, SJ. *It is the love that ended on the Cross...As Christ has loved us, even to laying down His life for us.*[91]

Every spouse appreciates the virtue of flexibility. *A person who is flexible adapts his behavior readily to the particular circumstances of each individual or situation, but without thereby abandoning his own personal principles of behavior.*[92] We are flexible when we can cheerfully change our plans to suit the problems or wishes of the other members of the family. For example, no matter how much we may have wanted to do lawn

---

[89] *Ibid.,* no. 179.

[90] *Christ Is Passing By, Op. Cit.,* no. 25.

[91] *The Catholic Family In The Modern World, Op. Cit.,* p. 33.

[92] David Isaacs, *Character Building, a Guide For Parents And Teachers* (Dublin: Four Courts Press, 1984) p. 254.

work or gardening on Saturday, if something more important comes up, we have to have the flexibility to put off the lawn work for another day.

In the midst of difficulties, peace can be found in the home if couples first seek God, then work to generate the virtue of cheerfulness. A smile means so much! Notice how one person's mood sets the atmosphere in the family. The happier you are, the happier your children are. When you are cross, your mood is transferred down the line to the children until everyone is snarling at each other and the baby is crying.

Kindness, thoughtfulness and warmth are not only to be appreciated when we are the recipients but are also to be given to our spouse and children by us. Likewise, teach your children how to show their love through their actions. Explain to them how to express their love by giving examples of how you live love for God, your spouse, parents, and friends. Teach your children that they are to act in a similar fashion toward God, their parents and friends. This is a very important point. If you do not verbally and by example teach them how to live love, when they mature they will most likely treat you in an indifferent, casual manner. There are thousands of residents of nursing homes who rarely if ever are visited by their children. Other children, once they leave home rarely call or come home for visits or holidays.

St. Paul writes so eloquently about the human condition: *I do not understand my own actions. For I do not do what I want, but I do the very thing I hate...For I do not do the good I want, but the evil I do not want is what I do...I delight in the law of God, in my inmost self, but I see in my members another law at war with the law of my mind and making me captive to the law of sin which dwells in my members* (*Rom.* 7:15-23). No matter how hard we try to be virtuous, at times we will fail. Consider your failings as opportunities to grow in humility. Without humility there can be no virtue. Bl. Escrivá points out in the *Furrow: Prayer is the humility of the man who acknowledges his profound wretchedness and the greatness of God. He addresses and adores God as one who expects everything from him and nothing from himself.*

Faith is the humility of the mind which renounces its own judgment and surrenders to the verdict and authority of the Church.

Obedience is the humility of the will which subjects itself to the will of another, for God's sake.

Chastity is the humility of the flesh, which subjects itself to the spirit.

Exterior mortification is the humility of the senses.

Penance is the humility of all the passions, immolated to God.

Humility is truth on the road of the ascetic struggle.[93]

When we value our own judgment over the judgment of others, we are proud which is a vice. In the common vernacular we can say the proud person is "a know it all." If one follows the vice of pride to its root one uncovers selfishness. St. Thomas teaches that selfishness is the source of all-evil. Isn't it the major factor in divorce? Aquinas writes: *Every sinful act proceeds from the inordinate desire for some temporal good. Now the fact that anyone desires a temporal good inordinately is due to the fact that he loves himself inordinately.*[94] In **Sirach** we learn: **the beginning of man's pride is to depart from the Lord. The beginning of sin is pride** (10:12-13). *Cure pride,* writes St. Augustine, *and you will eliminate all sin. In order to cure pride, which is the cause of all evil, the Son of God came down to earth and became humble.*[95]

The person who possesses humility not only listens but also seriously considers the opinions of others. He realizes that he is not superior to others.

Humility is not timidity or passivity but it is based on sincerity. How sincere, truthful, are we toward God, our spouse, and those we deal with daily? The degree of sincerity directly corresponds to the degree of humility we possess.

---

[93] *Furrow, Op. Cit.,* no. 259.

[94] St. Thomas Aquinas, *S. TH.* I-II, q. 77, a.4.

[95] St. Augustine, *In Ioannis Evangelilum tractatus 25, no. 16.*

Virtuous Couples Are Happy Couples

In the next chapter we are going to discuss marriage more in depth. Many difficulties in marriage involve our spouse's faults or vices as well as our own faults and vices. As Actor Ricardo Montalban contends, *Marriage is a tremendously difficult vocation...[I]t is two pieces of metal rubbing constantly, and sometimes sparks fly...Even with each little disagreement you go to levels—you go low and then you rise again—because you love each other so much. With another disagreement you conquer that and go to a still higher level. But if you quit, you will never know that great joy of marriage. Someone said you will never know the apex of sexual pleasure until you are faithful to one woman and one woman alone. Then, marriage becomes everything together—not simply sex but the love of the years, the history behind you, the looking into each other's eyes and being taken into the past—and you are brought to fruition. It's beautiful.*[96]

Since we are to help our spouse reach heaven we should consider our spouse's virtues. Do we know what they are? Do you have a plan to encourage your spouse's good habits such as prudence, justice, flexibility, generosity, etc? What are your spouse's vices? What is your plan to tactfully help your spouse to overcome these vices so as to grow in the opposite virtue? Remember, **be diplomatic**. Concentrate on a few areas at first then expand. What is loveable in your spouse is the good within him/her. Through marriage each spouse tries to help the other by drawing out that goodness while also trying to help the other fight particular vices. One can only help, not force.

Before you can tackle the vices, faults and limitations of your spouse, you first must begin with yourself. What are your strengths and weaknesses? What is your strongest virtue? What is your worst vice? What is your plan of attack to conquer vices? It takes humility to see oneself as one is. Don't forget, the only person you can change is yourself. Don't become discourage. Mother Angelica reminds us, *We all struggle with our faults and*

---

[96]"In The Heart Of Tinseltown, A Faith Lived Deeply," *Op. Cit.*, p. 6.

failings, and despite our efforts, it seems that we never advance. My friends, take courage! What we are unable to do in a lifetime of struggle, the Lord can accomplish in the blink of an eye. And He will, so let us remain faithful.[97]

Calmly consider how you are going to deal with your spouse's faults. In which areas can you help your spouse to improve and in which areas do you have to live with your spouse's faults? The definition of a fault is something that should be there but is lacking. It can also be described as a lack of generosity in some manner. There are two types of faults: subjective faults and objective faults. Subjective faults are simply things that irritate such as a husband who won't send flowers to his wife because he feels it is a waste of money. If sending flowers is not something he will do, then the wife needs the virtue of flexibility to accept the situation rather than pouting about it. An objective fault is a moral failing that harms the person. If the fault is a moral failing, it is necessary to work with your spouse to overcome the fault. Examples could be a drinking problem, pornography, dishonesty, gambling, anger, insincerity, gossip, or the lack of belief in God.

Besides faults, there are bad actions and limitations. Dr. Anna Maria Araujo, of the University of Navarra, defines a bad action as any action that brings one away from some good. A Catholic skips Sunday Mass to go golfing. This is a bad action because it takes the golfer away from the graces he would receive by attending Mass, as well as the graces received from the worthy reception of the Holy Eucharist. In addition, the golfer commits a mortal sin, which severs his relationship with God. Should the person die in the state of unrepentant mortal sin he would go to hell. By skipping Mass the golfer has withdrawn himself from countless graces along with the possibility of going to heaven. A spouse is obligated to point out bad actions in an attempt to help the person to overcome them so he can save his soul.

A limitation is a potential that one lacks which impairs a person's character and stops that person from relating better to people. An example would be shyness. When we love a person, we want

---

[97] Mother Angelica, *EWTN Familly Newsletter,* April 2000, #169.

them to be the best they can be. With kindness, each spouse should help the other to overcome limitations so as to become more perfect. That is why self-knowledge by both spouses is so necessary.

Dr. David Isaacs explains that within the human heart there are certain needs. *Among the first we find the need to be loved and respected by someone, to feel secure and be treated well, to communicate with another person, to gain satisfaction from having made an effort in something...[F]urthermore, if these needs have...not been fulfilled, it is probable that the person will not be in a position to help others, and, in the case of a married person to help his/her spouse.*

A person who enters matrimony with the experience or sensation of not having been loved, for example by his parents, or who has never had a real friend, may perhaps be able to receive from his spouse what he has never experienced before, but it will be difficult for him to express his love properly, at least at first...[T]he most important thing is to have a positive attitude, a desire to learn, and of course we can all improve little by little in some quality or ability which we lack. In a sense, a person who has never learnt to show his love, as he has no experience of the way love is expressed, can begin the learning process when he receives signs of love from another person...[W]hen a person receives love, he will respond by giving something, perhaps little in itself but a lot for him, and that he will progressively come to increase his capacity to give as the loving relationship develops.[98]

Part of our responsibility in marriage is to provide for the needs of our spouse. In developing virtues in ourselves we have to take into consideration the needs of our spouse and children. How can we better live charity/love? Women need frequent reassurance that they are loved. Most husbands are just content to have their wives physically present to feel loved. Both need to work to fulfill the needs of the other. This is the virtue of kindness. One person may need intellectual stimulation while his/her spouse prefers

---

[98] "Conditions for Giving and Receiving in Marriage," Dr. David Isaacs. *Course on Marriage Relationships*, (University of Navarra, Spain 1991-1992) p. 1.

passive entertainment. The virtue of generosity comes into play here for both spouses.

Fr. Hardon, S.J. observes: *Marriage certainly brings a revelation of many new beauties of character, but it also brings a revelation of many faults of character. It is fraught with disappointments even as with agreeable surprises...The Sacrament imparts all the courage, the energy, the refreshment, and the love needful to make the bond strong and lasting. It renews the youth of married life and makes it satisfying even in spite of years.*[99]

Additional Helps

- ✓ Which virtues do you need to acquire?
- ✓ Design a plan on how you will acquire the virtues you lack.
- ✓ Specifically, how can you help your spouse to grow in the virtues he/she needs?
- ✓ How are you living virtues in your married life such as cheerfulness, flexibility, thoughtfulness, justice, charity?
- ✓ Read books on how to acquire the virtues such as the classic **The Spiritual Combat** by Dom Lawrence Scupoli, **How to Live Nobly and Well** by Edward F. Garesché, SJ, **Humilty (Wellspring of Virtue)** by Dietrich von Hildebrand, and **Kindness** by Lawrence G. Lovasik.

---

[99] *Marriage and Parenthood, The Catholic Ideal*, op. Cit., p. 20.

Chapter 4

Life In The Married Lane

"The family you come from isn't as important as the family you're going to have." Ring Ladner

Remember driver's ed when you were sixteen? The course took months of classroom study then behind the wheel training. This was followed by a written test as well as a behind the wheel test given by a state employee. If you failed one of these tests you did not get your driver's license. This situation is not unique in life. To enter any type of profession a person needs experience or an apprenticeship. In business, a college degree is necessary. For promotion in many fields a M.B.A. or Ph.D. degree is required. In some fields such as medicine, engineering, law, and accounting extensive testing is compulsory for licensing.

For marriage there is neither training nor education provided. A couple can marry simply by paying a license fee. Yet, there is no greater impact on the body, soul, and psyche of an individual than a marriage. This permanent covenant of self-giving creates the basic unit of society, the family. The stability of society depends on stable families. Stable families depend in turn on stable marriages. The Church itself depends on families for continuation not to mention priestly vocations. Without marital training and education is it any wonder that 50% of marriages end in divorce? With few people realizing the responsibilities inherent in the marriage covenant is it any wonder that annulments are being granted?

Raising children becomes on the job training without a supervisor. In the past, extended family was present to give tips and help. Now families are geographically separated leaving young couples to muddle through the unknown on their own. Rather than dwelling on the unprecedented failure of many marriages, we need to learn how to enrich our own marriage. To avoid becoming a dysfunctional family, we need to study how to raise a happy, contented family. Once we apply what we have learned, we then have a moral obligation, through charity, to share what we learn with our friends. This is the theme of this chapter.

The Institute for Family Development, headquartered at the University of Navarra in Pamplona, Spain, has been addressing this situation for decades. In fact, this university has a department devoted to the family. Since the 1980's Dr. David Isaacs, of the University of Navarra, and Dr. Anna Maria Araujo De Venegas, professor at the University of La Sabana in Bogota, Colombia, have presented courses in Family Development in the U.S., Canada, Ireland, Africa, England, Europe, South America and Australia specifically for parents. In this chapter I am drawing material from two of their courses: *Marriage Relationships* held in Pamplona, Spain and *Happiness and Suffering in the Family* held in the Chicago area. In future chapters I will use material from their course in Washington, D.C. *Teaching Younger Children Virtues*. These courses enriched my marriage relationship and family life. My hope is that my notes from these courses will equally enrich yours.

"I Do" Is Only The Beginning

In fairy tales or romantic films the dramatic climax is the wedding. One is left with the warm feeling that the couple "lived happily every after." In life, the wedding is not the end of the story but rather the exciting beginning with the future yet to unfold. The drama of a relationship takes place in the progressing decades climaxing in eternity. How fitting that a popular wedding song is *"We've Only Just Begun..."*

Do you know what actually brought you and your spouse together? Actually your choice was a complex process. Physical appearance is probably what first attracted you. As you became more acquainted you found particular characteristics of your future spouse appealing. It may have been an outgoing personality or other qualities such as cheerfulness or thoughtfulness that you found attractive. Many times the characteristics you found loveable in your spouse are those, which you yourself lack or wish to acquire. Remember the saying about opposites attracting! As your relationship grew you began sharing your feelings, hopes and dreams. Some couples realize they are meant for each other almost immediately. My husband told me on our first date that he was going to marry me. Some couples take years, even a decade before making the commitment.

There are three stages each couple progresses through before deciding if this person is "the one." The first stage is yearning to learn all about this wonderful person you feel attracted to. This yearning leads to frequent dates, long phone conversations, and excuses to run into each other. As one learns more about the person, a decision is made to either end the relationship or move on to the second stage. The second stage is the desire to want the other person for one's own. The third stage is the desire to possess the beloved, the yearning for union. It is at this stage that the diamond is presented and the question of marriage asked. This final step is considered the perfection of love.

Besides the three stages of love, there are three different types of love: passionate love (strong sexual love), romantic love (intense idealization of the person) and conjugal love (intimate knowledge that leads to trust and security). Josef Pieper writes: *In all the cases of love imaginable, to love means to approve of...To love something or someone means to see them as, and to call them something good. To face them and to say to them: "It's good that you exist—it's good that you are in the world."*

Once married, our love flourishes if we work to keep the joy in our marriage. Each day our love should grow deeper. The love and joy we experienced on our wedding day should be minute compared to the growing intensity of love we experience as the years pass. Romantic love does not have to end with the honeymoon.

Prof. Manuel Gurpegui, Professor of Psychiatry at the University of Granada (Spain), believes that it is possible to build a good marriage in all situations. He finds that in successful marriages, spouses are willing to grow as a unit together. Committed to each other, they are willing to change over time. They share closeness, unity and the ability to communicate. Along with these characteristics the couple are physically (sexually) affectionate toward each other. St. Paul strongly councils: *Let the husband render to the wife her due [relations], and likewise the wife to the husband. The wife has not authority over her body, but the husband; the husband likewise has not authority over his body, but his wife. Do not deprive each other, except perhaps by consent, for a time, that you may give yourselves to prayer; and return together again lest Satan tempt you because you lack self-control* (*1 Cor.* 7:3-6).

John Paul II, in his *Theology of the Body*, teaches that the physical affection between spouses is a means of obtaining sanctifying grace as long as the marital act is open to pro-creation. *It would thus be certainly sinful, according to St. Thomas, to reject the pleasure of sex [in marriage] as something intrinsically evil".*[1] Dr. Gurpegui adds that sex is not just physical but encompasses the whole person.

Happily married couples not only express their love physically but also verbally. No one gets tired of hearing *"I love you!"* How often do you say those words to your spouse? The more you say them, the more your spouse will reciprocate.

Happily married couples are honest with each other. Each knows

---

[1] Rev. E. C. Messenger, Ph.D., *Two In One Flesh,* vol. 2, *The Mystery of Sex and Marriage* (Maryland: The Newman Press, 1948) p. 9.

what the other is doing. Money is not sheltered from the other. In addition, each spouse gives the other material and emotional support by showing appreciation and admiration toward the other. Love is expressed materially (through gifts) as well as by helping with chores, work or family obligations. Truly loving, each puts up with the shortcomings or the demands of the other. They create time to be together so as to grow even more closely united. Each of these areas will be discussed in greater detail later in this chapter.

The marriage relationship is the most unique of all relationships. It is a human and supernatural vocation (for Christian couples) founded on the physical and emotional faithfulness between the husband and wife. While procreation is the primary aim of marriage, marriage also serves to fill a psychological need for a love of one's own, for companionship. It is a total giving of one-self to one's spouse, to "become one flesh." It is the fusion of two natures into one forming a "joint personality." The husband serves his wife while the wife serves her husband since the two are one. *Moreover, this service is total and takes priority over all others (except the personal relationship with God.) It is total, because it is directed towards the spouse as a whole person...It takes priority, because it takes precedence over any commitment or bond forged in the past (for example, with parents), or in the future (with children, career, legitimate personal interests, etc.). This is the basis for all the norms—rights and duties—of natural conjugal morality...It is a relationship which calls for reciprocity— giving and receiving—between spouses, built on foundations of equality and free will.*[2]

Unfortunately, it is the lack of complete self-giving by one or both spouses that triggers marital problems. Those who have chosen the married state will find at times it can be a *hard knock life* precisely because it is a life of renunciation, of self-sacrifice, of service. St. Paul reiterates: **Yet such [as marry] shall have affliction in the flesh** (*1Cor.*7:28). That anticipated vacation might have to be scrapped due to pregnancy. A hobby or favorite

---

[2] "Some Aspects of Marriage" by Dr. Ana Maria Navarro Araujo , *Course on Marriage Relationships*, (University of Navarra, Spain 1991-1992) p. 1.

pastime may have to be dropped to spend more time with one's spouse and children. It could mean being up all night with a sick child or a colicky baby then having to contend with hyperactive toddlers the next day. Anticipated parties or business trips may have to be skipped if the sitter cancels out. At other times, bills mount and the income dwindles or a chronic illness strikes. Dad may have to work a second job or mom must work full-time. Thankfully as Christians we are not left to our own devices. We can turn to God for help in handling all the responsibilities and obligations that arise. Bl. Padre Pio told married couples: *In family life, have strong convictions; smile in the face of self-denial and in the constant sacrifice of your whole self. Self-denial must prevail in the home.*[3]

Every family is a gift from God, writes Bl. Pope John XXIII. The family is the community in which each person is accepted for what one is, not for what one does or can contribute. This acceptance is unconditional in spite of character flaws or personality defects. Family life is more than living in the same house or apartment. To develop family unity there are specific actions that family members must engage in together. *Centuries of Christian wisdom have shown that certain features are typically unifying, and their opposite are divisive,* remarks Fr. Hardon, S.J. He then lists the following points. Consider how well your family is living them. Note that to live these points members of the family must practice the virtues we have already discussed. To disregard these points is to court trouble.

- **Family members should live together**. When parents live separately for professional reasons, etc. the separation destroys family unity, spousal unity, and triggers behavioral problems with the children.

- **Family members should converse together**. This is the way to get to know each other, to exchange ideas, to teach values. *[T]he practice of sincere daily conversation is indispensable for sound family life.*

- **Family members must pray together**. *The corporate graces*

---

[3] Fr. Alessio Parente, OFM, Cap. "The Family: A Three Part Essay," *Echoes of Padre Pio's Voice*, Vol. 5 No. 1, 1998.

that families need, require corporate prayer. When Jesus said, **"where two or three are gathered together in my name, I shall be there with them"** (Matt. 18-19), He was giving us the most powerful motive possible for family prayer.

- **Family members must work together.** A sense of unity is formed when members of the family each contribute in their own capacity to the well-being of all. Each child should have set chores as his contribution to the family. Every member is personally responsible for keeping the home running and clean. Every member should be trained to pitch in with entertaining, cleaning, laundry, garden chores, running errands, babysitting, etc. When home is nothing more than a bed and breakfast, family unity is non-existent.

- **Family members should discuss issues together.** The husband and wife need to discuss family concerns together before arriving at a decision. It is also important to allow children to sit in on some discussions so they can learn how decisions are reached and why. It's an important aspect of their education.

- **Family members should worship together.** It's one thing to teach our children the faith, but another to show them how it is practiced though our example. United families attend Sunday Mass and at least monthly confession together. Spiritual habits acquired as children will remain when they become adults.

- **Family members should read together.** Television, computer games, and the Internet are not only addictive, but they dull people's minds/imagination. Turn these off during the week. Instead read stories or books to the children. (Note the example of the Martin family in the next chapter.)

- **Family members should eat together.** *During family meals, it is not only the body that is being fed, but the souls of those at table are nourished by their interchange of spirit."* Recall the example of Our Lord in Scripture. Many of His teachings took place at various dinners. This daily family interchange is more important than having your children in activities that disrupt family meals.

- **Family members should relax together.** *If you have no need for recreation for yourself,* St. Francis de Sales advised, *you must help to make recreation for those who need it.* Sunday outings, holidays, vacations are all opportunities to enjoy the company of family members in fun settings. Make the most of these opportunities to solidify family unity. Take turns letting children select activities or places to go. Include grandparents and extended family members.

- **Family members must bear one another's sufferings and joys.** Life is a mixture of the good and the bad. Recall the words of St. Paul: ***If one member suffers anything all the members suffer with it or if one member glories, all the members rejoice with it*** (*I Cor.* 12:26). So too in our families.[4] Teach the children to help each other, comfort each other, rejoice with each other.

Living the above points will not only unify your marriage and family but your commitment to care for each other will deepen through the years.

The Secret Of A Happy Marriage

Happy marriages do not simply happen. They are carefully nurtured every single day. *Happily ever after* means diligent work! As we begin our marriage, we are *so in love* that everything we do is done with our beloved in mind. It's a joy to serve the other. Unfortunately, as time goes by, it's natural to grow lazy, to slack off, to take each other for granted, to be more demanding of our spouse, to grow more self-centered. St. Peter Julian Eymard reminds us, *What are the proofs of genuine love? There is only one, it's sacrifices: the sacrifices it prompts us to do and those it accepts with joy. Love without sacrifice is but an empty name, a self-love in disguise.*[5]

John Gottman, Ph.D., author of **The Seven Principles for Making Marriage Work** claims *[w]orking briefly on your marriage every day will do more for your health and longevity than working out at a health club.*

But how does one work on a marriage? Begin by doing something daily for your spouse that is fun, thoughtful or romantic. Yes, this does take some thought and some effort but it does not have

---

[4] *The Catholic Family In The Modern World, Op. Cit.,* pp. 70-72.

[5] *The Real Presence, Op.Cit.,* p.59.

to be dramatic or expensive. It can be a love letter left on the pillow, put in a pocket, or packed in the lunch. It can be preparing a favorite dinner or bringing home a single, inexpensive flower. Design a card with a touching poem or make a special cocktail. Surprise your spouse with a special Saturday breakfast, Sunday brunch or just a special dessert some night. It can be offering to run an errand, giving a complement, extending a helping hand, sharing a quiet moment together, or surprising your spouse with a special treat. It's the smile and kiss at the door when you meet after work. It is the order in the home. Be creative. Use your imagination to spring simple little surprises on each other. It helps love to grow, puts the fun back into marriage, and creates the necessary good memories needed to keep your marriage healthy. Why not preface the activity or action by saying, *This is because I love you!* One husband, knowing how his wife enjoys champagne, surprises her with a bottle of her favorite vintage periodically. Another husband breaks up the week for his wife by taking her out for a sandwich on the days that are most hectic for her. Away from the phone and children they can talk in peace. His wife reciprocates by surprising him with a special cigar, a hunting magazine, or his favorite dinner.

Random acts of kindness keep our love fresh, along with developing the virtue of the spirit of service. If one partner is thoughtful and the other is not, the example and words of the thoughtful spouse should motivate the other to struggle to develop the virtue of thoughtfulness. On the other hand, if one spouse is always giving and the other only taking, the selfishness of the "taking" spouse spells trouble for the marriage. In order to continually give, a person must also receive. If a spouse never receives, eventually the giving spouse has nothing more to give and love dies.

Men, when you come home from work, don't rush to check the mail for bills. Give your wife your attention. Wives, get dressed up when your husband comes home. Fix your hair, put on make-up, surprise him by looking feminine—wear a skirt or dress just for him. My husband rarely recognizes many of his fellow employees on the weekends because the women do not wear make-up nor fix their hair. Remember ladies, it is more important to look good at home than on the job!

Men, give personal gifts to your wife. A vacuum cleaner will not cut it. Never give her a gift for the house unless she specifically asks for it. Listen for hints that she may be giving you. No hints? Then think jewelry, flowers (preferably cut flowers unless she requests a potted plant), candy, clothes (the wrong size will cause problems), perfume, or a weekend away together.

Men, help with or do the dishes to give your wife a break. Wives, keep the house up. It means a lot to a man to come home to order rather than chaos. Men, put the children to bed to give your wife a break. Wives, don't unload your woes until after your husband has a chance to unwind.

In today's world there is no set division of labor. Be a helpmate for each other. Laundry needs to be done? Work together to do it. Resentment builds when one spouse is overburdened.

Viva La Difference

Many times a man, once he wins the hand of the woman he loves, turns his attention to his profession leaving the young wife wondering *What happened?* On the flip side, many times a wife, once she snags her guy, lives in sweat suits letting herself go. This is an indication that one spouse is taking the other for granted...a deadly attitude for any marriage. Wives, your husband fell in love with you because he thought you were beautiful. Don't disappoint him. Look nice for him every day, not just when you go out. This shows your love for him as much as respect for yourself. Too difficult to do? Such an attitude is an indication of the vice of sloth (laziness). Besides looking nice for your husband, make the effort to prepare a nice dinner for him...even if you are not hungry. One woman I meet periodically for lunch opens a can of soup for her husband those days since she's not hungry. This is a selfish attitude.

Husbands, listen to your wife. Consider her opinions. When possible act on her wishes. Wives reciprocate. During the time couples court, they put their best side forward. This side is still there. So dust it off, then put it on again for your spouse.

With the birth of children, wives naturally tend to focus on them rather than their husbands. Increasing financial burdens caused by the growing family forces husbands to focus even more on their professions. Remember, your vows are centered on your spouse, not your children or your profession. After God, your spouse must come first. Couples, who live parallel lives, discover they have grown apart when their children leave home. With the children raised they no longer have anything in common. To avoid this happening to your marriage, plan time alone together. It's this time together that welds the man and the woman into the intellectual and spiritual unity we talked about earlier. Get a babysitter and do something together. Do not be overprotective with your children. It stifles them and your marriage. Husbands, take your wife out on a weekly date—to a Friday night fish fry, an ice cream parlor, a good movie, a play, a concert or museum. Courting during marriage builds happy memories, which in turn shapes a happy, fun-filled marriage. Happy memories are vitally important because they help couples to survive the difficult times. A marriage filled with unhappy memories will not last. Happy memories fuel hope. No one wants to face the future without hope.

Men and women express their love in radically different ways. Men show their love by doing things for their wives such as washing the car, filling it up with gas for her, buying her an appliance or bringing home a sexy negligee after a business trip. Women, more romantic by nature, are unaware that love motivated their husbands to do these things. Women view these actions as something expected. For the woman, there is no romance in a car wash while the negligee usually has an ulterior motive. Although the husband can be working hard to please his wife through these acts of love, the wife is totally oblivious because she views love from a different perspective.

Love for a woman means affectionate hugs, tender kisses, compliments, little surprises but most of all her husband's complete attention. Caring for children all day long, your wife needs an adult to communicate with in the evening. She waits patiently watching the clock hoping against hope that you will not only get home soon but will then take over for her. On the other hand, men are weary from communicating at work. Naturally when they arrive home, they simply want to relax, to be left alone. They are tempted to feel they have given enough at the office. So they seek refuge behind a newspaper, bury themselves in a hobby or channel surf.

Since marriage is the total giving of oneself, the husband needs to struggle to put aside his wants and needs to serve his wife, and the wife her husband's needs. Each should ask the other what help is needed. One husband has learned this so well that he never says, *I'm going to...* Instead he asks, *What would you like me to do for you now?* Each time we do something our spouse asks, we grow in different virtues such as patience, generosity, flexibility, order, industriousness, understanding, etc. If our actions are done for the honor and glory of God, we grow in holiness. This is why the Morning Offering is so important each day. We move so fast that there's rarely time to say, *God, I'm shopping for you,* or *Jesus, this obnoxious job is for you.* The Morning Offering takes care of everything. Happiness comes from loving our spouse and making him/her feel well loved and appreciated.

Communication In Marriage

Many problems in marriage are caused by the lack of communication. Communication is not simply words. It includes actions, gestures, emotions, facial expressions, body language, eye contact, memories, thoughts and feelings. Dr. Isaacs stresses: *[W]e have a twofold duty: to try to express ourselves adequately so that the other person can receive our message, and to make an effort to pick up the messages which the other is transmitting.*[6] This can become a bit tricky since women find it very difficult and at times impossible to express exactly what they want. They are more comfortable giving hints. Unfortunately, men, who tend to be brutally blunt, do not pick up hints. Yet over the years communication becomes such second nature between a husband

---

[6] Dr. David Isaacs, "Conditions for Giving and Receiving in Marriage," (University of Navarre, 1990) pp. 8-9.

and wife that they eventually learn to communicate by a look or a touch of the hand. One wife simply touches her husband's hand when he is driving and he immediately slows down.

To actually communicate, couples need to share the same values and interests, otherwise, they will simply be having an informational conversation, i.e. merely giving each other a daily report. This lack of communication can lead the couple to live parallel lives rather than one of unity. For unity to develop at least one shared valued is required. The shared values can be superficial ones such as an interest in sports and/or deeper values such as a concern to grow holy or to positively influence the culture they live in. The more values a couple share, the more they can communicate. This is also the basis of a united family. Doing everything together at the same time does not make a united family. It is shared values that unite family members.

To be happy in life we must be continually working to improve in all areas but specifically as a child of God; as a spouse; as a friend; as a citizen; and in our profession. The more each spouse improves in each area, the more the spouses will have to give to each other. This enriches their communication.

Another important aspect to communicating is timing. To communicate, a person has to be in the mood. When it's been a good day or something exciting has happened, it's easy to share the news. But if the day was a disaster there is a reluctance to talk. Some people cannot communicate until after the first cup of coffee in the morning. Trying to communicate when the baby is crying, children are fighting and the phone is ringing is impossible. Learn to be creative in finding opportunities to communicate. Locate a peaceful oasis, either in a room away from the children, outside in the backyard, or simply go for a walk. Once the cares of the day fall away it becomes easier to talk.

How do we react when our spouse tries to communicate with us? Do we close our book, turn off the TV, put down the newspaper? Or do we give curt answers as we keep one eye on the TV and the other on the person speaking? The last response kills communication.

While men would rather think over a problem than discuss it, women need to verbalize their concerns. Dr. Isaacs contends: *For a message to be communicated, it must be picked up in the same terms by the receiver...In marriage...the words used are never neutral. They reflect past events, the present situation, and even allude to future plans...[T]o the possible interpretations of the words we add the tone of voice used, the speed, [touch, look] etc., we shall see that there are many obstacles which make it difficult for us to ensure that the listener interprets our remarks correctly..*[7] Express yourself clearly. A couple were having problems with a new car. The husband was told to use premium gas rather than the less expensive grade. The husband told his wife, *buy the most expensive gas.* She did but it was diesal fuel that damaged the engine necessitating costly repairs. Dick had not communicated clearly and concisely to Sue.

In addition, to effectively communicate, one needs to develop sensitivity toward one's spouse so that you can read the person's mood. Learn to read your spouse's body language so that you can react correctly to the situation. Be aware of the signs your spouse gives to indicate tiredness, sickness, hurt, worry, or the need for affection. Then carry this same sensitivity over to the other members of the family. Listen to passing remarks that indicate a concern. For instance, a husband may drop the remark, *Sales are off at work.* He is actually saying, *"I'm afraid I'm going to be laid off."*

A husband can develop more sensitivity toward his wife by watching her facial expression as well as listening and trying to understand what she is saying. Learning to listen not only to the words but to the message is key. A husband may hear what a wife says but not understand <u>what</u> she is saying. My favorite example is that of a wife who told her husband that she would never, ever, under any circumstance want a pedicure. Her husband only heard "pedicure." When Mother's Day rolled around, he gave his dumbfounded wife a nonrefundable pedicure at Neiman Marcus. He was completely baffled by her angry reaction to his gift. The wife retaliated by giving her husband something she wanted for Father's Day rather than something he could use.

Besides listening, let the person complete what they are trying

---
[7] *"Conditions for Giving and Receiving in Marriage," Op. Cit., p. 3.*

to say rather than interrupting, cutting them off, or speaking at the same time. If it's a long involved story that you find distracting, ask questions to keep your attention on the issue. This will also show your interest. Watch the person's eyes as they speak. The eyes are the windows to the soul. They tell you even more than the words you are hearing. My friend Nancy and her husband, Jim, both wear hearing aids and read lips. She notes, *this forces us to face each other and look at the facial expression and eyes while trying to understand each other. I never thought of this hearing problem as a gift before but I do now!*

Sensitivity is also knowledge of a person. How well do you really know your spouse? Do you know your husband/wife's favorite color, favorite alcoholic drink, dress or suit size? What type of entertainment, music, books or activities does he/she enjoy? What is his/her favorite dinner, restaurant, play, dessert, vacation? What does he/she fear, dream about, wish for? Do you know what irritates your spouse? Do you avoid inciting your spouse to anger? Remember, when we goad someone to anger (an occasion of sin for the person) it is also our sin. Christ tells us: **You have heard that it was said to the ancients, "Thou shall not kill"...But I say to you that everyone who is angry with his brother shall be liable to judgment...and whoever says, "Thou fool!" shall be liable to the fire of Gehenna. Therefore, if you are offering your gift at the altar, and there remember that your brother has anything against you, leave your gift...and go first to be reconciled to your brother, and then come and offer you gift...** (*Matt.* 5:21-24).

Resolving Problems

To solve discord, problems need to be brought out into the open and discussed calmly. Situations that seem to produce the most conflict are how to spend money (his ideas vs. her ideas) and family relations. When there's a blow-up, Dr. Isaacs recommends looking deeper to discover what really precipitated the problem. It's usually not the proverbial "straw" that broke the camel's back as much as the main load on the camel. This is called "displaced aggression." Get to the root of the problem. Most couples know what irritates the other so they tiptoe around it rather than trying to resolve the problem. By ignoring the problem it keeps festering until one becomes angry. At other times our spouse may indicate a problem by teasingly telling an incident or situation in front of friends or relatives. Watch for such cues then change your conduct. Solve the problems when they are still solvable. Unsolved problems give birth to bitterness or resentment that leads to unhappiness. During your prayer time consider: as problems arise are you open to discussing them? Is your spouse comfortable bringing concerns to you or is he/she afraid to truly express himself/herself?

The best approach to handling a problem is to pray before discussing it. Pray to the Holy Spirit to infuse you with His gifts and enlightenment. Ask the Holy Spirit for guidance as to how to present the situation. Not meaning to sound superstitious, personal experience has taught me the power of one's guardian angel and the sacramental, holy water. Ask your guardian angel to intercede with your spouse's guardian angel so that you both can talk calmly without fighting. Angels have the ability to influence people's personality and their emotions. Ask for help in this sticky matter. Then find a quiet place to talk, away from interruptions. If the phone rings, don't answer it. If it's a real touchy subject, sprinkle the room with holy water before hand. Holy water is a powerful sacramental that seems to banish Satan from the premises. You don't want him stirring things up. Then calmly discuss what is bothering you in a respectful manner. Once the matter is discussed, drop it by changing the subject. Avoid nagging or harping on the subject. Dr. Isaacs and Dr. Araujo recommend avoiding the following devices when communicating:

✓ Avoid labeling the other person with defensive adjectives or adverbs such as "moody," "touchy," "unreasonable," or name-calling.
✓ Avoid being "in a mood." No matter how distasteful a topic, attempt to be cheerful or accepting of the criticism. No one is perfect. Everyone has faults.
✓ Avoid playing games such as sulking, not speaking, or hurling insults.
✓ Avoid negativity or a lack of enthusiasm. Listen with attention and a smile.
✓ Avoid a superiority complex or certainty. It is difficult to communicate with a "know it all" personality or a person who sneers, "What do you know?"

✓ Avoid going back over past arguments. Keep to the issue at hand.
✓ Avoid dragging other people into the argument such as in-laws or children.
✓ Avoid acting in haste. Think over all decisions then act calmly and prudently.
✓ Avoid making the other person appear to have bad will. This will only make the situation worse.
✓ Avoid leaving the situation at the status quo. Try to come to a resolution.

The famous quote from the book **Love Story,** *Love is never having to say I'm sorry* is terribly erroneous. If one loves, one readily says *I'm sorry.* As Christians we are called to follow the example of the Holy Father in acknowledging that as sinners we all do things for which we need to apologize. After saying *I'm sorry,* there should also be the will to change.

Other Considerations...

Dr. Isaacs considers it important for stay-at-home moms to have weekly outside activities for intellectual stimulation. When dad comes home from work, he brings along with him the outside world. Mom has little to discuss besides potty training, cantankerous children, household problems and "the soaps." Besides, moms need time alone, away from the home. The job of motherhood is a demanding one. The mother is constantly giving yet she receives little affection, little satisfaction, and no income for her work. Although mothers are raising future saints and citizens, homemakers lack prestige today. It's also difficult to see any results from the long hours of work. Isaacs insists that parents will not see results until their children are parents. It is then when you will see if you passed or failed "Parenting 101." To avoid stagnating, Dr. Isaacs recommends that women become involved in an outside activity that is disciplined, demanding, as well as goal orientated. Ideas could include volunteering to help in a pro-life center, helping in a political campaign, volunteering at a hospital, fundraising for worthy causes, working in a soup kitchen, driving for "meals on wheels," teaching a Catholic doctrine class, or holding an office in a club or organization.

Becoming involved in any of these activities will help Mom to grow in some, if not all of the five areas we discussed before. It will also give her something to communicate about besides the children. Otherwise moms will look for their enrichment in addictive soap operas or Internet chat rooms. Men also need to be enriched outside of their profession but in moderation, not at the expense of their wives and families. Remember to be able to give, each spouse needs to be enriched.

Working together on small and large projects stimulates conversation and creates memories. Select projects that result in warm memories such as planning vacations, holidays, a garden, remodeling, interior decorating, or shopping for furniture. The latter is especially important. If the wife does the decorating as well as the furniture shopping herself, it becomes "her home" rather than "our home." Each object in the home should bring fond memories for the couple. Study art, a foreign language or develop a hobby together. Avoid projects that cause friction such as wallpapering together! Remember, happy marriages have a wealth of good memories, few bad memories. Future projects keep our marriage vibrant. When couples plan future projects they have something to look forward to together, to hope for in the future. When people have no projects they tend to age and die. Recall how people who have no outside interests seem to die shortly after retirement. Future projects keep us youthful. If you want your own parents to stay young, sharp and vibrant, keep them involved with your children. It gives them a project to look forward too as well as providing wonderful memories for your children.

Good "memories" is a reoccurring theme in this chapter because an abundance of good memories are essential for happy marriages. When bad memories saturate a spouse's memory the spouse begins to mentally pull away from the other. The unhappy spouse can no longer see a future with his/her partner. Once the will decides there is no future together, it is difficult to move the will to change. That is why it is so critical for each spouse to provide good memories for the other. Fun memories are crucial for happy marriages. Go to the theatre, for a drive, or simply put a special picnic in a hamper for an afternoon together in the country. Rent a canoe or walk along a beach or nature trail. Once you and your spouse have a collection of warm, happy memories, problems can be more easily handled between the two of you.

Another way to stimulate communication is to develop a circle of friends together. Isolation is a strain on the marriage relationship. Rotate homes to socialize, play cards, discuss current issues, great books, or study family topics. An added benefit will be the acquiring of the virtues of hospitality and sociability, almost non-existent virtues in our culture. Defined by Isaacs, *the sociable person makes good use of and discovers ways of getting together with different people; he manages to communicate with them through the genuine interest he shows in them, in what they say, in what they do, in what they think and feel.*[8]

Christ, Himself, expresses the importance of hospitality: **For whoever gives you a cup of water to drink in my name, because you are Christ's, amen I say to you, he shall not lose his reward** (*Mk.* 9:41-42). Entertaining and socializing are fun ways to grow holy! In order to practice these virtues, develop friends who likewise are willing to grow in these virtues. If friends don't reciprocate, develop another group of friends who will. A person can only develop these virtues if they associate with similarly minded people who are willing to practice hospitality and socialization. Transplanted away from family and friends? Join the area Jaycees. They have activities for men, women and couples. Bring a pie or cake over to your new neighbors or have a neighborhood party. If your children are in school invite the parents of their classmates over. Select the ones who share common values, then work to develop friendships with them. Make an effort to develop friendships with a variety of different people.

We can never lump people, especially our spouse, into a category because people are always changing, and hopefully improving. Just remember that it's important to keep alive the excitement of trying to discover the depths of our spouse as we tried to do on our honeymoon.

---

[8] *Character Building, a Guide For Parents And Teachers, Op. Cit.,* p. 258.

Characteristics Of Happy Marriages

Happy marriages have four characteristics: **empathy, appreciation, congruence,** and **character.** Since the latter is self-explanatory, we will simply discuss the first three characteristics.

Empathy is defined as understanding, compassion, emotional identity, sympathy, insight and feeling. To be "one" we need to empathize with our spouse. This means to see things from the other person's point of view; to be objective rather than subjective. In order to empathize, we need information that can only be obtained through observation and listening. Once obtained, we need to create a calm situation that will put the person at ease so our spouse can open up to us.

To explain how empathy works, Isaacs gives the example of sadness. Why is my spouse sad? Rather than ignoring the problem or offering indifferent comfort until the person gets over the sadness, seek the cause through communication. Only then can you give a proper response.

- Is my spouse sad because of some unjust words or action he/she may have said or done to another?
- Is my spouse sad because of some inaction on his/her part? Was a promise or commitment not kept?
- Is my spouse sad because of the unjust words or actions of another person?
- Is my spouse sad because someone did not keep a commitment or promise? Did I forget his/her birthday, our anniversary?
- Is my spouse sad because of some fear, some situation, or something he/she has heard or seen?

Dr. Isaacs contends that a woman has a natural ability to quickly analyze what is bothering her husband because of the gift of intuition. Scientists believe that this is because women communication faster between the two sides of their brain. Men, on the other hand, think step-to-step before arriving at a conclusion. Women see the problem and can skip the different steps thereby coming to a conclusion faster. For instance, the baby is running 104-degree fever so the mother calls the doctor.

She knows this is a sign that the baby may have an ear infection. The father, on the other hand, may think calling the doctor is premature. He wants to wait to see if the fever drops because it may simply be the flu.

Men have a better overview of situations. Since they accumulate only a few pieces of information men can make quick decisions. Women, on the other hand, grasp all the specific details concerning the situation that men do not perceive. For this reason, it takes women longer to shift through all the possibilities before they can make a decision. A husband's "instant" decision without consulting his wife will frustrate her. Take the example of a couple trying to get away on a vacation. In trying to select a time to go, the husband checks his calendar and chooses a date. He neglects to consult his wife to see if the date is workable for her. She has to check to see if the children are in or out of school. Will the children be going along? If not, can a sitter be found to watch the children for those dates? What about the children's outside commitments? If they stay home with a sitter, who will drive them to these commitments? What about extended family birthdays or commitments, carpool obligations, doctors' appointments? Who will care for the house and grounds if everyone goes on vacation? What about social commitments? These are just some of the issues that the wife considers in the framework of leaving on vacation.

Appreciation means to esteem, cherish, value, admire, and prize a person for who he/she is. Happily married couples live this attitude. A smart husband values his wife as his best friend, confidant, fellow worker, social director and mother of his children. The smart wife values her husband as her best friend, confident, companion, fellow worker, breadwinner, and father of her children. In addition, each should value the other's talents such as: financial planning, gardening, business expertise, household maintenance, hunting, sports, playing bridge, etc. *When there is a rejection of one of these possible roles, or simply indifference, the possibilities of true appreciation decline.*[9]

[9] Dr. David Isaacs, "Conditions for a Developing Relationship in Marriage," Instituto de Ciencias de la Educacion, p. 4.

The husband needs to not only value the role of his wife in caring for and educating the children but also express his appreciation. Likewise, the wife needs to value the role of her husband in supporting and caring for the family by expressing her appreciation to her husband. Each role is equally difficult. It is a formidable task to raise, to care for, to educate, to teach virtue to toddlers, children and teens. It is equally challenging to financially support a growing family while at the same time making enough money to provide for doctrinally sound, moral schooling for each child. If one or both spouses do not express appreciation to the other, the couple will grow distant, seeking appreciation from outsiders which leads to marital problems.

Additional problems can arise when one spouse actually does not value what the other is doing or only partially appreciates the other's efforts. Sometimes one may value the spouse but not value what is most important to that person. My writing mentor is a brilliant author. Yet her husband refers to her writing as *Kath's typing*. While he says this in an affectionate manner, it indicates that he really does not take her work seriously. It is thoughtless little comments like these that wound the heart. Each of us needs to be valued in the area that is most important to us. When this does not occur, problems arise.

By stereotyping our spouse we indicate a prejudice which prevents the person from freely being himself. Some indications that we have categorized our spouse are no longer showing an interest in the other's opinion; not appreciating the other's interests; neglecting to inform the other about the activities of the children or financial matters because we feel he/she is not interested or would not understand; not recognizing the other's talents because we are not interested in that area or lack that talent ourselves.

Hurt feelings result when a spouse does not know how to communicate appreciation to the other. To appreciate another is to believe in their radical possibility for improvement; to believe that tomorrow they may offer something more than today, that they may achieve further maturity each day.[10] To reach this point

---

[10] *Ibid.,* p. 3.

of appreciation, each spouse needs to work to overcome ignorance of the role of the other and laziness. It takes effort to recognize the labors of the other. It's so easy to pass off what the other does as unimportant. To overcome this tendency each spouse should seek to develop oneself in the same areas as the spouse because until this is done, it's impossible to comprehend his/her laborious contribution to the family. The best way to handle this is to work together on the various aspects of running the home, caring for the children, and organizing outside social activities. If one or both spouses insist on a strict division of labor, appreciation for what the other does to contribute to family life will be lacking. If a spouse finds nothing in the other spouse to appreciate, the person becomes hollow and the relationship falters. By encouraging each to develop in all the areas of family life, appreciation for the other person grows. As mom takes on more of the household concerns, dad needs to be more actively involved with the children by helping to get them ready for bed, bathing them, changing diapers, babysitting, teaching them their prayers, reading them bedtime stories.

Mary, the mother of four little ones, went on retreat leaving her husband to care for the children. On Sunday night when she arrived home she had arranged for her mother-in-law to sit with the children so that she and her husband could have a quiet dinner alone. When she walked into the house she was greeted with complete chaos. The baby was running a high temperature. Dishes were stacked in the sink. The five year old proudly informed her that he had vomited on the newly cleaned carpeting necessitating a second carpet cleaning by her husband, Tony. Tony was in a state of collapse on the sofa unable to muster the strength to go out for dinner. He was so exhausted that he had to be helped to get up from the sofa and into bed. Delighted to have his wife back home, after the children were all in bed he candidly admitted, *Your life stinks, Mary. You need more help.* The young mom was thrilled with Tony's understanding. Mary's life has not changed but Tony appreciates the job she is doing as wife and mother. He's now more understanding of her fatigue when he gets home. Even more important, Tony picked up an important insight from the experience. He confided to her, *one thing that I learned from this weekend alone with the kids was that no matter what happens between the parents, parents cannot get divorced. You have to stay together for the sake of the kids.* Mary in return appreciates the efforts Tony makes to financially care for the family. He works two full-time jobs so that she can stay home with the children.

A wife needs to appreciate the sacrifices her husband makes to support the family by doing everything possible to help him to advance in his career, even if that means another move or attending more cocktail parties. Remember ladies, it's difficult working in a world without ethics and morals. There is no such thing as job security anymore. Your husband must give 100% every day at work or he's out of a job. Your home is your husband's safe refuge. Make it warm and inviting for him. Encourage and support him rather than being envious of his business trips or business dinners.

Avoid taking each other for granted. Pat learned just how much her husband was quietly doing when his foot surgery incapacitated him for six weeks. Suddenly she was shoveling snow, running to the bank to make deposits, calling repairmen, running errands, taking out the garbage, fixing items around the house, filling up the gas tanks in frigid weather. Pat developed a new appreciation for all of Michael's quiet help.

Years ago a very upset friend called. Jane was furious that her husband had sent her pink roses. *I hate pink roses. He knows I love yellow roses.* Now divorced, she would be grateful for even a dead rose from him. Nothing kills the spirit more than to be taken for granted or treated with a lack of gratitude. Everyone slips up now and again. When our spouse does, this gives us something to cheerfully "offer up" and grow in the virtues of patience and understanding.

Appreciation has another function. It indicates to the person that he/she is valuable. Psychiatrists find that many problems develop in marriages and personalities from the non-acceptance of self. One who knows that he/she is loved not only develops optimism but has something to offer to others. Isaacs emphasizes:

If one becomes impatient or even worse, if one becomes indifferent or scornful, a low degree of appreciation will be evident...As many of the other's virtues as possible should be appreciated because feeling a lack of appreciation even in an aspect of relatively little importance can easily produce an overall feeling of rejection because a person is one complete unity and if a person feels even partially rejected, it may produce a very delicate situation.

Where a high level of appreciation exists, the spouse will know that the other feels a real affection towards him/her; They will know that their spouses are interested in them as people. ...[A]ll this will be expressed in a series of acts in which each one is affectionate and attentive to the other.[11]

Congruence is defined in psychology as *[t]he ability to perceive the emotional state of the other with exactitude as though one were the other person, but without losing the observer's point of view.*[12] Isaacs adds that *congruence implies that a person acts in accordance with what he/she feels or thinks.* Jim can tell the mood of his wife simply by listening to her footsteps. Sara knows that when her husband whistles he is merely worried, but when he puffs up his cheeks he is upset!

If we possess congruence, not only are we keenly aware of how our spouse feels at any given time even if the spouse cannot articulate the concern but we are able to transmit our awareness, our concern to our spouse so that he/she knows that we are not indifferent. Our individual pace is fast. Each spouse is hit with personal problems, emotional upsets, and demands on time. Make a daily effort to empathize with your spouse so that your marriage relationship develops. To be indifferent to the feelings or concerns of your spouse is to severely damage the marriage relationship. Without empathy your spouse will feel isolated, not understood, unloved, insecure. *If this becomes a recurrent feeling, the memory might become "saturated" with these feelings and the result may be a serious breakdown in the marriage relationship.*[13]

---

[11] *Ibid.,* p. 4.

[12] C. R. Rogers, "The Necessary and Sufficient Conditions of Therapeutic Personality Change," *Journal of Consulting Psychology.* 1957, 21, 94-103.

[13] "Conditions for a Developing Relationship...," *Op. Cit.,* p. 3.

Congruence is also defined as harmony, balance, constancy, and regularity. In marriage, congruence should be applied by thinking before acting. It is keeping emotions under control. It is the practice of self-control by both spouses. To raise it to a higher plane, it is living in a prudent manner so that one's well-formed conscience guides actions rather than one's emotions. Problems enter marriage when one or both spouses have strong wills but weak reason or strong reason but weak wills or mixed-up minds motivated by strong wills.

Concluding his discussion on congruence, Isaacs points out: *There should be a general feeling of openness and sincerity, but there are also times in which it will be convenient to mention certain subjects or not....*

Lack of congruence can be noted when there is a sensation that the other is not being him/herself; that they are playacting; when he/she is uncomfortable when asked about certain topics or gives the impression that their exterior actions are different from their internal feelings.

The spouses' congruence...will be noticeable if they are sincere and don't elude important topics, if they express their feelings and if they feel comfortable with the relationship as a whole.[14]

Love And Authority

In the family, both the husband and wife share aspects of leadership. Yet shared leadership sometimes can lead to friction. (In Chapter 6 we will discuss in depth the specific roles of husband and wife, as well as the authority of the husband.) *Each couple has to define the different areas of their dependency in each particular circumstance. If one partner realizes that the other partner does not have any initiative, and that he or she cannot count on his or her help to solve a problem, then the partner has to realize that this is a cause for alarm. In order to continue a relationship, a personal style must exist in each partner...This personal style is reflected by [one's] behavior in everyday life. We can then say that a person who behaves in an unpredictable way*

---

[14] "Conditions for a Developing Relationship...," *Op. Cit.,* p. 6.

does not have a personal style. [Personal style] is not just a way of behaving, it is also the result of some kind of previous decision. A person who just lets himself be carried along and does not make personal decisions will have little personal style...[Personal] style can only be developed if each partner is responsible and accepts the consequences of a decision that he or she has made. Responsibility must be taken by each partner.[15]

Be alert to how children play one parent against the other. A child who is grounded by his mother may go to his father to ask permission to go out. The father, unaware that the son is grounded, gives his permission. To avoid situations such as this, parents need to keep each other informed as to the happenings and problems in the family so that both can work together, supporting the decisions the other spouse makes. Should you disagree with a decision your husband/wife made, do not express your opposition in front of the children. Support your spouse in front of the children but discuss the issue together when the children are out of hearing range.

For a couple to make a decision that is agreeable to both parties, each must have the same objective information. The next step is to agree on the same criteria for the best solution. This can be tricky if values are not shared. Problems develop in marriages resulting from bad secondary decisions made by one of the spouses. He blames her for a decision she made in regard to a child. She blames him for a bad career move. *Difficulties in communication don't always arise from the relationship itself, but rather from decisions made by the couple together or separately.*[16]

Each couple has to find the system that works best for them. Most couples split the division of labor. The husband takes care of one area and the wife the other depending on the skills or abilities of each. Yet it is important that each is able to substitute for the other in time of sickness or absence.

As mentioned at the beginning of this chapter, when we marry

---

[15] Dr. David Isaacs, "Communication and Decision Making In Matrimony," Instituto de Ciencias de la Educacion, 1985, p.5, 6.

[16] *Ibid.,* p. 1.

we become one body. All serious decisions affecting the marriage (our children, the individual spouses, relocation, professional work or the values you are trying to live as a family) cannot be made by one spouse independent of the other. Both spouses need to consult together before making a decision. Such decisions invoke the virtues of prudence, charity, humility, and justice. Dr. Isaac advises consulting if the commitment is permanent, or difficult to abandon. Consult on new issues such as a promotion that may entail the father living in another country or state for several months. How will this impact the marriage, the children? Topics that should be consulted between spouses include:

- family budget and how to handle it
- aspects related to leisure time
- aspects related to religion
- ways of showing love
- friends
- intimate relationships
- norms of social behavior
- philosophy of life
- how to treat parents and grandparents
- important objectives
- amount of time spent together
- the system followed in order to make important decisions
- sharing of housework
- hobbies
- decisions related to professional work.[17]

Isaacs insists that some professions or jobs are not for the married such as the work of the perpetual scholar or the sailor who is always away from home.

In the realm of marriage there are also personal decisions to be made; decisions that will be made personally but explained later to one's spouse; and decisions regarding one's own area of autonomy within the family taken after consulting with the spouse. Each spouse can make his/her own personal decisions in relation to God and friendships without any consultation. In many

---

[17] "Communication and Decision Making In Matrimony," *Op. Cit.*, p. 4.

cases a spouse will act on a decision and then explain why because the action does not affect the spouse in any manner. Examples could include dropping a friendship, changing a hobby or a career move within the same company. If the wife is autonomous in the area of interior decor, she will still want to consult her husband before she throws out his favorite chair.

Decisions which should be made together include the *basic questions of the nature of the marriage relationship and the fundamental values of a child's education...These are common objectives that require a common effort, and they have to be shared. In other situations, if there is disagreement, one partner can always give in. However this should not always be the same person because a permanent state of dependency can be created.*[18]

Other areas that are a source of marital problems include:

- When there is undue competition to make use of limited resources, money, time, space, etc.
- When there is a desire to control activities that belong to the personal autonomy of the other person.
- When there is disagreement about the goals people want to achieve, or about the manner in which these goals should be achieved.
- When one of the partners does not recognize the area of autonomy of the other partner.
- When there is no agreement in the basic objective of matrimony, or in the ...means to obtain these objectives.
- When one of the partners does not know how to give in in trivial matters. [19]

The Question Of Suffering

"A crushed heart becomes the throne of grace."

Bl. Marie Thérèse Haze

God created us to be happy. The traditional catechism question: *Why did God make me?* is answered by, *God made me to know*

---

[18] *Ibid.,* p 8.
[19] *Ibid.,* p. 4, p. 8.

Him, to love Him, to serve Him in this world so as to be happy with Him in the next world.   Happiness is not just a far off goal to be achieved only through union with God after death. In the state of innocence, before the commission of original sin, our first parents lived in a state of happiness. Original sin opened a Pandora's box of pain, suffering, and unhappiness. Yet God turns this evil into good. John Paul II notes: *It is suffering, more than anything else, which clears the way for the grace which transforms human souls.*   When some suffering hits, we tend to reevaluate our priorities. Only nine weeks after taking over the presidency, an assassin shot President Ronald Reagan. With the *bullet lodged less than an inch from Reagan's heart...the surgeon who operated on him said he was "right on the margin" of death.*[20] During his time of recuperation President Reagan told one of his visitors, Cardinal Cooke, *I have decided that whatever time I have left is for Him.*[21]

The more united we are to God on earth, the less suffering will have a hold on us. Likewise the happier we become. *Happiness means knowledge of and love of truth, and the more we open up to the Supreme Truth, even in this world, the happier we can become.*[22] Life on earth then becomes a foretaste of heaven.

C. S. Lewis adds: *The Christian doctrine of suffering explains...that settled happiness and security which we all desire, God withholds from us by the very nature of the world: but joy, pleasure, and merriment He has scattered broadcast. We are never safe, but we have plenty of fun, and some ecstasy...The security we crave would teach us to rest our hearts in this world and propose an obstacle to our return to God: a few moments of happy love, a landscape, a symphony, a merry meeting with our friends, a bath or a football match, have no such tendency. Our Father refreshes us on the journey with some pleasant inns, but will not encourage us to mistake them for home.*[23]

---

[20] *Ronald Reagan, How An Ordinary Man Became An Extraordinary Leader, Op. Cit.,* p. 205.

[21] *Ibid.,* p.207.

[22] Professor Francisco Altajeros, "The Denial of Happiness," Instituto de las Ciencias de la Educacion, 1982, p.5.

[23] C. S. Lewis, *The Problem of Pain* (NY: MacMillian, 1962) p. 115.

Conversely, *[i]t can be said of no individual and no family that they are entirely open to happiness at a given moment, if their horizons are not open to God.*[24]

One of our main goals as parents is to raise happy children—not pleasure seeking, egocentric children but children who know how to love and how to suffer. Only then can they be happy. Of course, to do this, we as parents must provide an example for our children. *The second aspect is the external one, namely to transmit happiness, and this can be done in a very natural way from one family to another during social intercourse...thus effectively helping the human race.*[25]

The ability to love is one component of happiness. Yet, the more we love, the more we suffer. *[T]o say that love is a cause of pain means two things: (1) the more we love something concrete, the more we will suffer if it is lost; (2) the more we love generically, the more capacity we have to suffer...[T]he more we try to educate [our children] for love—the more we are preparing our children to endure things, to suffer—although this is not our intention.*[26]

The virtue of hope helps us to endure suffering. Professor Altarejos explains: *As a virtue, hope refers to supreme happiness; as a human attitude...it refers to earthly happiness. From this point of view, despair, loss of hope, means giving up the hope of happiness.*[27]

Suffering is a component of happiness and love. Unless we are willing to suffer, we can never be happy. Sounds almost like a riddle, doesn't it? If you had a pet as a child you remember how much you loved that pet. But when the pet died, you suffered. Remember how you suffered when your best friend either moved away or dropped your friendship? Happiness is composed of lights and shadows, highs and lows. Cardinal Joseph Ratzinger explains that *suffering accepted and endured in communion with Christ*

---

[24] "The Denial of Happiness," *Op. Cit.,* p.5.

[25] Ibid., p.4.

[26] Professor Francisco Altajeros, "Pain and Love in Education," Instituto de las Ciencias de la Educacion, 1982, p.4.

[27] "The Denial of Happiness," *Op. Cit.,* p.1.

crucified and resurrected, finds profound meaning for the person and for others; what is more, it can become a curing force. This is not theological speculation, but a very realistic position, since a program which does not help man in suffering but promises to eliminate it altogether, lacks realism.[28]

Our culture frantically pursues happiness while at the same time seeking to avoid suffering. It's like a dog chasing after its tail. Success is futile. To avoid "suffering," couples do not marry, instead they "live together." Their "love" is conditional—until one or the other tires of the relationship. Then the sorrow they tried to avoid comes crashing down on them. If couples do marry, many seek to avoid "suffering" by not having children or putting them off until the biological clock almost runs out. By avoiding the "suffering of having children" these couples suffer by missing the happiness of family life. In life suffering cannot be avoided. It is part of the human condition.[29]

According to Dr. Isaacs, St. Thomas Aquinas has some very human tips for handling life's miseries:

✓ Find something joyful to do or contemplate.
✓ Share some pleasure with another person.
✓ Contemplate truth (pray).
✓ Have a good cry to release tension.
✓ Take a bath and go to bed.

We could add, when one suffers it helps to talk it out with a sympathetic listener. One day my daughter, Marianne, received a call from a terribly depressed friend. Annie worked hard throughout the conversation to boast the girl's spirits. At the end of the conversation the friend told her, *I call you whenever I'm stressed and depressed. You make me feel that it's ok to have a miserable life.*

Since we are composed of body and soul, suffering affects both. In fact, spiritual suffering can actually make one physically ill.

---

[28] Zenit, March 12, 2001.

[29] For a deeper understanding of suffering consult the booklet "Why Suffer?" by Mary Ann Budnik. Scepter (800)322-8773.

Physical suffering impacts one spiritually. It's difficult to pray when one is ill. Pope Paul VI explained: *Behavior in suffering varies. One can suffer with rebellion in his heart. The unbeliever, the man who does not pray, suffers thus, even if he says nothing. How often, in passing through the wards of the sick, one hears, one sees this fearful silence—people who repress within themselves a sense of despair, of rebellion, of unconsoled doubt.*

There is a second form of suffering: it is that of patience.

But there is another way (and it must be yours, as loving believers in Christ): to suffer with love and for love—not only with patience, but also with love. And this can be done always, even when there is no strength to say prayers or perform other practices. As long as there is life, the heart is capable of loving, this act so sublime, which sums up our whole spirituality: "Lord, I weep, I suffer, I lie here inert and immobile, but I love You, and I suffer for love, for You!"

From this it can be seen that our actions acquire value through the thought which accompanies them, that is, through the intention which ennobles them.[30]

Since suffering is part of life, it is important to learn how to deal with it in a cheerful, upbeat manner. The saints joyously suffered terrible illness, setbacks, contradictions and horrendous martyrdoms. Can we do less? Besides the saints, this is a lesson I have learned from the example of my husband. At one time he was going through a difficult work situation. When one of my friends asked our eleven-year-old daughter, Marianne, about the state of affairs, she replied *My Dad always came home laughing. Now he just smiles.* Even when the world comes crashing down around us we need to keep a smile on our face.

Some people seek happiness in incessant activity. Perpetual activity simply keeps us from thinking about how truly miserable we are. Happiness does not come from possessing money or things. Once we possess what we desire, we no longer desire it. It has lost its appeal. One cannot buy happiness because it is not

---

[30] Pope Paul VI, audience, August 22, 1963.

material. One cannot look for happiness because it is spiritual. As such it is not physically attainable. Isaacs insists that happiness comes from contemplation, the contemplation of happy memories such as your wedding, the birth of your first child, moving into your first home, walking along the beach holding hands. When these events were actually happening to you, you were so involved in the happening that there was no time to contemplate what was occurring. After the event, thinking about it, remembering who said or did what makes one happy. Happiness is knowing and discovering the good; then possessing it. Being in union with God brings happiness. Helping someone brings happiness.

As parents it is important to consider if our children are happy. Is each one happy? If they are not happy, why? Are they as happy as they could be? If your children are not happy consider these possible causes:

- ✓ Are the children ignorant of good things? Are they exposed to God, beauty, culture, and goodness or only the TV?
- ✓ Does your child lack the will to pursue the good?
- ✓ Is your child's time spent only pursuing pleasure or incessant activity?
- ✓ Is your child involved in too many outside activities that prevent him from pursuing the good?

As a family what values do you really want to live? Write them down. Then decide if you have the will to live those values. It does take the virtue of fortitude united with constant effort. In the previous chapter and this chapter the importance of virtues has been stressed. As Dr. David Isaacs insists we all need good operative habits (virtues) in order to have a happy, fulfilling marriage and happy children. A virtue is that characteristic that we love to see or experience in others but which takes a great effort to perform ourselves. But remember that not only will the acquisition of human virtues perfect your personality but they will also help you to handle the sufferings of life. Recall the words of St. Paul (**Romans** 5:3-5) *[W]e can boast about our sufferings. These sufferings bring patience, as we know, and patience brings perseverance, and perseverance brings hope, and* *this hope is not deceptive, because the love of God has been poured into our hearts by the Holy Spirit which has been given us.*

The Stages Of Married Life

Each marriage is a vibrant, living organism since spouses are continually growing, maturing and changing which in turn changes the quality of their relationship. *We are going to analyze love as a moving from a me to a you, from a you to an us and from the us to the them, in a process which is also the process of emotional maturity...[It is a] moving from the concept of individual to that of spouse, from spouse to that of parent, from parent to one's home open to others.*[31]

Happy marriages are united when each spouse gives continuous attention to the other. It is the gift of self to the other, as well as the acceptance of the gift by the other. Married love grows through the actions and deeds of the spouses while marital love is expressed in its fruitfulness, the children born into the family. This love deepens through the sufferings and contradictions the couple weathers together. The school of suffering matures the spouses while enriching the marriage itself. Remember, it is a mixture of suffering and joy that brings happiness.

As an act of the will, love *can be channeled, fostered or killed off...At first [physical manifestations of love] are urgent but then gradually become less important as there develops a deeper communication between two hearts and wills. Mature love is found in mutual help, respect and acceptance of the parties, in making each other better people through being together.*[32]

Just as the human person goes through stages, so does the married couple. The first stage of human development is called "infantile" because it is "narcissistic" and "egocentric." As the person grows into youth, romantic is added to egocentric opening the person to jealousy, individualism, ideals, and the desire to

---

[31] Dr. Anna Maria Araujo de Vanegas, "The Stages of Married Life," Instituto de Ciencias de la Educacion, 1987, p. 1.

[32] *Ibid.,* p. 2.

possess. The third stage is adulthood in which the above is overcome by learning to serve, dealing in reality, and becoming generous rather than egocentric. An adult learns to accept another person as that person is, *not as one would like him to be.* [33]

Dr. Araujo divides the stages of marriage into the young couples (1-5 years of marriage until the children go to school); the adult couple (10-15 years from the time the children begin school until the children are independent); the senior couple (when the children leave home and the couple are again alone).

The main focus in the first stage of young couples, is learning to live as a couple, the interdependence on each other. The first years together are filled with firsts: maybe the first apartment, the first house, the first baby, the first professional job. Life is completely different from the carefree days of being single. Araujo equates it with the growth of children up to the age of three *wherein we find the greatest qualitative and quantitative changes of the entire human life. Conflicts can be found here regarding the couple's relationship...[F]or example the typical **jealousy** on the part of the wife for the time that her husband's profession occupies him. There is also the famous **two-year crisis**, brought about by an absorbing maternity which dictates the wife's duties...[T]his is the moment to learn how to bring one's dreams down to earth, to grow in love, learning to move on from idealism to realism, from understanding, to doing, from egocentrism to fruitfulness. One must not...fear tensions, if these are proportional to the causes.* [34]

In the "adult couple" the couple gives way to being parents who are concerned about their children be it the children's health, friendships, growth in virtues and faith, and academic education. But rather than abandoning the role of spouse, each must balance his/her role as parent and spouse. Now rather than being fixated on each other, the couple runs into the temptation to live parallel lives making communication difficult. Dr. Araujo recommends taking special measures to promote unity between husbands and

---

[33] *Ibid.,* p. 3.
[34] *Ibid.,* p. 4

wives such as the *"healthy selfishness of a trip or some activity together"* to continually renew marital love. She warns that while conflicts are less volatile, they are easier to ignore in the hectic pace of each day. But if ignored, they are harder to resolve. *They can be manifested in behavior, reproaches and complaints, or developed within each person.*[35] The wise spouse will not judge on mere appearances but take the time to learn all the particulars before making snap decisions.

In this period of the relationship one of two types of silence are introduced into the relationship. Active silence is communication without words. Each enjoys just being with the other. A smile, the touch of the hand, a glance is wordless communication. On the other hand, passive silence is a danger signal. It says that the spouses no longer enjoy one another's company. Each is living in his/her own world.

This stage of marriage brings about the maturity of the spouses along with their love for each other. There is more self-giving, more realistic expectations, hopefully more growth in faith and virtue. The downside is that couples can fall into a routine of taking each other for granted which lacks charity along with justice.

During this stage of marriage the "midlife crisis" and "the change of life" occur. James Stenson reminds us that *there are three periods in life when hormonal interactions in the body produce psychological reactions, a kind of mild temporary insanity: mood swings, crankiness, lack of self-esteem, resistance to correction, unreasonable worries, stubbornness, escapism, and other unpleasantries. The first of these occurs between the ages of two and four. The second...takes place in adolescence, from 13 to 17 or later. The third, much more subtle and subdued, occurs around the age of 40, plus or minus a few years. This last stage is not universal and varies a great deal, but it is quite common.*[36] Things can get rather tense in a household in which the husband is having a midlife crisis, the mother is going through "the change," and the children range in age from two years through

---

[35] *Ibid.*,p. 5.

[36] James Stenson, *Upbringing* (NY: Scepter Publishers, Inc., 1999) p.131.

the teens! It helps to know that it is the messed up hormones, not the people who are causing the problems.

Is the so-called "midlife crisis" actually a crisis or a time to review the past and consider the future? The stage of life between forty and fifty years old should be used to rectify faults and misdirection so one can *leave good deeds behind through love, sowing happiness for others...With this attitude both husband and wife, parents and children, will find themselves motivated to polish their rough sides, lessen conflicts, find occasions to serve each other, and enjoy things together...because the memory of one's love will leave a lasting mark on the children."*[37]

Rev. José M. Pero-Sanz, of the University of Navarra, has some interesting observations on the "mid-life crisis." He believes that people who face life with human and supernatural maturity make the transition smoothly. Key signs of mid-life are physical changes which include weight gain, hair loss, less energy, fatigue, and sleeplessness. Professional work loses its appeal and practices of piety seem to become more difficult, less spontaneous.

Maturity itself has more positives then negatives. The adult's life is emotionally and intellectually full. There is an ability to work with all types of personalities; there is less prejudice; people are accepted with their defects and good qualities. It also brings the awareness of one's limitations; the humility to ask for help; the ability to collaborate with others.

The mature person deals with realism. *His objectivity, if he does not lack faith, includes supernatural outlook with which he evaluates persons and events. Being realistic, he adapts to change. He is flexible with regard to inconsequential details while remaining firm on principles.*

Although not having the same energy level as individuals in their 20s, the mature person is endowed with wisdom, strength, and experience. This allows the person to resolve problems calmly, in an easy manner. *The teacher can give a class on the spur of the moment. The housewife does not go into shock when she has to*

---

[37] *Ibid.,* p. 7.

come up with a meal unexpectedly.

In mature adults loyalty is lived along with responsibility and fidelity. The mature person gives good example by faithfully fulfilling his obligations. He's not a slave to his emotions or passions. *The mature individual appreciates freedom without confusing it with spontaneity. The mature person is faithful to the commitments he has freely taken on even when he doesn't particularly feel like keeping them. Although he may lack enthusiasm at times, or even often, his fidelity is serene. He doesn't see external circumstances at home or at work as obstacles to his fulfillment: but neither does he foolishly refuse to acknowledge the existence of difficulties. He sees them as opportunities for doing good. Finally, the mature person resists the temptation to avoid reality, the temptation which is at the root of the "crisis of the forties."*

Fr. Sanz believes the heart of the mid-life crisis is stocktaking. There is the temptation to think that our life is irreparable or a failure. *At most there may appear the possibility of salvaging what might still be saved from the onset of a definitive decline.* This leads to two false options. One is passivity, a *selfish position implying a lack of real effort.* The person is given good advice but laziness prohibits one from making the effort to change or improve. The other option is to flee, in the case of marriage to divorce and start a new life with another. *The individual regards his situation as a mistake. He attempts to free himself from anything that might tie him down and restrict his freedom: the bonds are felt to be the cause of his unhappiness.*

These options blame external circumstances for one's present unhappiness. This unhappiness can trigger *harsh criticism of individuals or institutions that until then had represented an ideal.* It can lead to incessant activity so the person can avoid thinking about himself, his unhappiness and others. It can lead to rationalizing one's behavior so as to avoid responsibilities and excuse oneself from duties.

The attempt to reconstruct self-identity is frequently accompanied by a resurgence of passion. The desire for sensual satisfaction takes its mildest form in an unhealthy concern for physical well-being. This can be the hair transplants, the face-lifts, tummy tucks, and the red sports car.

To avoid turning the mature years into a full-blown "mid-life crisis" we have to carefully avoid flight and passivity. Instead, maturely consider your vocation in the light of faithfulness to God, spouse and to self. Begin with a fresh spiritual start, particularly with the Sacrament of Reconciliation. View your situation with humility and humor. Then follow the three steps that Fr. Sanz recommends:

- ✓ Recognize one's limitations and mistakes; take responsibility for personal misuse of freedom without blaming others or circumstances;
- ✓ Be prudent in keeping with one's age. Physically, this includes moderation in food and drink and periodic rest. Mentally, it includes being modest in the face of success (which in large part is due to others anyway) and detachment from personal opinions;
- ✓ Forget self. Two ways to escape self-centeredness are service to others and sincerity in spiritual direction: this last especially helps to be objective and provides a necessary sense of proportion.

If a friend or spouse is going through the mid-life crisis you can help by being understanding, optimistic and encouraging without being indulgent. The person in crisis may mistakenly believe that he cannot change for the better or go on with his life as it is. *Those who help must be convinced that the difficulties will indeed pass. They should facilitate sincerity, enabling the person to unburden himself. It takes patience not to get upset or to feel hurt by another's outburst of anger or at his critical comments. The years of faithful service should be recalled and they should look forward to many more years of the same once the present difficulties have been overcome.*

To be understanding, however, does not mean allowing those in crisis simply to speak about the temptation without doing something about it. With fortitude full of affection, the person must be helped to adopt the attitudes of appropriate response: realism, supernatural outlook and humility.

True understanding involves taking the problem seriously, realizing that there is a risk of losing if the crisis is not resolved successfully. Therefore sincerity with the individual is required. The words can be pleasant and warm, but have to be crystal-clear, for a person who is confused needs light.

Finally, to help others who are having a hard time, we have to pray to the Holy Spirit for the gift of counsel. In truth, the prayer of the person in crisis, the prayer of those trying to help him, the prayer of those who know and care for him--the prayer of them all constitutes the most effective means to make the "crisis of the forties" a time for growth in human and supernatural maturity.[38]

The Senior Years

The final marital stage is the "senior years." There are three parts to this transition. The first is when the children marry and begin their own families. For the sake of the young marrieds the parents must let go, allowing the couple autonomy without strings attached. To truly love a child is to teach the child to be independent. To keep a child dependent is a self-seeking love. For the young couple to grow together, parents need to avoid the tendency to become indispensable to the husband and wife. One marriage broke up simply because the husband's mother insisted that the young couple come over for dinner every night. After several years of this unreasonable demand the young wife, completely fed-up, divorced her husband saying, *He'd rather be with his mother anyway.*

Other parents, trying to assume control of the young couple, will place a "guilt trip" on them by reiterating all the sacrifices that they as parents have made. Again, this is a selfish love that is very destructive for all the parties involved. True love gives, and then forgets. There are those parents who focused all their attention on their children rather than centering it on the spousal relationship. When the children leave home, the parents cannot cope. They feel deserted. Without any other outlets, they tend to meddle in the new marriage causing serious problems for the

[38] Rev. José M. Pero-Sanz, "Maturity" *Palabra* #214, May 1983.

young couple. To avoid this temptation, develop outlets of interest aside from your children before they leave home.

The second part of this transition is forming the interrelationship between the parental home and children's families that includes in-laws as well as the families of the in-laws. As the young couple begins having children, their time is more limited. Visits to see the grandparents may not be as frequent. Grandparents may become more demanding, even childish over the lack of attention. This is called "psychological regression." If a grandparent truly loves, he/she helps but does not meddle. The young couple has to fight the temptation to isolate themselves from their extended family by refusing to spend time with their parental families.

The final segment of the senior years is to redevelop a relationship as a couple again. Think of your marriage as not winding down but rather becoming more enriched. Schedule a "date night" each week to keep the spark in your marriage. Dress up for each other. Do something spontaneous and maybe just a little silly like having a picnic at the beach. Develop a common interest together such as gardening, playing bridge, golfing or traveling. Attend auctions just for the fun of it. Take a drive or walk in the country. Entertain other couples at your home. Have a candlelight dinner for special occasions. Volunteer together for a political action committee. This is the opportunity to take on leadership positions in the community. To avoid the tendency to grow selfish, learn to serve each other as well as others. Each day consider, *how can I make life more fun or more enjoyable for my spouse? What would he like right now? How can I make her smile?*

As the years take their toll, *the calm acceptance of the deterioration of one's physical and mental faculties will be the best lesson of detachment which the senior citizens can bequeath to society, together with the profound conviction that love transcends all limits of temporal life.* [39]

Living in a world dictated by technology, if we hope to protect

---

[39] *Ibid.,* p. 10.

our marriages and families we must heed the words Pope Pius XII issued almost a half century ago: *[W]herever the technical concept of life gains sway, the family loses the personal bond of its unity, it loses its warmth and stability. It only remains united in the measure imposed by the demands of mass production, towards which there is more insistent progress each day. The family is then not a work of love and refuge for souls, but rather, according to circumstances, the dreary deposit either of manpower for production, or of consumers of the material goods produced.*[40]

To counter such negative situations Blessed Padre Pio advises: *Form a Christian family if you want a little bit of peace in this life.*

Additional Helps

- ✓ Read **The Catholic Family in the Modern World** by John A. Hardon, SJ (Leaflet Missal Company (800) 328-9582).
- ✓ Plan a date night with your spouse and discuss how to enrich your marriage.
- ✓ Plan a fun project to do together with your spouse.
- ✓ Plan a fun family outing on Sunday after Mass.
- ✓ Put together a schedule for family prayer.
- ✓ Do something extra special for your spouse.
- ✓ Plan a set time weekly to discuss your children together.
- ✓ The four characteristics of a happy marriage are empathy, appreciation, congruence and character. How are you living them?
- ✓ Are you and your children happy? If not, why? If so, why?

---

[40] Pius XII, "Christmas Message," December 24, 1953.

Chapter 5

Why Is The Family So Important?

"...The fruitfulness of conjugal love is not restricted solely to the procreation of children...: it is enlarged and enriched by all those fruits of moral, spiritual and supernatural life which the father and mother are called to hand on to their children, and through the children to the Church and to the world."

John Paul II [1]

Attending a luncheon, I found the atmosphere lovely but the conversation disturbing. Present were the wives of executives. Their conversation centered on their husbands, their husband's profession, and the difficulty of raising their children alone. After listening to the women's conversation I added this and the next chapter to this book. It was startling to learn how many couples do not understand their individual duties as mothers and fathers nor the critical role of the family in raising moral and responsible young adults.

---

[1] John Paul II *Familiaris Consortio #28.*

Mothers, for the most part, understand that their role is to nurture their children and care for the home. Unfortunately, many are putting their careers first with devastating results. St. Paul reminds wives that they are *to love their husbands and children, to be sensible, chaste, domestic, kind, and submissive to their husbands* (*Tit.* 2:4-5). This is a fulltime job if done correctly. Fathers, unfortunately, tend to equate their role solely with working for their families. They are to provide a suitable home for the children God sends in addition to providing money for their education and holidays. This is part of their role but there are equally important aspects to fatherhood that many men are totally oblivious to. One woman laughingly told us, *When my son was asked what his father did he told people, "He makes money." I think he actually thought his father printed the money!* Her comment struck me as sad, not humorous. *Making money* must have been the focus of conversation in their home for her son to respond in such a manner. What a distorted, valueless, humanistic education he received from his parents!

Each of the women discussed how they not only handled the full responsibility of raising their children alone but also how their husbands were not involved in any of the details of running the home, not even changing light bulbs. These intelligent, articulate women have no clue that part of their vocation is to help their husbands grow holy through the fulfillment of their duties as husbands and fathers. By shouldering their husbands' rightful responsibilities these wives helped their husbands cultivate the vices of selfishness, self-centeredness, laziness, intemperance, and so forth...all in pursuit of greater earning ability. Yes, these couples are very wealthy but as Jesus Christ asks in the Gospel, *What does it profit a man to gain the whole world but lose his soul?* (*Lk.* 9:23-26)

Now their husbands are nearing retirement age. They are trying to make up for what they missed raising their own children by becoming involved in their grandchildren's lives. While it's necessary to be involved with one's grandchildren, our primary responsibility before God is for our own children, not our children's children. In focusing exclusively on their profession, these men lived their will, not God's. Furthermore, they provided bad example to their children. By not being available to their wives and children these men were not able to give their families strength and moral support. Without a truly Christian model of father and husband, how will these children know how to parent in a Christian manner?

But it is not fair to simply single out these men. While avarice (greed) has been with mankind since the Fall, it seemed to particularly invade the generation of Christian families during the Great Depression. The children who lived through that difficult economic period emerged with the Scarlett O'Hara syndrome swearing they would *never be hungry again!* Following World War II the race began for financial security, which resulted in wealth and luxuries for the average person. But families paid a high price for climbing the corporate ladder. Frequent moves away from family and friends were required. Dad was expected to spend more and more hours at work or on business trips. Mom took over the role of mother and father. As fathers abdicated their role, feminism, fueled by neo-Marxist ideology, gained a foothold in the family. Wives and daughters, witnessing the success, power and wealth of their husbands and fathers began leaving their families for the corporate world. Self-gratification replaced the traditional self-sacrifice expected of both parents. While orphanages were closed down, daycare centers opened. Neglected children triggered a rise in emotionally disturbed and violent children. Understandably there are situations in which both parents must work to put bread on the table but in many families living more simply would provide a stay-at-home mom and a father who is available for his children. A full-time mother available to the children is more important than a larger home, fancy vacations or the latest electronic toys. In the words of Alice Von Hildebrand: *Women who prefer to do boring types of work outside of their home rather than to remain with their children, bear witness to the fact that we have lost sight of one of the deepest human values, the value of the family. Not only is the family one of the highest goods in the hierarchy of human values; but it is in and of itself of such pivotal importance that society as a whole depends on it. A society in which families hold together is a sane society; a society, like ours, in which families go to pieces, is a society which is threatened by collapse, even though the façade can still give the impression of health.*[2]

Consider the rich young man in the gospel. He was a good, moral young man. He was doing everything right until God asked more of him, as He asks more of our children and us. This young man could not give up his riches to follow Christ. Sadly, he turned away. On the other hand, St. Katherine Drexel gave up her huge pharmaceutical fortune for God. Which legacy do we want for ourselves and our children?

The Family

"Without a family, man, alone in the world, trembles with the cold."
                                                            André Malraux

When Cardinal Juan Luis Cipriani Thorne, Archbishop of Lima, Peru, became the first player of a national basketball team to become a Cardinal he was asked, *How did you decide one day to leave behind what you had, basketball, your engineering career, to follow Christ into the priesthood?* He replied, *In the first place, I think that everything is born in the family. We are 11 brothers. My father was a doctor...a surgeon, a specialist in ophthalmology, [who] manifested in his very career a great concern for others, and a desire to help them. [M]y mother [was] a homemaker. I can recall a thousand details of daily life. For example, when we went to bed at night, my mother used to come to each one's room to help us to thank Jesus and to offer our day...All this was shaping my soul a bit...God knows more...In my home we simply breathed Catholicism. I had been taught to have a certain discipline of work...*[3]

---

[2] Alice Von Hildebrand, "Women At Work," (NY: Scepter Publishers, 1985) p.13.

[3] Zenit, Feb. 27, 2001.

The family is the creation of God. As such its composition cannot be touched by social engineers, court rulings, nor UN proclamations. Despite the various aberrations the media insist constitute a family, John Paul II explains that *the family is a community of persons: of husband and wife, of parents and children, of relatives. Its first task is to live with fidelity the reality of communion in a constant effort to develop an authentic community of persons...Without love the family is not a community of persons and...without love the family cannot live, grow and perfect itself. The love between husband and wife...between parents and children, brothers and sisters and relatives and members of the household—is given life and sustenance by an unceasing inner dynamism leading the family to ever deeper and more intense **communion**, which is the foundation and soul of the **community** of marriage and the family.*[4]

*[T]he family has the **mission to guard, reveal and communicate love**, and this is a living reflection of and a real sharing in God's love for humanity and the love of Christ the Lord for the Church His bride.*[5]

The four tasks of the family are:

1. forming a community of persons;
2. serving life;
3. participating in the development of society
4. sharing in the life and mission of the Church.[6]

Each family not only forms its own community or society but it also becomes an individual domestic Church. How each family lives the faith determines the depth of faith in their domestic Church. Consider for a moment the depth of the faith in your domestic Church. Is it liberal, orthodox, indifferent or fallen away?

The future of the Catholic Church depends on our faithfulness to this task of spiritually forming our domestic churches.

---

[4] John Paul II, *Familiaris Consortio* #18.

[5] *Ibid.,* #17.

[6] *Ibid.*

Dr. John Haas, a convert to Catholicism, observes that *[t]he family is the principal means of our insertion into society and the means through which we laity make our witness to the world.*[7]

Each of our homes is a seedbed for marriage, religious, priestly, and celibate lay vocations. The future of the Church rests with the vocational choices of our children. Bishop Michael J. Sheridan, of St. Louis, reminds us that *the Eucharist needs priests.*[8] If priests do not come from our families we will not have the Sacrifice of the Mass nor the Holy Eucharist. If we are not training our children to become saints, they will not have the capacity to respond should God call them. Bl. Escrivá insists that *we must strive so that these cells of Christianity may be born and may develop with a desire for holiness.*[9]

John Paul II points out that *[a]ll members of the family...have the grace and responsibility of building, day by day, the communion of persons making the family "a school of deeper humanity"; this happens when there is care and love for the little ones, the sick, the aged; where there is mutual service every day; when there is a sharing of goods, of joys and of sorrows.*

A fundamental opportunity for building such a communion is constituted by the educational exchange between parents and children in which each gives and receives. By means of love, respect and obedience towards their parents, children offer their specific and irreplaceable contribution to the construction of an authentically human and Christian family...

Family communion can only be preserved and perfected through a great spirit of sacrifice. It requires, in fact, a ready and generous openness of each and all to understanding, to forbearance, to pardon, to reconciliation. There is no family that does not know how selfishness, discord, tension and conflict violently attack and at times mortally wound its own communion: hence there arise the many and varied forms of divisions in family life. But, at the same time, every family is called by the God of peace to have the

---

[7] "Marriage and the Priesthood," *Op. Cit.,* p. 25.

[8] Homily June 26, 2000 on the 25th Anniversary of the death of Blessed Escrivá.

[9] Bl. Escriva, *Conversations,* #91.

joyous and renewing experience of "reconciliation," that is, communion reestablished, unity restored. In particular, participation in the Sacrament of Reconciliation and in the banquet of the one Body of Christ offers to the Christian family the grace and responsibility of overcoming every division and of moving toward the fullness of communion willed by God, responding in this way to the ardent desire of the Lord: "that they may be one."[10]

God could have chosen innumerable ways to send us a Savior but He chose to send His Son in the framework of a family, the Holy Family. Likewise, God wants His adopted children to be born and raised within the stable, firmly established institution of the family. It is within the family that we find the school of virtues and how to live them: *first, the theological virtues, and then all the others: prudence, loyalty, sincerity, humility, industriousness, cheerfulness...*[11]

St. Thomas Aquinas compares the vocation of parents to the vocation of priests since Christian families provide *corporal as well as spiritual life: this is done through the sacrament of matrimony, in which man and woman unite to bear children and educate them to worship God.*[12]

As a community of love, there exist rights, duties, and responsibilities that can only be lived through ongoing daily sacrifices by each member of the family. *Husband and wife are called to sanctify their married life and to sanctify themselves in it. It would be a serious mistake if they were to exclude family life from their spiritual development. The marriage union, the care and education of children, the effort to provide for the needs of the family as well as for its security and development, the relationships with other persons who make up the community, all these are among the ordinary human situations that Christian couples are called upon to sanctify.*[13]

---

[10] John Paul II, *Familiaris Consortio* #21.

[11] *Christ is Passing By,* #23.

[12] St. Thomas Aquinas, *Summa contra Gentiles,* IV, ch. 58.

[13] Bl. Escrivá, *Christ is Passing By,* #23.

Part of the duties of the parents is to pass on cultural values and norms to their children. These values and norms include love and consideration toward other people: *the love of truth; respect for life; peaceable solutions to conflicts, respect for the dignity and freedom of others, a love of justice and equality, compassion and solidarity with other people; cooperation and a willingness to help others, tolerance and the readiness to contribute with one's own efforts towards the well-being of all men. These values are instilled in the family. They have their origin there. It is here that man develops his personality and forms his social nature. Of overriding importance here are the child's first interpersonal relationships. It is here that the inner value system is formed which later enables a person to cope with very burdening crisis situations.*[14]

This education is ongoing as the mother and father interact daily with their children and the children with each other. Daycare children are physically managed not emotionally and intellectually trained in virtues. My daughter, Marianne, has been teaching catechism to kindergarteners for the past eight years. She can tell by the child's conduct whether the mother is a stay-at-home mom or if the child goes to daycare. She finds that *children with full-time moms are better disciplined, brighter, and exhibit self-control. Daycare children are hungry for attention so they are disruptive, have short attention spans and are demanding of my attention.*

At the World Congress of Families II, which took place in Geneva, Switzerland November of 1999, Dr. Annemarie Buchholz and Dr. Eva-Maria Föllmer presented a thought-provoking paper on the role of parents in raising their children. They maintain that *[i]f value concepts become emotionally anchored in a child, that child can later build upon them and develop the necessary resistance...against attack on his and other people's dignity, whether this is in the form of violence or other, finer forms of abuse, for example in commercial advertising or political manipulation...*

Imparting values in the family requires guidance from the

---

[14] Dr. Annemarie Buchholz and Dr. Eve-Maria Föllmer, "Imparting Values in the Family," *Current Concerns*, (Zurich, Switzerland) No. 1/2000 Jan. 2000, p.7.

parents. The parents act as role models, and positive parental authority is necessary...Children observe and sense very clearly which values are crucial for their parents in their lives, how they live them and how they assume responsibility for others. The child takes them as an example. The parental model is mirrored in both outward appearances and the attitudes and emotional reactions of children.

In addition young people must acquire knowledge and become capable of solving conflicts peaceably and constructively; they need common sense. Further pre-requisites of moral behavior are human interest, self-confidence and courage.

It is through the identification with parents and grandparents that cultural values and norms are imparted to the next generation...[G]randparents can set children an example with their wisdom and calmness, their possession of a broader perspective of life and as a result a better-balanced temperament, and with other qualities which parents are perhaps more lacking in. If not only parents but also grandparents or even great-grandparents participate in the educational process, culture and history will be passed on. This in turn constitutes an essential contribution towards safeguarding and protecting life.

This passing on of cultural norms and values produces a feeling of solidarity with one's origins, of affiliation with one's people, culture, nation and history; this is likewise a prerequisite for the development of a mature personality. This feeling also safeguards one against indifference, irresponsibility and spinelessness, and forms a basis for a real understanding of other cultures.

"The seeds of humanity" are sown within the family. Family life based on love and trust is the anthropological model for co-existence within society and the state, promoting the development of everyone. Constructive cooperation and actively working towards resolving conflicts peaceably begins with family upbringing. In the family, the principle of subsidiary, solidarity and public welfare are kept alive. Within the family, the foundation for co-existence in a liberal democracy is laid.

The reciprocity in the parent-child relationship, its deep emotional attachments, the bonds that are forged by a common future, and a shared life under one roof is what distinguishes the family and makes it so irreplaceable. Democracy begins at the dinner table, the social focal point of the day.

Children and young people orient themselves on those in their immediate vicinity who function as role models. A generation of adults, actively committed in their own lives to finding a way to establish peace and protect their fellow human beings, and who follow that path—even with all the unsolved problems and insecurities that this entails—can provide the rising generation with strong roots that will sustain them in their own similar efforts. The family is the life nerve of each individual as well as of the entire society.[15]

Besides the parents, children, as an integral part of the family, also have a role to play. They are called to be affectionate toward their parents, obedient, docile, helpful, as well as hardworking in study and work. Just as their parents are called to serve, so are the children. St. Paul exhorts, **Children, obey your parents in the Lord, for this is right. "Honor your father and mother" (this is the first commandment with a promise), "that it may be well with you and that you may live long on the earth"** (*Eph.* 6:1-3.). Fr. Raoul Plus, S.J. addresses the sad lack of loyalty of grown children toward their parents: *There are some who do not make enough of the part of the home in their lives. How strange it is that children can be so loving when they are little, so demonstrative, and when they grow up so adept at saddening their parents.*[16]

When each member of the family fulfills his or her obligations with love, society is built-up as well as the Church. It is love that turns living together into family life. It is love that makes self-denial joyful. It is family love that fosters understanding, loyalty, confidence, and respect for one another. It is this love, which is a

---

[15] "Imparting Values in the Family," *Op. Cit.*, p.7.

[16] Raoul Plus, SJ, *Christ In The Home* (NY: Frederick Pustet Co., Inc., 1951) pp. 339-340.

foretaste of heaven. The detail which one decorates the home, plans interesting meals, dresses with *"personal elegance,"* and works to find fun ways for family members to rest all add to our earthly happiness.

The Question Of Upbringing

"The first thing that a person finds in life and the last to which he holds out his hand, and the most precious that he posseses, even if he does not realize it, is family life." Bl. Adolph Kolping

Shaping the character of one's children is time consuming. It requires long and short-term planning, preparation, patience, and effort. If one or both parents are too busy outside the home this formation will not be given. It is important to begin by developing a friendship with your children. This probably sounds basic but many times children love and respect their parents but lack confidence in them. To develop this friendship, talk to them frankly, as you would to a friend. Listen to their concerns and opinions. If you treat them with respect, kindness and understanding, they will know that they can talk to you about any topic and be understood or ask your advice with their problems. If you project constant stress or treat them brusquely, they will avoid confiding in you or worse yet, fear you. At the same time, when they behave badly you must correct them, forgive them, and then help them to improve.

As a society, everyone in the family can contribute to the common good by helping with the various jobs that keep the family running smoothly. Even toddlers can run and get a diaper for mommy or throw items in the trash.

Fatherhood and motherhood mean renunciation of personal ambitions and desires. As Fr. Raoul Plus, S.J. insists, *the true rewards of marriage are called work, duty, responsibility... **Marriage is a sacrifice.***[17] For instance, a father may want to play the stock market but instead puts the money into tuition for

---

[17] *Christ In The Home, Op. Cit.,* p. 93.

a private school that protects the faith and morals of his children. His return will be children who are morally upright and responsible adults.

Another father travels frequently during the week. He makes an effort to take early bird flights so he can be home in the evening with his children. It would be easier for him not to have to bounce back and forth each day but his wife and children are top priorities with him.

Zelié Martin, the mother of St. Thérèse, ran her lace-making business from her home so that she could still care for her daughters. She became so successful that her husband, Louis, eventually closed his jewelry shop to work fulltime in his wife's business. Zelié balanced her priorities by putting God first, her husband next, then her daughters with her business last.

There are women today who are on a career fast track but give it up to be stay-at-home moms. Dr. Laura Schlessinger, popular radio personality, is such a mom. She gave up a promising career to become a fulltime mom. When she and her husband faced financial reversals they worked together to keep the family unit intact by working part-time, then fulltime from her home with her son playing at her feet. When her son went to school, she worked the same hours as he attended school. She writes her books when her son is in school and after her husband and son go to bed. Not wanting to be away from her family, Dr. Laura refuses to do personal appearances. She and her husband refuse to bring work home because the evening is strictly for family time. Although she puts her husband and family first she still has managed to have a successful career. [18]

When I covered the UN Population and Development Conference in Cairo, Egypt, a radio station in Utah called my hotel and asked if I would be willing to give its listeners periodic updates on the Conference. Figuring the radio program must be pro-family/ pro-life I agreed. The first evening the announcer permitted me to explain and interject my viewpoint in regard to

---

[18] Read Dr. Schlessinger's book *,Parenthood By Proxy,* for her background.

the various family and life issues being discussed at the Conference. The following evening I discovered the program was actually a call-in talk show that was *not* pro-life nor pro-family. The final caller of the segment was an enraged feminist. She shot question after question at me: *Did you give up a career to be a stay- at- home- mom? Yes. How many children do you have? Three adult daughters. You really think women should give up their ambitions to put their families first? Yes I do.* As the woman began to verbally slice me to ribbons the Holy Spirit intervened and I heard myself saying, *As a career feminist you are sitting in Salt Lake, Utah while I am covering the UN Conference as a foreign correspondent in Egypt. Need I say more?* When we put our spouse and family first, God does the rest. In His time and according to His Will our talents will be used for His honor and glory. Fr. Raoul Plus, SJ insists:*[T]he duties of the home remain [the wife's] principal work: To plan, to arrange, to mend, to clean, to sew, to beautify, to care for the children. Insignificant duties? But what would that matter if they represent the Will of God? Are we not too often tempted to want a change?*

Would not the greatest charity in such a case be…to remain faithfully at home and devote oneself to works which no one will speak of and which will win no one's congratulations? Later when the children have grown up and settled, there may be leisure…[19]

In the **Chicago Tribune,** writer Michele Weldon confessed that being a career woman did not bring her happiness. *I was such a jerk in my 20's…It has taken marriage of five years and the arrival of two children to forge this opinion of myself…That I was so aggressively shallow is what disturbs me…What I had was a belief system that deified career advancement, Ann Taylor suits, and boyfriends with summer homes in Marblehead, Mass.*

The only thing that saved me from complete self-absorption was that I met my husband when I was 25, and only halfway through my decade of superficiality. Thankfully, he had the tenacity to watch me outgrow it…I kept whirling in these narrow circles of

---

[19] *Christ In The Home, Op.Cit.,* pp. 341-342.

self-fulfillment, feeling the future was only as promising as I looked in person or sounded in print...[then] on the brink of parenthood I was beginning to see how petty my own career seemed in the larger scheme of things...I'm still a writer...but it's not all I am anymore and it's not the most important thing. That I so fervently tried to make it so, at the expense of everyone and everything else, is what embarrasses me...I want to apologize publicly for being such a fool.[20]

If the work of home is not beneath the dignity of Our Lady, Queen of the Universe, it's not beneath the dignity of women today to spend themselves for their husbands and children. Still, raising children does not rest solely on the shoulders of mothers. Likewise , it is a privilege to be shared by fathers. Quality time is a myth. Parenting takes quantity time. Charity, which is true love, is not doing the easiest thing at the moment but rather the right thing at the right moment no matter how tired you may be or how inconvenient it is. Parents need to be available to disciple, love, teach virtues, give guidance and supervision, to share a joke and laugh together with their children. Family members need time together for family meals and fun interaction in the evenings. If you do not give this time to your children Dr. Laura insists that children not raised by dedicated parents will not only do poorly in school but will also do poorly as adults.[21]

To raise a child to face the challenges of life that includes everything from love to death you must be available to give your child quantity time that is more than just the couple of hours mom has after work. You must be available when you child suffers the loss of a friendship, the death of a pet, and when school seems overwhelming to your child. Your daily supervision and guidance protects your children from dangerous relationships, the opportunity to try drugs, or worse yet, suicide if the child feels that he has no one to turn to for help.

In my research for this book I picked up **Don't   Make   Me**

---

[20] Michele Weldon, "Out of the Shallows," Womenews, *The Chicago Tribune,* Sunday, Oct. 6, 1991, section 6, p. 8.

[21] See p. 34 of Dr. Schlessinger's book, *Parenthood By Proxy*

Stop This Car! by Al Roker, the weatherman on the *Today Show.* His third wife, Debbie, is a correspondent for ABC News *20/20.* It did not take long to realize that Roker's book is the antithesis of this book. The reader learns that in Roker's second marriage the couple was unable to conceive a child although his wife, Alice, did have a teenage son from her first marriage. So they decided to adopt a little girl. The foster family of the five-month-old little girl the Roker's selected also wanted to adopt her. The family and baby had bonded together. Roker relates: *That said, we wanted this baby. Hey, these people already had kids of their own. I know this sounds selfish, but you got yours, lemme get mine.*[22] Couples do not have a "right" to a child. A child is neither a possession nor a trophy. In Roker's description of the adoption, what was best for the little girl was not even considered. The little one's natural mother *wants to make sure this baby is taken care of by a good family.*[23] While Roker feels he gives the best to Courtney, he is not a fulltime father because the couple is now divorced and Alice has custody of their daughter. Before the couple even divorced, Courtney was raised by working parents and a sitter. Roker's third wife, Debbie, had a daughter through in-vitro fertilization. Again, both parents have hectic professional schedules. Roker explains: *Our biggest concern with Leila was that we'd both miss the moment [she took her first step]. With Deborah's travel and my schedule, the odds were that our baby-sitter, Evette, would get to see Leila walk before we did. In fact, we've come to an understanding. If Leila performs some milestone, Evette knows to let us discover it on our own.*[24] Is this pathetic or what?

We read so much about child abuse, *yet 46% of child abuse is simply neglect according to a 1993 study cited by the* Los Angeles Daily News.[25] Psychiatrist Dr. Bruce Perry of Texas Children's Hospital in Houston claims that *if an infant misses out on two*

---

[22] Al Roker, *Don't Make Me Stop This Car, Adventures in Fatherhood* (NY: Scribner, 2000) p. 103.

[23] *Ibid.,* p. 102.

[24] *Ibid.,* pp. 140-141.

[25] April 27, 1997.

months of crucial brain stimulation, you will forever have a disorganized brain.[26] In the same article a 1998 University of Michigan study on parenting was cited. That study concluded: *When parents can't find the time to hug, encourage and develop relationships with their children...the damage can be enormous, affecting everything from brain development to future relations with spouses or children. Without such interactions children become withdrawn, antisocial and insecure, and have difficulty making friends and maintaining relationships. They also tend to do significantly worse at school—from elementary through high school—than children who were physically or sexually abused.*

Show affection and appreciation with hugs, smiles, gestures, affectionate nicknames and winks. Teens, sometimes rather difficult to love, need just as much physical affection as the baby.

Neglect causes more problems in school than physical or sexual abuse! *In Israel, experts warned last year about mental neglect of infants and toddlers in day nurseries. According to experts, the employees of such nurseries deal almost exclusively with the physical care of the children...Emotional care is grossly lacking. This is especially true of infants grouped with more than six babies. The babies there often experienced serious emotional traumas because their environment neglects their feelings*[27]...

Parents encompass the whole universe for a child. Watch a four-month-old baby happy gurgling in a bouncy chair. But let the mother leave the room, the baby begins to fuss and cry. Watch a little one when mom and dad have to go out together. There are tears and tantrums as the parents leave.

When our eldest daughter, Mary Kate, was expecting her fourth baby she was so ill that her husband brought their three children down to Springfield for us to watch. Michael, the eldest at four-years-old, was so homesick that we had to return the children within twenty-four hours. The youngest, Margaret Mary, not quite a year old, usually so smiley and happy, never smiled until she heard her mother's voice on our speakerphone. Then she

---

[26] *Detroit Free Press*, March 20, 1999.

[27] "Imparting Values in the Family," *Op. Cit.*, p. 7.

became happy and animated. This year we again babysat for the four children now ranging in age from 18 months to six-years-old in their own home, hoping they would feel more comfortable with us in familiar surroundings. While we had a great time together, it was obvious that we could not replace the security they felt with their own parents. Our weeklong experience reinforced for me the importance of children being raised by their own parents, not daycare workers or even other family members.

While children have to learn to trust that when their parents go out they will return, the trauma to the emotional well being of little ones who are separated from their parents on a continual basis is significant. Olaru Otunno, the UN emissary for children in war zones, found that half of the refugee children in Kosovo were separated from their families in 1999. *These children show signs of severe trauma.*[28] Later in this same article Otunno insists that without a strong, viable family children grow up emotionally scarred so that they are unable to love or form attachments. They become irresponsible, indifferent, apathetic, depressed, and violent toward others. This is the root cause of the growing violence in young children, not guns.

A recent study on the importance of mothers bonding with their children is thought provoking. This study did not discuss the family bed nor breast-feeding but rather how involved we are with our children. This involvement does not mean driving our child from activity to activity but actually interacting with each other by praying, talking, working together and of course, sharing an experience. If a child does not bond with its mother through these activities, that child cannot develop moral values. We only have to click on the TV to see immoral public officials lying about their latest scandal. Have they no morals because their mothers were too involved in other activities to be involved with them? It's something to consider.

John Paul II, seeking to stress the importance of fulltime mothers, writes in *Familiaris Consortio #23: Society should be structured in such a way that wives and mothers are not in practice compelled to work outside the home, and that their families can*

---
[28] *Ibid.*, p. 6.

live and prosper in a dignified way even when they themselves devote their full time to their own family.

Still not convinced that fulltime moms are important? Then I urge you to read Dr. Laura Schlessinger's book, **Parenthood By Proxy**. It's a fast but profound read. One word of warning though, Dr. Schlessinger, an orthodox Jew, does accept contraception, which is contrary to the teachings of the Catholic Church and the views expressed in this book.

Take a moment and consider what you do to bond with your children. What can you do to increase your bonding time and activities? Keep a record of how much actual time you spend interacting with each of your children in your weekly planner. Along with the time spent, write down the interaction. Was it conversation, reading stories, running errands together, chores, fun activities? Note the number of meals eaten together as a family. How often do you have family outings? Do you go to church together? How do you spend Sundays? Do you live it as the day of the *Creator's Joyful Rest*?[29] Is this a day for family, prayer, outings, nature, visiting, cultural activities as the Holy Father recommends or do we use it to catch up on chores and shopping? (Remember Our Lady appeared at La Salette specifically to warn people not to work on Sunday.)

The Role Of Parent/Leader

The role of parent is that of leader. When parents do not lead, the children take over and become tyrants. Barbara Falk,[30] Director of Oakcrest School for Girls in Washington, D.C., explains that leadership and control are two different things. One leads by appealing to the heart and intellect, particularly the heart with girls. One controls through force. The power of control is limited to the short term, when your children are in your presence. Once out of sight and sound of mom and dad everything is up for

---

[29] *John Paul II*, Dies Domini (On Keeping The Lord's Day Holy) *#11*.

[30] This information is from the audiotape *Family Leadership: A Woman's Perspective* by Barbara Falk from R.B. Media, Inc.

grabs. Leadership on the other hand extends its influence when mom and dad are out of sight or when the kids are away at college.

A good parent/leader brings out the best in each person in the family; sets goals for the family and each child; strives to keep calm; and cultivates a sense of humor to survive the difficulties. A leader leads with the tone of voice at the right time. *Seize the moment.* For instance, rather than screaming at a child to clean his room (which brings resentment and stubbornness anyway) try appealing to the child's sense of fairness. For example, *Jill, come over here and sit down honey. Have you checked out your room lately? What grade would you give it? Go up and clean it now.* If there is still resistance, a threat can be added *only* if you fully intend to carry out the punishment. *Jill, you are grounded one day for each day your room remains a mess.*

Miss Falk also recommends that it is important in our interaction with our children to name the good and evil, the virtue or vice involved so children can seek the good and avoid the bad. Rather than saying, *Stop that!* or *Don't do that!* instead name the problem so the child can learn what he is doing wrong. If the children are yelling at one another you can say *You are being impatient and uncharitable.* If a child will not share a toy, *You are being selfish, share your toy. You can play with it later.* When a child does something good, compliment him to reinforce the good behavior. *Thank you for sharing your cookie. You are being charitable toward your friend.* Parents also lead when they monitor carpool conversations by stressing to the children if you can't say something nice about a person don't say anything.

Parent/leaders stress loyalty toward the Catholic Church, priests, religious, teachers, friends, and family members. Falk relates the story of a mother and daughter who had a terrible argument right before the daughter was to go out. As the daughter was about to leave the mother put her arms around the daughter saying, *Honey, I know you will be tempted to tell your friends about our fight but I beg you to be loyal and not discuss it with them.*

A parent/leader does not ask permission or try to reason with children. Instead, the leader tells the children what to do. Rather than *Jody, should we go home now?* The parent/leader tells the child, *Jody, mommy is leaving now. Say good-bye.* Don't ask children what they want for dinner. Instead tell them, *Boy, you are lucky. We are having meatloaf for dinner.* When you go out for dinner, encourage your children to try new foods rather than the standard chicken fingers, hot dog or hamburger. This will prevent them from becoming picky eaters. If a child insists on ordering something but when it arrives refuses to eat it, do not order something else or share your food with him. If he is truly hungry he will eat what he ordered. It is amazing how food becomes more appetizing when there is no other option available.

Allow your child to be responsible for his actions. Do not save the child from suffering because of his irresponsibility. If the child forgets his lunch, do not run to school with it. Let him scrounge items from his classmates. The next time he will remember to take his own lunch.

Let me digress a bit to discuss the importance of permitting our children to suffer. To allow our children to handle the consequences of their actions is a suffering for both parents and children. But if we truly love them, we will consider the long term allowing them to suffer while at the same time accepting the cross that their suffering brings to us. John Paul II insists that *It is suffering, more than anything else, which clears the way for the grace which transforms human souls.*

We want our children's souls to be transformed. C.S. Lewis explains why: *We are not merely imperfect creatures who must be improved: we are, as Newman said, rebels who must lay down our arms. The first answer, then, to the question why our cure should be painful, is that to render back the will which we have so long claimed for our own, is in itself...a grievous pain...We can rest contentedly in our sins and in our stupidities...[b]ut pain insists upon being attended to. God whispers to us in our pleasures, speaks in our conscience, but shouts in our pains: it is His megaphone to rouse a deaf world.*[31]

---

[31] C.S.Lewis, *The Problem of Pain* (NY: MacMillian, 1962) pp. 91-93.

How does suffering help our children to grow? Each time our child suffers and learns to accepts the cross, his soul becomes better developed and capable of greater deeds. Self-control strengthens and interiorly the child is at peace. There is a feeling of freedom because the environment no longer controls the child. Rather, the child learns to carry his own environment. Courage grows and fortitude is strengthened. Who can be proud when cast down? Humility takes root then begins to grow. *Hence along with humility comes the strength and the resolution to adapt oneself to the force of circumstances.*[32] Each cross brings with it the virtue of detachment. The things that were so important before, no longer matter. New priorities are set and there is growth even if we do not perceive it.

Trust in God grows when one learns to accept God's actions in one's life without question, with acceptance, even if it is a bit reluctantly. There is an ability to look at the events through the eyes of God. This is the beginning of wisdom. Charity grows and with it the ability to forgive oneself and others. Actions begin to revolve around the will of God. In effect, our child is becoming Christ-like, which is the foundation for his personal happiness.

The value of suffering and shouldering one's daily cross is something that our children must learn. Otherwise, when our children experience an unexpected blow, and they will, they will run away like the apostles did on Holy Thursday night. Their escape will be through drugs, alcohol, premarital sex, divorce, and/or suicide. If we truly want our children to be happy, not only must we form them in the various virtues, but we also have to teach them to suffer in a cheerful, supernatural manner.

We do not help our children when we give them everything they desire or protect them from disappointments and heartaches. Instead, we emotionally and spiritually hurt them. Columnist William Raspberry observes: *Our young people, no doubt learning from the behavior of their elders, are well-schooled in their rights as citizens, but are functionally illiterate when it comes to*

---

[32] David P. McAstocker, SJ, *The Joy of Sorrow* (NY: Bruce Publishng Co., 1936) p. 52.

responsibilities.[33]

Parents must lead in the area of choosing entertainment and social activities. You are the adult with the sound moral criteria. You have the responsibility to decide what you think is appropriate for your children to read, see and listen to. Children should ask permission to watch TV, not turn it on automatically. Barbara Falk relates the story of how one daughter asked her father if she could watch a TV show. The father paused a moment then said, *Sure you can watch it if you can give me one good reason for watching it.* The girl thought and thought but could not come up with a reason so she did not watch the show.

When pressured by your children to allow them to do something you know they should not do, recall that saints do not give in to peer or any other type of pressure. Practice fortitude by sticking to your guns. When you do, you will be repaid in spades. Our youngest daughter, like her sisters, attended high school several hundred miles away from home. In her junior year it was decided that she would attend a public high school in Springfield and return to The Willows for her senior year. It was a difficult year for her because the people she knew from grade school all had new friends. Mary Terese was stuck with mom as her only friend. Toward the end of the first semester she came home all excited. She was invited to a party with kids from her honor classes. The boy who was hosting the party was the son of one of the high school teachers. Teresie picked out a cute outfit to wear and was happily looking forward to the party that evening. What a relief to finally have her happy again! On the way to our daily evening Mass together, she happily chatted about the party that evening. She was thrilled she was finally accepted into the top clique at school. As she chattered away it suddenly dawned on me (my guardian angel?) that I had not asked THE question, so I did. *Are his parents going to be at the party?* Dead silence. Then the rationale began. *No, his parents are divorced and his mother is going out of town but Mom, you can trust these kids. They're all straight. They're all in the honor society. They would never do*

---

[33] William Raspberry, "Teaching Youngsters to Volunteer," *State-Journal Register,* 8/26/91.

anything wrong...Besides, kids don't have parties if the parents are around. You can trust me. I won't drink. The discussion ended when I told her, *Let's ask your father what he thinks.* I knew exactly what he would think. Bob explained to her that while we trusted her, we did not trust the other teens. *Besides, we cannot permit you to attend a party that is not chaperoned.* With tears streaming down her face, she went up to change and spent another lonely weekend with her parents. After school on Monday I asked about the party. Her reply was a pleasant surprise: *Thank you, thank you, thank you for not letting me go to the party!* It was a drinking party that got out of hand. When the boy who hosted the party could not get the teens to leave, he grabbed a butcher knife to force the teens to leave. It was a miracle that no one was hurt.

A parent/leader prepares his/her children in advance for what can happen in different situations such as slumber parties, dances, mixed parties, babysitting, job situations. Lay down specific rules. For example, a Catholic politician hosted an after-prom party at his home which a friend's daughter attended. Her parents warned her that should her date bring alcohol to the party or if alcohol was served at the party and her date drank, she was to call her father to pick her up. The politician served alcohol. The girl's date became drunk. She called her father and he picked her up.

A parent/leader teaches his children how to live the spiritual and corporal works of mercy. Burying the dead comes to mind because some people are squeamish about taking children to wakes and funerals. It is important for children to understand the concept of death and eternity. Death is never an end but a beginning. We should live so when we die we are born into heaven. Still, sometimes children are embarrassed to go to wakes and funerals because they do not know what to do or what to say. Explain that this is a normal feeling but we go to cheer up the people who are sorrowing over the loss of a loved one. Prompt your children on what to say and do.

A parent/leader helps his children to rebel against the pagan culture we live in. A leader makes the important choices such as how the family lives its faith and what schools the children attend.

Remember, teens are children in transition. They are not equipped to decide which school will help them to grow holy, to become saints. Schools have a profound effect on children. Teachers can change the direction of a child's life. It was the youth minister of her Methodist Church who changed Hillary Clinton from a Goldwater conservative to a radical leftist.[34] While a teen may protest a parent's decision to send him to a particular school or home school, a hassle for a month or so may save your child's soul for eternity. The hassle is a small price to pay for eternal happiness.

Wise parent/leaders give their children the bare necessities and few luxuries. Necessities do not include TVs, a walkman, computer games, stereos, personal phones, cars, fad or expensive clothing, electronic games, or funding for excessive activities. A friend related an experience she had at dinner with a family of 15 children. The older children, now established, are all upright, responsible young men and women. One is an engineer, another a doctor, the third a scientist, then there's a lawyer, and the fifth son is studying to be a priest. The other ten are still in school. The father explained that he and his wife only gave the children the bare necessities, nothing beyond that. While his children suffered for not having "things" their friends had, my friend observed what a happy family they are. "Things" never buy happiness and contentment. Besides, when a parent allows a child to have his own TV set, VCR, and car, the parent is teaching him the vices of consumerism, selfishness, greed and intemperance.

When Mary Terese spent her junior year at the local public school she told us that she was the only 16-year-old in the school without her own car. We laughed. As the months went by we discovered that she was not exaggerating. Some mothers actually leave the home and join the work force in order to pay for Kindra and Zach's cars and insurance. Teachers at the high school gave class time to complete homework so that the teens could get jobs to help support their car payments. This is nonsense. Parent/

---

[34] Barbara Olson *Hell To Pay* (Washington, DC: Regnery Publishing, Inc., 1999) p. 31.

leaders have the obligation to fight this type of mentality.

If we are serious about raising our children saints—and if they do not become saints they will not go to heaven—we must begin from a young age to teach them the spirit of poverty. This begins by checking out our own homes and cutting back on luxuries. There is no need for multiple TVs. Besides, you can better control what is viewed if there is one TV and you can monitor it easily in the family room. By limiting objects, children are taught to share. Psychologist John Rosemond is convinced: *Parents have to separate wants from needs. We're to give them [our children] all they truly need along with a small amount of what they want. Doing this gives children the opportunity to figure things out for themselves without any parental help. For instance, organizing time, occupying oneself, and solving academic and social problems are all situations children need to handle, for the most part, on their own. In the process, the child learns to persevere and to be resourceful, the two keys to success in any endeavor. If you give excessively to your children, they not only don't have to figure anything out by themselves, they can't. You're doing it all.*

He goes on to say that most five-year-olds have hundreds of toys yet are bored. *Why? Because they haven't learned how to play independently occupying their time, or to do a lot with a little. Overall, the key to the obligation stage of parenting is a willingness to say "no" more often than "yes."* Independence is a process in which we encourage our children to confront reality. *The opportunity to figure things out, which comes by courtesy of parents who meet all of a child's needs and deny most of his or her wants, provides a child with incredible self-sufficiency. And that's the essence of self-esteem, which will lead your child to succeed where others will fail for lack of resourcefulness and purpose.*[35]

When a parent does the science project for his child because it is the night before it is due or because the parent can help the child get a better grade, the parent is depriving the child of learning the virtues of order, steadfastness, patience, fortitude, perseverance, and humility. The parent also teaches the child

---

[35] John Rosemond, *Better Homes and Gardens,* April, 1991, p. 39.

that irresponsibility pays off.

Parent/leaders have a daily plan, are flexible, and work with schedules. Family dinnertime is important. Every member of the family should be there. Explain your weekend plans ahead of time so children do not make other plans. Leaders point their children in the direction of the good. Be strict but not mean.

It is also helpful to keep reminding yourself and your spouse that no person is perfect, particularly the children. There will be fewer surprises in your family if you expect flaws. Each family deals with the imperfections of each of its members. The Martin family struggled with Léonie, one of St. Thérèse's sisters. Mrs. Martin told Pauline, another sister, *I don't know what to do with Léonie. She does exactly as she pleases.* In a letter to her sister-in-law, Mrs. Martin again expressed her frustration: *The poor child worries me; she has a very undisciplined nature, and mentally she is underdeveloped... As for Léonie, only God can change her— and I am confident that He will.*[36]

When mom is home with the children she leads them. When dad comes home from work, he takes over as leader. When parents lead, children are happy. They feel secure and loved. But to lead, one has to know where one is going. **Proverbs** tells us, **Without vision the people perish.** One wouldn't think of going on a road trip without a map or directions. Parents cannot successfully parent if they do not have a concrete image of what they want for their children. Wise and prudent parents have a plan, a vision of the type of adults they want their children to become. I'm not talking about Jane becoming a lawyer or John winning honors in medical school. Where do you want each of your children to be five, ten, fifty years from now?

If you weren't interested in the best for your children, and striving for holiness is the highest calling in life, you would not be reading this book. In view of this, your long and short-range plan should center on how you can raise Jane and John to become

[36] Sr. Mary Christine Martens, V.H.M. "Léonie Martin: The Forgotten Sister of St. Thérèse" *Apostolate of The Little Flower*, May/June 2000, Vol. 68, No. 3., p. 9.

saints. Once you determine that you truly want to raise your children saints than each day begins with this in mind. Remember, good character is formed, it doesn't just happen. Parents who are determined to raise happy, holy children shape their personality and character by helping them to develop virtues day in and day out. Each activity, each project, each problem, each interchange has this as its end. Will this school raise our children saints? Will this sports activity or hobby help my child to grow holy or self-centered? Will this friend hinder or help my child to get to heaven? Will this gift help or hurt my child spiritually? Work together as a couple to define your family plan then support the decisions of each other. Let your children know the vision you have for your family and each of them individually. When everyone knows the ground rules, the purpose, and the plan, people work together. The children see there is a reason behind each of your actions and decisions even if they do not agree. They realize you are not being arbitrary in your rules. When everyone is headed in the same direction things go more smoothly, there is more understanding, more willingness to cooperate, a feeling of security for everyone.

Stephen R. Covey finds that *[w]ith a clear sense of shared vision and values, you can be very demanding when it comes to standards. You can have the courage to hold your children accountable and to let them experience the consequences of their actions. Ironically, you will also become more loving and empathic as you respect the individuality of each child and allow your children to be self-regulating, to make their own decisions within the scope of their experience and wisdom.*[37]

A shared vision is also a commitment. *When children feel this level of commitment—and when it's communicated consistently through words and actions—they are then willing to live with limits, to accept responsibility and be accountable for their actions. But when the price has not been paid in making the deep decisions that are contained in these mission statements, parents can easily be uprooted by the social forces and by the pressures they will*

---

[37] Stephen R. Covey, *The 7 Habits of Highly Effective Families* (NY: St. Martin's Griffin, 1997) p.95.

continually get against taking the responsible course, moving toward interdependency, maintaining standards in the home, and carrying out agreed upon consequences.[38]

Developing A Catholic Family Culture

Part of our plan of action in raising our children to be saints is to develop our own Catholic family culture. The dictionary defines culture as *the act of developing the intellectual and moral faculties especially by education; expert care and training; enlightenment and excellence of taste acquired by intellectual and aesthetic training; the integrated pattern of human behavior that includes thought, speech, action, and artifacts and depends upon man's capacity for learning and transmitting knowledge to succeeding generations.*[39] Our culture is chronicled in our novels, poetry, music, films, news, media and art. These reflect what is important to us as a society.

Fr. Frank Hoffman, Doctor of Canon Law and chaplain of Northridge Prep in Niles, Illinois, speaking on the Christian influence on culture emphasizes that Christ calls us to be the salt, light, and leaven in our culture.[40] It is precisely our task as Christians to speak the truth and set an example. People may not like to hear the truth but when we speak it, it settles into their consciousness. Rather than following the current styles, we, as Christians, are to set new trends. Father Raniero Cantamaessa, O.F.M. Cap. observes: *the divine truth...acts through reason, not contrary to it; not destroying it but saving it.*[41]

When Cardinal Francis George met with John Paul II, for his Ad Lumina visit, the Pope asked him, *How is the transformation*

---

[38] *Ibid.,* p. 99.

[39] *Webster's New Collegiate Dictionary* (MA: G.& C. Merriam Company,1980) p. 274.

[40] Fr. Frank Hoffman, "The Christian Influence on Culture," Willows/Northridge Seminar, March 2000. Audiotape from R.B. Media.

[41] Fr. Raniero Cantalamessa, *The Mystery of God's Word* (MN: The Liturgical Press, 1994).

of culture going in the U.S.? As families we evangelize by developing a Christian culture within our homes then exporting it to our extended family and friends. Fr. Hoffman reminds us that St. Francis of Assisi had a profound effect on the culture of Europe through his actions that were based on prayer and devotion to the Holy Eucharist. We can do the same within our families. Holy people, people striving to become saints, bring about reform. Bl. Escrivá insisted that *these world crises are crises of saints.* Christian culture is formed by a Christian family culture.

The values we cling to and the object we worship are reflected in our customs, which creates our culture. In the U.S. we tend to worship success rather than God. To turn our culture around we must instill moral values and the love of God into everything we do. Begin by deepening your family devotion to the Holy Eucharist. *[T]he Eucharist is the chief means of progress in spiritual life, the light which shows the way and supplies the needed strength to follow it,* according to St. Peter Julian Eymard.[42] This explains the growing trend of Perpetual Adoration. Archbishop Rigali of St. Louis asked the pastors of his diocese to implement some form of Eucharistic Adoration for priestly vocations. He has 90% participation. In the Chicago Archdiocese there is a movement to imitate St. Louis. In my own diocese of Springfield, Illinois, during the Jubilee Year, Bishop George Lucas spent the Sundays between Easter and Pentecost leading Eucharist Adoration at each of the deanery churches in the diocese. His newspaper columns address the various aspects of Eucharistic Adoration. It is through these endeavors that a truly Christian culture will replace our pagan culture.

Our present culture is labeled the *culture of death.* One out of ten people are missing because of abortion. We have the highest percent of suicide in the world. While we are 5% of the world population we use 50% of the cocaine. In 1900 our divorce rate was 7%. Now it is 50%. From 1960 to today *illegitimate births grew by 523%. More than two-thirds of all black children are now illegitimate, as are 42.1% of Hispanics, and 22% of whites...More than 80% of black women will be single heads of*

---

[42] *The Real Presence, Op. Cit.,* viii

households at some point in their lives. The median family income for a two-parent married family is four times that of a never-married woman with children.[43]

As mentioned at the beginning of this chapter, work has become our god with many executives putting in 65-70 hours a week working. We no longer read because it takes work. Our attention span is 7 seconds on the Internet. While we believe in science and technology, we have lost the sense of truth and beauty. Art now makes a political statement. The pursuit of money drives our culture. All ideas are accorded equal status but that of truth. Our national sin is envy. We want what other people have.

The truly Catholic family can change this culture. The family is not only the place for acceptance and rest, but also the place where our faith can permeate every area of family life. For our children to grow holy we need to teach them that our faith is not simply attending Sunday Mass. The Catholic faith embraces how we furnish our homes, how we talk, how we dress, how we amuse ourselves and how we act. Catholic family culture should dictate acceptable behavior, manners, appearance and speech, courtesy, spirit of service, standards for entertainment, and specific practices of piety. When there are set rules, standards and customs that everyone is expected to adhere to everyone knows what is expected of them. There is less arguing and misunderstandings so there is more peace and cooperation within the family.

Where To Begin?

Let's begin with the look of the home. People should know when they enter your home that you are Catholic. I discovered that Springfield, Illinois is a largely Catholic city simply by house hunting. There was either a statue of Our Lady in the garden, or crucifixes in the bedrooms in almost every house I viewed. Why should we have visible signs of our faith around our home? When we love someone, we keep reminders of them around us. We have pictures of our family in our homes. Likewise we should have statues or pictures, in good taste of course, of Our Lady,

---

[43] Zenit, April 2, 2001.

Our Lord and the saints scattered throughout our house or apartment. These images are reminders to periodically to raise our minds and hearts to God. They also remind us that our lives on earth are simply a pilgrimage to the House of Our Father. While our homes are not to look like chapels or religious stores, to relegate signs of our faith out of sight of visitors, indicates a lack of spiritual affection. It indicates an unconscious shame to be branded a follower of Jesus and child of Mary. This attitude will then be passed on to your children. Images are a means to evangelize. Visitors may not acknowledge what they see, but they will think about it.

Our children take the presence of Our Lord and Our Lady, represented by statues and pictures, as part of their home-life, their culture, and their faith. It is also a way to introduce little ones to the mysteries of our faith by explaining who each statue or picture represents and why they are important to our lives, our family. Teach little ones to say "hi" as they pass by Our Lady or Jesus. Prayer than becomes a natural part of their lives. Place a statue or picture of Our Lady where all can see her and say aspirations as they pass by. One evening a priest was visiting a large family. As he talked with the parents he could hear a lot of commotion going on upstairs among the children. Suddenly there was a yelp and a young boy started to run downstairs sobbing. As he hit the landing the crying stopped for a few moments, then began again as he ran down the rest of the stairs. After the parents comforted the child, the priest inquired what happened that the child would stop crying at the landing but resume crying the rest of the way down. The parents explained that there is a statue of Our Lady at the landing. The children are taught to always stop and say a little prayer to Our Lady as they walk up and down the stairs. *What a beautiful custom to teach our children!*

Barbara Falk, tells the story about a family that had sacred images in their home. One day the little boy had a friend over. They went into the bathroom to get something. The friend pointing to the unusual scale asked what it was. The little boy replied, *It must be something religious because every time my*

Mom gets on it she says, "Oh, my God!" (The Mom wasn't taking God's name in vain. It was a petition for help!)

Consider enthroning the Sacred Heart in your most public room such as your living room or family room. The image can be a picture or a beautiful statue.[44] One of the earliest memories that I have as a child is a priest coming over to enthrone a painting of the Sacred Heart over our living room mantle. That made such an impression on me that when I got a dollhouse I enthroned a miniature picture of the Sacred Heart over my miniature mantle. When we married, my parents presented Bob and me with an exquisite Sacred Heart by Pattarino, which is enthroned in our living room.

A father can enthrone the Sacred Heart with his family in attendance. If the father is not available, the mother can do it. The prayer is very simple:

Family Consecration
To The Sacred Heart Of Jesus

Oh most Sacred Heart of Jesus, we come to you as a family and consecrate ourselves to Your Sacred Heart. Protect us through Your Most Precious Blood and keep us pure and holy.

Oh Dear Jesus, we are so far away from Your most pure and Sacred Heart. As a family we need Your help. Heal all the quarrels that exist in our famly due to our unforgiveness and lack of love for You. Heal our unbelieving and unconverted hearts and lead us to Your Sacred Heart with love. Unite us as a family and remove all stain of sinfulness from our souls. Help us to be a prayerful and loving family, so that through our example we may lead other souls to Your Most Sacred Heart.

We give You our hearts Dearest Jesus, and consecrate our family through the fourth generation. Through the prayers of our Dearest Mother Mary, may we live this consecration every day of our lives. Amen. Most Sacred Heart of Jesus, have pity on us.

---

[44]Pictures and images can be purchased from religious bookstores or contact the Priests of the Sacred Heart, Sacred Heart Monastery, PO Box 900, Hales Corners, WI 53130-0900.

The Sacred Heart, through St. Margaret Mary, gave twelve promises to those who are devoted to His Sacred Heart and enthrone His image. They are:

1. I will give them all the graces necessary in their state of life.
2. I will establish peace in their houses.
3. I will comfort them in all their afflictions.
4. I will be their secure refuge during life, and above all at death.
5. I will bestow a large blessing upon all their undertakings.
6. Sinners shall find in My Heart the source and the infinite ocean of mercy.
7. Tepid souls shall grow fervent.
8. Fervent souls shall quickly mount to high perfection.
9. I will bless every place where a picture of My Heart shall be set up and honored.
10. I will give to priests the gift of touching the most hardened hearts.
11. Those who shall promote this devotion shall have their names written in My Heart, never to be blotted out.
12. I promise super-abundant mercy of My Heart that My all-powerful love will grant to those who communicate on the First Friday in nine consecutive months the grace of final penitence; they shall not die in My disgrace nor without receiving their Sacraments; My Divine Heart shall be their safe refuge in this last moment.

Note promise #2. Jesus will protect your marriage. Each year renew your family consecration on the Feast of the Sacred Heart that falls toward the end of June. Make a family consecration to the Immaculate Heart of Mary as well. Renew that consecration on her feast day which is the day after the Feast of the Sacred Heart.

Divine Mercy is another powerful devotion to teach your children. On February 22, 1931, Jesus appeared to a young Polish nun, St. Faustina Kowalska. He asked her to have an image painted of Him as the Merciful Savior. Radiating from His heart are red and pale rays representing the blood and water that flowed from His pierced Heart as a fountain of mercy for all of us. At the bottom of the picture is the aspiration *Jesus I trust in You.* The image reminds us of God's unlimited mercy towards us. It is an invitation for sinners to return to the mercy of God while reminding us to show mercy by actively living the spiritual and corporal works of mercy. Place an image of Divine Mercy in your home. It should be exposed in a place where the members of your family can see it as they come and go during the day. This image is a source of graces from God. Jesus told Sister Faustina, *I am offering people a vessel to which they are to keep coming for graces.*[45] It is a means to re-Christianize your family. *I cannot punish even the most hardened sinner, if he appeals to My Mercy. He is immediately granted pardon through My incomprehensible and unfathomable Mercy. Tell them, My Daughter, that I am Love and Mercy Itself. When a soul draws near to me with confidence, My generosity fills it with an abundance of graces far greater than its capacity to contain them—thus overflowing on others.* This devotion is a powerful means to spiritually and physically protect your family. It was the image of Divine Mercy that, during World War II, saved the city of Krakow, Poland from the merciless German bombing. Our Lord also promises to provide the physical means of support to those who venerate His image of mercy. Say the Chaplet of Mercy at the bedside of the dying to bring consolation and peace for those suffering. Pray it at 3PM for special intentions. Unite your intensions with Christ's Passion .

Act Of Consecration To Divine Mercy

We consecrate our entire life from here on to you without reserve. Into Your hands we abandon our past, our present, our future. Jesus, we ask you, from this day on, to look after this family. Help us to be true children of God and children of Your Blessed Mother Mary. Through this image may your Divine Mercy triumph over all the powers of evil the world over. May all who venerate it never perish. May it be their joy in life, their hope in death and their glory in eternity. This we ask through Christ our Lord, Amen. Jesus I trust in You.

As Catholics, we are blessed with many powerful sacramentals besides statues such as crucifixes, Holy Water and blessed medals.

---

[45] St. Faustina Kowalska, *Divine Mercy in My Soul,* (Stockbridge, MA: Marian Press, 1987.*Diary* 1, #138.

Place a crucifix in each bedroom. Use holy water. It is such a powerful sacramental. Teach your children to bless themselves with holy water at bedtime and when they leave home. Many families have a holy water font near the door so as people come and go they can bless themselves. Again, not to sound superstitious, I have found that when children are fighting or when teenagers are moody, sprinkling them with holy water seems to resolve the problem.

Teach your children the power of the miraculous medal and the scapular medal. Encourage them to wear the medals or cloth. Each child who has made his First Communion should be enrolled in the brown scapular. It's like having Our Lady's arms wrapped around them. Even infants can wear miraculous medals pinned to their onesies.™

Pious practices are also part of a Catholic family culture such as morning prayers, evening prayers, grace before meals and, the family rosary. Remember the words of Fr. Peyton, *the family that prays together stays together.* Develop the custom of going to weekly confession and Sunday Mass as a family. In May and October go on a family pilgrimage and invite other families to join you. Bl. Escrivá's parents joined a group of families each Saturday morning for Mass then stayed after to say the rosary together. Family prayer is a vital component in raising happy children. Other pious practices include making visits to the Blessed Sacrament and giving alms to the poor. Louis Martin took his daughters for daily visits to the Blessed Sacrament. He also gave money to St. Thérèse to give the poor. Mr. Escrivá likewise gave money to his son, Bl. Josemaría, to give to the poor on their walks through town.

Develop religious family customs and traditions for Advent, Christmas, Lent, and Easter as well as for other feastdays. Our religious holydays have become too secularized with Santa Claus and the Easter Bunny. Ronda De Sola Chervin and her daughter, Carla Conley, wrote a book entitled **Catholic Customs and Traditions.** Maybe you can incorporate some of their ideas into your family. While in Medjugorja I interviewed an eleven-year-old girl for an article. When I asked if Santa Claus brought their Christmas presents she looked at me perplexed and replied, *No.*

The Christ Child brings our gifts. Did I feel like a fool! When I returned home I threw all my Santa items and secular ornaments away. Now angels decorate our tree with a nativity set that encompasses a large part of our living room. Consider starting a beautiful nativity set for Christmas adding different pieces each year. Read the Christmas story to your children. Bring back St. Nicholas and the custom of putting shoes outside the bedroom door on December 6th. Participate in a yearly Corpus Christi Procession. If there is none in your area, organize one at your parish. Take the children to novenas and Holy Hours. Expose them to the faith in all its forms.

The Importance Of Correct Language

Since children learn how to talk from their parents, most parents have an embarrassing story to tell about a toddler repeating "naughty" words they overheard them say. Never ever, use the name of Jesus, God, Our Lady or anything holy in anger or jest. These names are to be used only with the highest respect and in prayer. The Jewish orthodox treat the name of God with such reverence that they do not even say or write His name. Instead they write G-d. Teach your children, when they hear others taking the name of God in vain, to say an aspiration in reparation for that offense against God. Teach your children to stand-up for God, to correct people who take God's name in vain. It is especially important to teach this to young boys so that as they grow older they will not follow the example of their peers.

Teach your children to avoid crudity and coarseness in language and subject matter. It's disturbing to listen to conversations that degenerate into sexual innuendos or other unsavory topics. Many people seem to have lost the ability to enjoy discussing the good, the beautiful, or anything uplifting.

Fr. Andrew Apostoli, C.F.R. tells a story about driving down a highway and seeing a police car off on the side of the road shooting a radar gun. A fellow priest humorously observed, *What a witness that police car is. It got everyone to slow down!* That's the type of witness our children and we have to be. When people are in contact with us, they should know to watch their language, their conversation, and their conduct. When they see us it should immediately trigger right conduct in their mind that is pleasing to God.

Appearance Tells A Lot About Us...

When we are in the state of sanctifying grace, we are temples of the Holy Spirit. As such our appearance should be that of a son or daughter of God. To disfigure God's creation with weird hairstyles in glow in the dark colors, tattoos and body piercing (I'm not taking about pierced ears unless it's excessive) comes from another spirit, not God. One family author I listened to on audiotape calls it "body noise" and told parents to ignore it. I disagree. It's rebellion. It's a visible cry for attention. Teach your children to respect their bodies, to rebel against our pagan culture. Strengthen their character so that they *dare to be different.* It may save their lives. A priest told me of a family of seven who vacationed one summer in Southern California. The five older children, teens and young adults spent a day in Mexico. On their return their parents were flabbergasted to see that they had all gotten tattoos and in time AIDS. What had begun as a lark ended in death.

How we dress expresses who we think we are. We also act the way we dress. Rent the video *Mr. Holland's Opus.* Note the appearance of the students and their accompanying conduct as the film progresses through the decades. It's rather shocking.

According to well-known author and consultant John Molloy [New Dress for Success], aside from ability, how one looks on the job is the single most important factor in a person's professional success. And how successful one is in his or her job directly impacts how profitable a company can be.[46] Molloy also maintains that *[r]esearch conducted by two companies independent of each other (one with blue-collar workers and the other with office workers) found that employees who were neat and well put together performed better than employees who were not. It may be due to the fact that [the neater] employees have a*

---

[46] Debbie Leaper, "The Dollars and Sense of Image," *People & Productivity,* Vol. 21, Dec.-Jan. 1998-1999.

better self-image, and therefore performed at a higher level.[47]

While people claim that clothes don't make the man or woman recent findings disagree. It was found that the most effective managers dress well. Here's what top executives of 100 corporations think about dress:

- ✓ 96% said companies have a better chance for success if their employees know how to dress.
- ✓ 100% said dress affects the general tone of the office.
- ✓ 92% said if given presentations of equal weight when forging an alliance with a new company, they would choose the more professionally attired one.
- ✓ 78% said they'd hold up a promotion if an employee didn't dress properly.
- ✓ 65% said they'd tell someone if they were inappropriately attired ...
- ✓ 84% turned down applicants at job interviews and sales pitches based upon improper dress alone.
- ✓ 92% said they would not hire someone who did not dress appropriately.[48]

Tom Monaghan, founder of Domino's Pizza, keeps the same dress standards for his Ave Maria Foundation as he had for his company. Men wear suits and women wear skirted knee length suits or dresses. Why not dress down? Robert R. Flaconi believes that *if dressing down has an effect on productivity, it's only negative. If you look sharp, you're more likely to act sharp. I suspect that's one reason our military requires a certain standard of dress.*[49] A survey was done with CPAs on dress-down days. Here is what these employees observed.

- ✓ Employees act lazily and unprofessionally.
- ✓ There is a definite noise level increase in the office on dress-down days.
- ✓ Another candidly reported that he is more inclined

---

[47] Robert R. Falconi, "If you want to move up, don't dress down," *Financial Executive,* vol. 12, #1, Jan/Feb. 1996.

[48] "The Dollars and Sense of Image," *Op. Cit.*

[49] "If you want to move up, don't dress down," *Op. Cit.*

> to leave to play golf when dressed in casual clothing.
> ✓ That day might turn into a "free" day that is unproductive.[50]

Now change the scene to Sunday Mass. Dressing sloppy casual encourages

> ✓ Churchgoers to act irreverent from half-hearted genuflections to none.
> ✓ A definite noise level increase from talking to yelling across the church to friends.
> ✓ People coming to Mass late and leaving at communion time.
> ✓ People tending toward casual posture such as lounging in the pews, putting their arm around their "honey," and talking and laughing throughout the Mass.
> ✓ People acting as a distraction for others by acting bored by checking out their watch, leaving to go to the restroom, and squirming during the homily.

Critics maintain that dressing well is very expensive. Actually, dressing well is not anymore costly than dressing slovenly. The same styles, colors, patterns and textures are available in less expensive clothing as the more expensive clothing.

Why am I spending so much time on quotes about dress? It's simply because the richest country in the world, the U.S., has become the land of slobs. As my mother observes, one needs only to have a pair of jeans and a tee shirt with a message on it to be dressed for any occasion. This dress is not based on financial need but rather laziness, the vice of sloth and the love of comfort, which is a lack of the virtue of temperance. It's too much work to get dressed up, to look nice, to have to change one's clothes several times a day. As Christians, it's time to get back to a dress code and this begins within our families. *Knowing how to dress successfully is not information with which one is born; it is a learned skill.*[51] So set a dress code for each occasion, and then stick to it. A young doctor in town puzzles why golfers are required

---

[50] Terri Gutierrez and R. John Freese, "Benefit or Burden? Dress Down Days," *The CPA Journal*, April 1999.

[51] "The Dollars and sense of Image," *Op. Cit.*

to wear collared shirts but there is not a dress code for church. This past Easter we had brunch at the Grove Park Inn in Ashville, North Carolina which is a resort, country club and spa. Guests are informed that the dress code for the main restaurant requires men to wear a jacket while women are required to wear dresses or comparable dress slacks. For their other restaurants, patrons are permitted to dress casual but it is noted that jeans, cutoffs, shorts (for either men or women), tee shirts and halter-tops are not acceptable. Here in Springfield, Illinois there is even a dress code for bars that call themselves "nightclubs."A sign outside one such bar reads:

- No nylon pants or sweatpants.
- No gang-related clothing.
- All oversize necklaces and pendants must be tucked in.
- No visible undergarments.
- No ripped or torn clothing.[52]

This is all clothing worn to the Holy Sacrifice of the Mass. The following Sunday I made reservations for brunch at the American Club in Kohler, Wisconsin. When I made the reservations I was told that the dress code was business casual. There is a dress code to feed our faces but no dress code for feeding our souls with God. Something is wrong here!

What a person wears for play or for lounging around is not appropriate for Holy Mass, social events or school. Teach your children the correct manner of dressing for each occasion. When everyone in the family knows the rules and expectations there are few arguments. If children complain, *nobody dresses like this*, exhort them to *Dare to be different!* Teach them to set the tone, to lead rather than to follow. James Stenson maintains that *a great many parents give in to their children's wishes about fashionable dress and gadgets because they don't want the kids to suffer from being **different**...Why don't they see the dangers of this outlook? What could happen to the kids later in high school, when alcohol or drugs are being passed around at parties? Or in college, when "everyone else" is sexually promiscuous? Or as young*

---

[52] Jayette Bolinski, "UIS student: Nightclub dress codes cloak racial bias", *The State Journal Register,* May 12, 2001.

singles, when most of one's acquaintances are "living together" with someone?...Anyone who aims to live a moral life has to become accustomed to being "different." A habit of mindless conformity can lead to endless personal suffering.[53]

The first criteria for clothing is that it should always be modest, i.e. not revealing. Revealing clothing can tempt others to commit sins against purity and chastity. Remember, should a person, through dress, words or actions cause another to sin, the person who triggered the sin is also guilty of a sin. I overheard a couple talking on a beach. The wife asked her husband why he didn't wait for her around the pool. He replied that after she left two women in bikinis came and sat down right next to him even though the whole pool area was empty. *I felt uncomfortable sitting next to naked women so I waited here on the beach for you.* Think carefully before you and your children leave home: *Will my appearance or the appearance of my children cause anyone to sin against chastity or purity?*

Moms, explain to your daughters that when a woman is scantily clad men look at her body, not at her as a person. Skimpy, revealing clothing makes your daughter a sex object. Help her to understand that she wants to be viewed as a lovely young woman rather than the object of a man's lust. Dads have a keen sensitivity as to what arouses other men. So Dad, it is your job to utilize the virtue of fortitude (backbone) to give your wife and daughters the once over before they go out. Do not allow them to dress immodestly. Guidelines for women and girls should be: skirts no shorter than knee length; swimsuits that are one-piece; avoid plunging tops, spaghetti straps, and short-shorts. Sleeveless tops should fit snuggly so underwear does not show. Just to be on the safe side wear a tee shirt under or a light sweater over the sleeveless outfit. Camisoles should be worn under see through tops. Slacks for men and women should be loose rather than tight fitting. Men should wear shirts. Recall the words of St. Paul: *I wish women to be decently dressed, adorning themselves with modesty and dignity...*(*1 Timothy* 2:9). This also applies to men.

Before John XXIII was elected pope, he was the Papal Legate to France. Attending a sumptuous banquet in Paris, he was

[53] *Upbringing, Op. Cit.,* p. 157.

seated next to a woman with a plunging neckline. When the apples were passed around the table, Pope John graciously offered one to the woman next to him. She refused. *But you must eat it,* he insisted, *for it was only after Eve ate the apple that she realized she was NAKED.*

Aside from modest clothing, appropriate clothing also needs to be addressed. What to wear when? Let's begin with church. A good indication of how much we love God is visible in how we dress. When people trail into Mass in jeans, tee shirts, shorts and other picnic attire it shows an indifferent relationship toward God. At a Sunday evening Mass at our Cathedral, a gentleman in his 60s rushed into Holy Mass wearing shorts, a Hawaiian shirt open to his waist, a fortune in gold chains hanging down his hairy chest and no socks. He was perfectly dressed for seduction on the beach but certainly not for Holy Mass.

Are you aware that non-Christian faiths have strict dress codes for honoring God? The Jewish Temple in Jerusalem was built on Mt. Moriah, which tradition claims is the place that Abraham was prepared to sacrifice his son, Isaac. Presently this area is under Moslem control and called the Dome of the Rock. It is the second most sacred shrine for Moslems. A strict dress code is enforced for anyone wishing to enter this area. Floor length blue skirts are actually lent to men and women who try to enter wearing shorts.

Adjoining this area is the Wailing Wall; the only remaining wall left standing of the Temple. It is here that the Jews come to pray. A dress code is likewise strictly enforced. Jewish guards handout large black cloths with ties to be used to cover shorts or sleeveless tops for men and women. Should we not likewise honor God with appropriate dress? Note that the executives in the survey quoted found that dress set the tone. Inappropriate dress leads to inappropriate behavior.

In *1 Paralipomenon* 16:29[54] we are told to worship God in festive garments. *Festive* translates into our finest clothes. In other words we are to really get dressed up to go to Mass,

---

[54] Some Bibles refer to this book as ***Chronicles***.

particularly Sunday Mass since that is the day of the Lord. For women this means a suit, dressy dress, or something comparable. Dress for men is suit and tie, or sport jacket, shirt and tie. Little girls should wear dressy dresses while little boys should wear shirt, tie and a jacket or sweater if available. Too strict of a dress code? Go to the poorest section of town and watch the Protestants leave church. This is exactly how they dress to worship God. This is how the Jehovah Witnesses dress to honor God. Can we, as Catholics, who participate not only at the Last Supper but also at Calvary do any less? We receive the actual Body and Blood of Jesus, who is God! This is the most stupendous event in the world yet our dress equates it with the same importance as a ballgame. Our lack of respect in dressing for Holy Mass leads to the loss of faith in the Real Presence. Studies claim that less than 30% of Catholics believe that Jesus is really present in the Blessed Sacrament. I would wager that the percentage that believes in the Real Presence is the same percentage that dresses up for Holy Mass. If one believes, one shows it in dress and by reverence. St. John is not depicted at the foot of the cross wearing his fishing attire, nor Mary Magdalene wearing sweatpants. Casualness in our treatment of God leads to the loss of faith. In 1964 78% of Catholics attended Sunday Mass. In 1990 only 30% attended Sunday Mass. Seven out of ten Catholics do not go to Holy Mass on Sunday. Many who do go to Mass leave right after communion.

Each Sunday we go out for brunch. The Protestants come in beautifully dressed and say grace before they eat. Catholics come in from church dressed for the beach and chow down without saying grace. What's wrong with this picture? Rather than building up and refining our culture, we Catholics are helping to destroy it by our careless actions.

For weekday Mass, dress standards are a little looser. If going to work or coming from work, work dress is appropriate as well as business casual. Shorts are not appropriate. Shirts should be tucked in and socks should be worn. Altar servers should wear dress shoes rather than gym shoes.

When attending wakes, funerals or business functions men wear dark suits, shirts and ties. Women wear tailored dresses or suits. For weddings men should wear suits and women wear dressy dresses or suits. Other social events depend on the situation. Ask the hostess if the event is casual or dressy, then comply. Black tie affairs mandate a tux for men and a formal gown or cocktail dress for women. Black tie optional indicates a dark suit or tux for men and a cocktail dress or formal gown for women.

Even schools are getting into the discussion about dress. Public schools are talking about requiring uniforms or instituting a dress code so that the kids are *more regimented and ready to learn.*[55] Martha Blue, a teacher at Hillcrest Middle School in North Carolina notes, *Students look at how a teacher is dressed and act accordingly. If the teacher is dressed in jeans and tennis shoes, it's difficult for the student to take him or her seriously. The way you dress affects student behavior. They look at you as a role model, and you must dress the part."* Mallie Monroe, a math teacher at the same school comments, *As a student, I was always affected and impressed by the way a teacher dressed and presented himself. It has a domino effect on the child to not only dress professional, but act professional.*[56]

Noting the comments of the teachers, dress your children to learn. Have different clothes for school than for play. If uniforms are not utilized, insist that your children wear clothing that is neat, pressed and clean. Shirts should be tucked in. Socks should be worn. Before you and your children leave the house consider this criteria:

- ✓ Are we dressed modestly so as not to cause another impure temptations?
- ✓ Do we look clean, pressed and put together so as to give good example?
- ✓ Are we dressed appropriately for the occasion?

At a lecture, an elderly gentleman next to me began talking about his life's experiences. Although dressed in a sports shirt

---

[55] *The Topeka Capital-Journal,* "Are we too casual?" Sept. 4, 1997.

[56] Jeffery Womble, "Dress The Part," Fayetteville *(NC) Observer-Times,* Oct. 8, 1997.

he told me he was a 90-year-old Franciscan priest. As he chatted on a group of priests entered the room dressed in clericals. The Franciscan priest put his hand on his shirt and said, *Oh, those priests are wearing their clerical garb. I should have worn mine. See that priest over there? He's a Franciscan and he wore his clerics.* The point of this story is to show how positive peer pressure can even influence the elderly.

Rather than trying to fit in, stand out by making a positive statement with your family's appearance. Start a positive fashion trend at work, at church, at school, at social functions. One executive upon changing jobs discovered causal dress at his new corporation. He continued his custom of wearing business suits to work. Within a month his division managers began wearing business suits. Within a few months, the rest of the executives, including the CEO began wearing suits. This influenced lower level managers throughout the corporation who also adopted suits. By dressing professionally this man altered the dress code of his corporation. We can have the same effect on our sphere of influence.

On The Topic Of Manners...

Manners and courtesy toward one another are also part of a Catholic culture. It reflects the virtues of kindness, consideration, charity, spirit of service and thoughtfulness. Children are not born refined but rather self-centered "barbarians." Part of our role as parents is to train our children to behave properly and to correct them firmly when they stray.

Teach each child how to answer the phone in a friendly, cheerful, courteous manner. It is always a pleasure to call one of my friends because no matter what traumas she is facing, she is always bubbly and happy on the phone. When I complimented her on her cheerful phone voice she replied, *I don't think it's fair to burden callers with my problems. After all they have problems of their own. So before I pick up the phone I stop what I'm doing for a moment, smile, and then answer the phone.* Remember the phone is a window into your home. A cheerful greeting is a way to evangelize callers.

Greeting people outside the home is equally important. Teach your children how to shake hands, open doors for others, pull out chairs for women, and make eye contact while saying *hello* with a smile. One family who attends daily Mass at the same chapel as I do has a young son, Nicholas, who never fails to greet me with a smiley *Hello, Mrs. Budnik, how are you today?...* This experience is rare. Most of the time children, school age through college, cannot make eye contact, smile or say hello. This is poor breeding besides a lack of virtue. It's the "sullen child syndrome." Rather than telling children how they should act, have them practice with you and each other until it becomes second nature.

The Topeka Capital-Journal had an interesting editorial on the casualness of our society. *And what gives those strangers who call you up and immediately start calling you by your first name? Or what about your children's friends using your first name? Some of us still believe that even such intimacy, as the use of a first name should be earned—by age and maturity, by familiarity and by permission. But such notions seem sadly quaint and out of date. And the more we put on khaki, the more we may put out tacky...Comfort is good, but not if civility becomes a casualty.*[57]

As a way to show respect for adults, teach your children to call them by Mr., Mrs., Miss, or Ms. This formality teaches children that they do not have the same rights or privileges as adults. St. Margaret of Scotland became a saint by raising her children well. It is written of her that *even as children her boys and girls often had better manners than many of their elders. They were polite and respectful to each other. They were affectionate and able to get along with one another. Margaret taught them how to behave and then expected them to do so.*[58]

Bl. Barbe Acarie, a wealthy matron, also emphasized good manners with her children. The servants were not allowed to respond to any child's request unless the child spoke respectfully with humility prefacing their request with *please* and ending with

[57] *The Topeka Capital-Journal, Op.Cit.*
[58] Wendy Leifeld, *Mothers of the Saints* (Ann Arbor, MI: Servant Publications, 1991) p. 82.

thank you.

Equally important is teaching your children table manners for home, for restaurants, and for social gatherings. At one restaurant I watched as the man at the next table noisily licked every one of his ten digits. His parents apparently never taught him to wipe his fingers in the napkin. Teach your children to refrain from slurping soup, licking plates, fingers or silverware as well as how to stifle belches. Explain how to use utensils, napkins, and Kleenex. Likewise, train them to remain seated until everyone is finished eating. Explain that it is bad manners to complain about food or to refuse to eat something *because I don't like it.*

Barbara Falk contrasts the pizza feeding frenzy in the film *Home Alone* with dinner scenes in the older films such as *Father of the Bride, It's A Wonderful Life,* and *The Sound of Music.* The grabbing, pushing, and selfishness exhibited in *Home Alone* is a perfect example of what mealtime should not be like. Children should be taught to sit and not to get up during meals until everyone is finished. Grace should be said before any food is consumed. Food should be quietly passed, first to any guest, next to the adults and then to the children. Moderate portions should be taken so as to leave enough for everyone at the table. *I don't like this. I'm not going to eat this* should not be permitted. Everything served should be sampled at least once. If someone will not eat a certain dish, another meal should not be prepared. The child can eat the side dishes.

In the home of St. Thérèse, meals were not prepared according to the different tastes of the girls. They were expected to eat what was placed in front of them. The Martin girls were also schooled in the various human virtues by their parents. They were to be polite, courteous, humble, clean, orderly, and punctual. Vulgar language was not permitted. When her daughters attended social activities Mrs. Martin enjoyed having her daughters attractively dressed.

As a bonus James Stenson finds that *[c]hildren who are taught considerateness and good manners at the youngest age grow up to be chaste in high school and young adulthood. They respect other people, and people respect them. Eventually, and usually unwittingly, they wind up marrying spouses who are similar to their own parents in outlook and character.*[59]

Holidays

Catholic culture should infuse our holidays. Saint Patrick's Day should be for celebrating the gift of the Catholic faith and the Irish culture rather than a drunken bash. Easter is more than Easter baskets and the family brunch. It begins by participating in Holy Week services and concludes at the beautiful Mass of the Resurrection on Easter. Mother's Day should include Our Lady by attending a May Crowning, making a pilgrimage or some other sign of affection toward our Heavenly Mother. Consider how you can incorporate God the Father into Father's Day.

Sanctify secular holidays by attendance at Holy Mass as a family. It's fun to have family picnics on Memorial Day, the Fourth of July, and Labor Day but begin the day with Mass. Pray for the repose of the souls of the dead on Memorial Day. Thank God for the blessings He has bestowed on our country on the Fourth of July. Thank God for the job He provides to feed, shelter and clothe your family on Labor Day.

On Halloween dress your children as saints or virtuous, well-known historical figures. Don't permit them to dress as witches, devils, or other despicable characters. On All Saints Day read stories of the saints and visit a shrine of a saint. On All Souls Day visit a cemetery as a family to pray for the souls of the faithful departed. In New Orleans, All Saints Day is a public holiday. Families take a picnic to the cemetery where they pray for the dead then clean up the family plots.

Thanksgiving should not focus on a dead turkey and football games, but rather on giving grateful thanks to God for His countless blessings beginning with the air we breathe.

Christmas should center on the birthday of Jesus, family unity and the spirit of generosity rather than on Santa Claus and *gime*. Use your imagination as to how you and your family can better

[59] *Upbringing, Op. Cit.* p. 156.

infuse Catholicism into holidays and holydays.

Entertainment . . .

Teach your children to seek out the good, the beautiful, and the uplifting by exposing them to nature, good music, plays, museums, cultural activities, literature, and poetry. Keep Sunday holy by putting God first then planning to do something as a family in one of the above areas. Bike or walk the nature trails. Take your children to a concert in the park. Acquaint them with classical music. After Mass on Sundays, the Martin family would picnic in the country and then return to church later in the day for Vespers.

Introduce your children to musicals such as the *Sound of Music, Brigadoon, My Fair Lady, Oliver, Kiss Me Kate, Camelot, Annie Get Your Gun, The King and I, Fiddler on the Roof, You're A Good Man, Charlie Brown, Oklahoma! Hello, Dolly, The Music Man, Irene, Bye, Bye Birdie, Calamity Jane, Cinderella, Show Boat, Kismet, George M, The Student Prince, Peter Pan, Annie, Seven Brides for Seven Brothers, Singing in the Rain, Hans Christian Anderson, Pirates of Penzance, Big River, Meet Me in St. Louis, Phantom of the Opera, The Will Rogers Follies, State Fair, 42nd Street, The Wizard of Oz, Going My Way, The Bells of St. Mary's, Thoroughly Modern Millie, Friendly Persuasion, Pete's Dragon,* and *Scrooge (musical version)*.

In addition to secular music, introduce them to Christian music. It spans all genres. With our family spread hundreds of miles apart with few connecting radio stations between we began listening to tapes and CDs of Dana. My teenage daughters told me that at different points in their lives, the words of her songs came back to help them. Rather than having your children singing risqué songs, introduce them to music that praises God and His creation. If you like easy listening get *Vince Ambrosetti Live.* The orchestral background music along with his beautiful lyrics are uplifting. Listen to Catholic radio stations. Watch EWTN as a family. Get the video from them entitled, *The Path of the Messiah,* an outstanding tour of the Holy Land.[60] Bob and I viewed

---

[60] To order call (800) 854-6316.

this video after our return from making a pilgrimage to the Holy Land. It was an exact replication of our pilgrimage. Show your children their spiritual "roots." St. Luke Productions has fabulous videos and audiotapes of the lives of the saints such as St. Francis, St. John of the Cross, St. Maximilian Kolbe, St. Thérèse's **Story of a Soul**, The Passion of Our Lord, and the first six chapters of St. Luke's Gospel.[61] You could also bring their live presentations to your parish or diocese.

Watch good videos together such as *Mr. Smith Goes To Washington, The Robe, The Scarlet and the Black, The Assisi Connection, Boys Town, Ben Hur, The Ten Commandments, IQ, Father of the Bride (original version), Father's Little Dividend. Shop Around the Corner, Beau Gest, Trouble with Angels, Jane Eyre, The Apple Dumpling Gang, Anastasia, Papa's Delicate Condition, Doctor Dolittle (original version), The Devil and Daniel Webster, Alexander Bell, Yours, Mine and Ours, Silas Marner, Secret Garden, Little Match Girl, It's a Wonderful Life, Gazebo, Bednobs and Broomsticks, The Lion, The Witch, And The Wardrobe, I Remember Mama, Daddy Long-Legs, Life With Father, Rear Window, Dial M for Murder, Vertigo, The Man Who Knew Too Much, The Longest Day, Anne of Green Gables, Swiss Family Robinson, Green Dolphin Street, Toy Tiger, Come to the Stable, The Miracle of the Bells.*

Expose your children to historical, natural science, art and science museums; planetariums and aquariums. Introduce them to different cultures through ethnic festivals and ethnic restaurants. Plan vacations so that they can see different sections of the country, to meet different people, to see historical sites. Try the mountains one year and the coast the next. Camping is a low cost way to vacation.

Read poetry and good literature to your children. Encourage them to read good books by selecting classics for them but remember, children will only read if you turn off the TV.

By instilling a Catholic culture in your family you will be cultivating class. Class is defined as elegance, high quality.

---

[61] For information contact Saint Luke Productions (800) 683-2998.

Fr. Groeschel, C.F.R., adds that it is always *doing everything right.* This is how to give your children the very best.

Bl. Escrivá advises parents: *The secret of married happiness lies in everyday things, not in daydreams. It lies in finding the hidden joy of coming home in the evening; in affectionate relations with their children; in everyday work in which the whole family cooperates; in good humor in the face of difficulties that should be met with a sporting spirit; in making the best use of all the advances that civilization offers to help us bring up children, to make the house pleasant and life more simple.*

*I constantly tell those who have been called by God to form a home to love one another always, to love each other with the love of their youth. Any one who thinks that love ends when the worries and difficulties that life brings with it begin, has a poor idea of marriage, which is a sacrament and an ideal and a vocation. It is precisely then that love grows strong. Torrents of worries and difficulties are incapable of drowning true love because people who sacrifice themselves generously together are brought closer by their sacrifice. As Scripture says, a host of difficulties, physical and moral (**Cant.** 8:7) cannot extinguish love.*[62]

 *Additional Helps*

✓   Together with your spouse put together goals for the family and goals for each child. Over the coming weeks check to see how your goals are being met.

✓   Using a notebook, jot down how much time you spend this week talking and interacting with each child.

---

[62] *Conversations With Msgr. Escrivá de Balaguer, Op. Cit., #91.*

✓ Devise a plan to implement a Catholic culture in your home.
✓ How is your family living these tasks?
1. forming a community of persons;
2. serving life;
3. participating in the development of society;
4. sharing in the life and mission of the Church.[63]
✓ Organize a group of couples to read and discuss **Upbringing, A Discussion Handbook For Parents Of Young Children** by James Stenson. (Scepter (800) 322-8773).
✓ Check out www.ottawacatholichome.ca\little flowers for more on modesty.
✓ What customs can you begin to incorporate in your family for feastdays and holidays?
✓ Consider listening to the audiotapes by James Stenson such as "How To Be A Successful Parent;" "How Successful Families Raise Responsible Children;" "The Intellectual Formation Of Children." "The Challenge Of Being A Good Parent & Teacher In A Consumer Society," "Communication In Marriage," and the series "Happiness & Suffering In The Family," or "Marriage Relationships," by Dr. David Isaacs are excellent as well as "Shaping Your Children's Cultural Values" by Dr. William Thorn. Other excellent audiotapes are "The Christian Influence On Culture" by Fr. Hoffman and "The Effects of Music, TV and Movies on Youth," by Fr. Hoffman and Fr. Armenio. All the above audiotapes are available from R.B. Media, Inc. *(rbmediainc.com)*

---

[63] John Paul II, *Familiaris Consortio* #17.

Chapter 6

Mom & Dad, Do You Know How Important You Are?

"The family does not exist merely for the sake of the love of the husband and wife; nor for the love of parent and children; nor for the acquistion of worldly fortunes; nor for the promotion of the children in business; nor for the material prosperity of nations. All these are lawful and subordinate aims, subordinate to the final aim which is to help immortal souls to get to heaven.
Fr. Thomas J. Gerrard

It seems outrageous that an explanation has to be given as to why a man and woman are necessary to form a family. Yet, this is indicative of the insane world we live in today. The Venezuelan Ambassador to the Holy See, Alberto Vollmer and his wife Christine, presented some interesting observations at a Symposium entitled **The Paternity of God and the Paternity in the Family**. They propose that *the security that the perceived strength and wisdom of his or her father gives a child is immeasurable...*

Fathers today are suppose to be as much like mothers as possible, to the great detriment of children...In fact, the strength, kindness, and support, which are such masculine attributes of fatherhood, are shown in this beautiful way by the modern fathers in aprons...

The new fathers are supposed to only provide comforts for their children. Robbed of their masculine properties and increasingly feminine, fathers are becoming dispensable. As substitute mothers, men can fill in nicely, but...studies now demonstrate that in trendy families where mother goes out to work and father looks after the children the children develop verbal skills and learn to read much later than when brought up by their mothers.

*Children of course need mothers also. [T]he mother's unique and instinctive approach is **vital** for correct development, not only physical and emotional, but even neurological. The tones of a woman's voice, the particular light in her eyes and other distinctive womanly traits are now proven to have an effect on the baby's brain development that a man, or even a group of women, cannot achieve.*[1]

In order to do the intense, intricate and indispensable job of forming her children's neurology and spirit, a mother must have the support and the security of her job.

Mothers are not only indispensable...but are essential for mediating, softening and explaining the rougher aspects of the world as the child encounters them. Not infrequently, these rougher aspects are clashes with the law-giving capacity of their father!![2]

Judge John A. Frusciante of Broward County, Florida wrote a decision in 1997 forbidding homosexuals in Florida from adopting children for the same reasons. He points out: *The evidence established that exposure to male and female role models is of particular significance in child development. Traditionally,*

---

[1] See Allan N. Schore, *Affect Regulation and the Origin of the Self The Neurobiology of Emotional Development*, (Hillsdale, New Jersey: Lawrence Erlbaum Associates, Publishers, 1994).

[2] Ambassador and Mrs. Alberto Vollmer, "Paternity and Maternity, Human and Christian Values," Symposium on The Paternity of God and Paternity In The Family.

children receive primary role modeling through the parent/child relationship. The child's gender identity is shaped through years of interaction between the child and his/her parent or parental figure...

The relationship between the mother and father figures also plays a significant role in the healthy development of children. From that relationship, children learn their role within the family unit and the necessary skills to form meaningful relationships outside the family structure... [T]he overwhelming evidence suggests that children need male and female role modeling for healthy development.[3]

To develop emotionally, children need to experience both the masculine and feminine temperament in family life along with the different role God has entrusted to each parent. Dr. Annemarie Buchholz and Dr. Eva-Maria Föllmer concur: *Studies show that the **natural family**, consisting of mother, father and children, offers the best conditions for the development of a child. Mother and father are of equal importance. However, naturally they are responsible for different emotional domains. This includes their task as same-sex or opposite-sex role model and identification figure. **It is essential for a healthy mental development that the child can identify positively with its same-sex parent.** The child identifies naturally with the character traits and life attitudes of the same-sex parent... Mother and father are role models for the children in the way they shape their female and male roles.*

*[P]arents impart in the way that they co-operate in their long-term relationship...of the family [in a manner] that is qualitatively completely different from other forms of cohabitation or collectivist **educational facilities.** [i.e. daycare, kibbutz, etc.)*

...[M]odern ideas which propagate dividing up parental care and attention according to quotas between man and woman, grossly contradict what a child necessitates from its parents...[4]

---

[3] See reference in *Parenthood By Proxy,* p. 149-150.
[4] "Imparting Values in the Family," Op. Cit., p. 7.

Let's examine some of the differences between men and women. First of all, Adam was created from the dust of the earth while Eve was made from Adam. As such, Fr. Raoul Plus, S.J. finds that man is coarser, *more vehement in passion, more readily excited to physical desires. This is understandable because of his role in generation...Woman...is more soulful than man...Might it not also be explained by the fact that, born as she was from a living human being, the beginnings of her material being were nobler than Adam?*

...God wanted Adam and Eve to be different from each other. It is a mistake for man to become effeminate, for woman to play the man. They are not made to resemble each other but to complement each other.[5]

Woman is called to refine man, not imitate his coarseness. A truly feminine woman not only brings out the best in a man but also forces him to rise above his earthiness. She teaches him how to dress-up, to guard his language, to improve the subject matter of his jokes and conversation. The woman who *wants to be one of the guys* lowers herself as she brings the men in her life even lower with her coarse conversation/language and masculine dress. Consider the negative example of the popular play and movie *Grease*. Sandy Dumbrowski, the heroine of the story is a refined, moral young lady. Her heartthrob is Danny Zuko, a greaser. Their summer romance is perfect until Sandy unknowingly transfers to the same high school. Suddenly Sandy's morals come under attack from Danny and his friends. They make fun of her unwillingness to smoke, drink, or dress like a slut. The tension in the story builds as Sandy stands firm while Danny struggles to improve so as to win her heart again. At the conclusion, Sandy succumbs to peer pressure, gives up practicing fortitude and sinks to Danny's level to become a sluttish-looking greaser complete with all the vices to show her "love" for him. Sandy failed in her role as a woman to challenge "her man" to improve. She loved too little. As Ambassador and Mrs. Vollmer contend, *beyond fertility, man senses a need for a real woman in order to be more man; and woman senses the need for a real man in order to be*

---

[5] *Christ In The Home, Op.Cit.,* pp. 52-53.

more woman. And if this were not so, there would be very little literature![5A]

Wife And Mother

In the encyclical **Women's Duties in Social and Political Life**, Pope Pius XII explains the unique role of women as *motherhood. Every woman is called to be a mother, mother in the physical sense, or mother in a sense more spiritual and more exalted yet real nonetheless. To this end the Creator has fashioned the whole of woman's nature; not only her organism, but also and still more her spirit, and most of all her exquisite sensibility.*[6]

The role of a wife and mother is to love and sacrifice. Dr. John M. Hass insists that *[t]remendous sacrifices are required of those who embrace the Catholic vocation to marriage and an openness to children...The woman goes so far as to risk her very life fulfilling her vocation. She endures the pain and discomfort of carrying the child in her womb; the distended stomach, the leg cramps, the morning nausea, the stretch marks on belly and breast. She suffers incisions, scars, and the shedding of her blood...Each of us is indebted to our mothers for the sacrifices they endured in their vocation to life...Our mothers have given their blood to bear us, their milk to nourish us and their tears to save us. Their life is one of sacrificial surrender to their husbands and their children in union with our Lord's own life of surrender.*[7]

But this does not mean that motherhood is a grim, grit-your-teeth experience. The joy of self-giving is rich in unexpected blessings even in seemingly hopeless situations. When Teresa Gorsage, whom you met in Chapter 2, introduced me to her nine-week old son, John Michael, she joyfully told me, *he's a gift from God!* While all children are a gift from God, "Jack" the youngest of David and Teresa's seven children, is a special baby. He is her sixth c-section and as such her pregnancy was considered high-risk. Teresa found herself in an even more complicated situation than her high-risk pregnancy...she had no maternity insurance.

[5A] Symposium on Paterinity of God & Paternity of Family, *Op. Cit.*

[6] Pius XII, *Women's Duties in Social and Political Life,* p. 8.

[7] "Marriage and the Priesthood," *Op. Cit.*, pp. 14-15.

The company that employed her husband, David, did not include pregnancy in its coverage. Faced with a $12,000 medical bill and no insurance, she felt compelled to leave her OB doctor who had cared for her through her previous high-risk pregnancies. Her only recourse was to seek prenatal care from a charity clinic where she could pay on a sliding scale after enduring the humiliation of filling out countless forms.

Each appointment she saw a different doctor and faced indifferent care. During the first couple of months Terese fought resentment as she waited several hours to see some unknown doctor. Then one day as she was waiting at the clinic, she looked at the unwed mothers waiting with her. Suddenly she was inspired to use the time to pray for each of these young mothers-to-be. She prayed that each would carry her baby full term and then would do what was best for the baby, either placing the child up for adoption or caring for the baby with affection and dedication. This became her mission at each appointment.

To complicate the situation further, during her pregnancy, the Gorsage's daughter, Alex, needed major surgery to correct her scoliosis. Alex is a child with special needs that necessitates continual care and home health nursing care. Unable to communicate to her daughter what she was about to endure, Teresa and David turned to their friends for prayers and blood donations. During the eight hours of surgery, friends rotated praying before the Blessed Sacrament at an Adoration Chapel. Little Alex came through the surgery well, came home from the hospital five days earlier than expected and needed less than a half cup of blood during the surgery rather than the expected 8 pints. Her pain was minimal for what she had endured.

As her due date grew closer the hospital requested that she schedule an amniocentesis. Concerned, Teresa called her regular OB doctor to discuss her situation. In talking with Teresa, her doctor questioned her as to why she had changed doctors. Upon hearing that it was because of the lack of insurance, the doctor told her, *I will take care of you. We'll talk about the fee later.* At the same time, her husband received an unexpected job offer from a Catholic employer, which gave him pregnancy medical coverage in time for the birth of the baby. Her c-section went well without complications. Her recuperation was swift and free from the usual pain and discomfort. The hospital even sent her flowers, something that had never happened before. All in all it was a most incredible experience. When the photographer came in to photograph Jack, Teresa had a sudden inspiration. She ran down to the hospital gift shop to get a large blue bow. She put the baby in just a diaper, with the blue bow on one side, then in calligraphy wrote on a card, *Gift From God*. The photo, done in a sepia finish, is so precious that the diocesan Right To Life Office is considering using it for billboards. Certainly there is pain, suffering, sacrifice and contradictions in motherhood but oh, there is also spiritual growth, the loving help of God and lots of exciting surprises along the way as well!

The Importance Of Mothers

Drs. Annemarie Buchholz and Eva-Maria Föllmer stress the importance of the mother's total involvement with her children: *The quality of attachment is crucial. It is of eminent importance for the healthy development of the child, in all areas of the personality: for its physical, emotional, intellectual, social and moral development... The question is how does the mother react to the signals of the child? If the mother is positive towards these signals, if she can react to them joyfully, a love of humanity can evolve. The mother's respect for the child and its first attempts to communicate and her perceptive interaction provide the child with the feeling of security. The child experiences that, even if it is still small, it already has significance and can have an impact in its relationships to others. It is in this situation that trust in other people and the child's own abilities can form, and the child can experience respect and dignity. The child is able to develop a stable core to its personality, a sense of basic trust, i.e. that emotional solidarity with others that is basic to a healthy personality development.*[8]

Equally important is the mother's role to spiritually and culturally form her children. Fr. Bill Stetson, the former vicar

---

[8] "Imparting Values in the Family," *Op. Cit.*, p.7.

general of Opus Dei in the Midwest, notes that women *have the qualities of generosity, warmth, piety, loyalty, constancy, and love. In their role of mother they use these qualities to form the image of Christ in each child while at the same time equipping the child with natural virtues. The purpose of life is to give glory to God. Women, you fulfill this purpose when you care for your children and make your house a home where peace and the joy of Christ reigns. Your home should reflect the openness and warmth of Nazareth and Bethany.*[9]

Teaching and living the Catholic faith are critical components of motherhood. Do you realize that God's call to holiness is so strong and compelling that it is believed that infants in the womb sense this call to sanctity?[10] A study by Columbia University found that if a mother has a strong religious commitment, her children are less likely to suffer from depression later in life. Mothers with a strong religious commitment were also found to be less likely to suffer from depression. So striving for sanctity is good for the mental health of your children and for yourself!

John Paul II speaking on the Feast of the Mother of God explains that *the immense privilege and lofty mission of being Mother of the Son of God did not change her [Mary's] humble behavior, submissive to the Father's plan. Among the other aspects of this divine plan, she assumed the educational endeavor implied in her maternity. The mother is not simply the one who gives birth but also the one who actively undertakes the formation and development of the son's personality. Mary's behavior undoubtedly had an influence on Jesus' conduct. One can assume, for example that the act of the washing the feet (Jn 13, 4-5), which was left to the disciples as a model to imitate (Jn 13, 14-15), reflects that which Jesus himself had observed in Mary's behavior during His childhood, when, in a spirit of humble service, she washed her guests' feet.*

According to Gospel testimony, during the period Jesus spent in

---

[9] Fr. Bill Stetson, Homily on the 50th anniversary of Opus Dei women's apostolate in the US, May 24, 2000.

[10] Rev. Dick Schent, retreat of March 6, 1998 at Shellbourne in Valparaiso,IN

Nazareth he was "subject" to Mary and Joseph (Lk 2:51). He thus received from Mary a real education that marked His humanity...[11]

God has given us children to be formed in the same manner that Our Lady educated Jesus. However, to form our children in the faith we have to be constantly growing in the faith ourselves. Too busy for spiritual growth? St. Briget of Sweden raised eight children. Conchita Cabrera, born in 1862, was the mother of nine children. At the same time that she cared for her husband and raised her children, she founded two religious Congregations, two lay works, and a priestly fraternity. Despite her acute illnesses, she also published several books on the interior life. At 39 she found herself a widow in dire financial straights. After her death, Archbishop Luis María Martinez of Mexico City, her spiritual director during the last 12 years of her life, said that *[s]he is a great mystic at the level of the greatest in the Church.*[12] Conchita died in 1937. Moms of large and small families can become great saints as they strive for sanctity for the sake of their spouses and children.

Wendy Leifeld, the author of **Mothers of Saints**, wrote her book to show the powerful spiritual influence of mothers. From her research she observed, *[m]otherhood was much more than I had previously suspected. More important, for one thing. These mothers really made a difference in their kids' future ability to do God's will...I couldn't help noticing that character formation was second only to religious instruction in the priorities of these women.*

Working with my children's pride or selfishness, their reluctance to help one another, or their eagerness to fight took a lot of time and energy, but I found it was the heart of mothering...Christian charity and works of mercy must become an established part of my life and that of my children.[13]

Motherhood is a profoundly powerful profession because *the hand that rocks the cradle rules the world.* It is not politicians

---

[11] John Paul II, talk, Jan. 1, 2000.

[12] "Conchita Cabrera: Wife, Mother, And 20th Century Mystic," *Zenit,* March 7, 2000, p. 11.

[13] *Mothers of the Saints, Op. Cit.,* pp. 2-4.

who will change the world but dedicated Christian mothers and fathers who raise upright, responsible, Christ-like children. T*here is a famous French saying, "The worth of a country is to be gauged by the worth of its women," which is very true indeed; and women are the heart of the family. Once women freely abandon this bastion of love, society is headed for destruction,* warns Dr. Alice Von Hildebrand. [14]

Dr. Von Hildebrand calls the work of the home *mostly a work of love, which is to my mind the highest type of work that one can accomplish; women have been the great educators of mankind.*

In her family a woman works so hard that her work never comes to an end. It is a type of work dedicated to the loving care of her family. And this type of work, humble as it might seem to be, is one of the deepest and most meaningful types of work that exists...It calls for alertness, foresight, flexibility, patience, and wisdom...

The work that a woman is called upon to perform calls for an array of not only skills, but also virtues which constantly remind one that the purpose of human existence is holiness, not mere efficiency... [15]

Dr. Paul Vitz, a father of six, a practicing psychologist and a professor at NY University finds that motherhood develops the personality and maturity of women. But more important than personal fulfillment is the mother's effect on children. A psychiatrist from Boston disclosed that disorders in little children have become horrendous. *Little children are terribly disturbed.* A female psychiatrist in New York, observing the same phenomenon, left the New York Medical School to devote her full attention to teaching mothers how to mother. She feels so strongly that if mothers were taught how to mother correctly, mental intervention for children would be unnecessary. A headline in the **The Wall Street Journal** screams "Teen-Agers End Up In Psychiatric Hospitals In Alarming Numbers. Family Turmoil and 2 Careers Are Factors in the Trend: Results So Far Are Mixed."[16] St. John Chrysostom reminds us *a neglected youth is*

---

[14] "Women At Work," *Op. Cit.,* p. 13.

[15] *Ibid.,* pp. 7-8.

like uncultivated terrain, which can yield only thorns.[17]

Lillian Katz, a child development expert, when asked about working mothers, expressed this insight: *How can you say to a well-educated woman, "Stay home all day"? It's intellectually unstimulating. It's difficult...But there's another way to look at it. Children are small for a very short period of time. My real worry is the first three years...*

What very young children need is very personal care, lots of one-to-one. That's the big critical thing. Once children are about 3, spending half a day or even a full day in a really good center-based program is all right.[18]

A government study found that *the more hours toddlers spend in day care, the more likely they are to turn out aggressive, disobedient and defiant by the time they reach kindergarten. Researchers said the correlation held true whether the children were from rich or poor homes, whether they were cared for by a relative, a nanny or day care center.*[19]

Doctors Stanley Greenspan and T. Berry Brazelton in their book **Irreducible Needs of Children** stress the importance of *parents staying home with their young children..."The simple solution—I don't think it's going to be very popular—is that we make children come first and make everything else work around it. A warm, loving human relationship is very important for intellectual development. Children form their capacity to think and self-image based on these back-and forth-interactions...Having too many people to identify with, too many choices can be a deficit for a child.*[20]

---

[16] James R. Schiffman, "Teen-agers End Up In Psychiatric Hospitals In Alarming Numbers," *The Wall Street Journal*, Feb. 3, 1989.

[17] St. John Chrysostom, *In Matth. Hom. 49, 6.*

[18] Debra Landis, "Kids According to Katz," *The State-Journal Register*, July 5, 1992, p. 17.

[19] "Unteaching Toddlers," *Spotlight*, May 7, 2001.

[20] Katy Kelly, "Child docs to parents: Stay home and save your kids," *U.S. News & World Report*, October 30, 2000, p. 65.

Doctor Brazelton also believes that school children and high schoolers need a mom after school. *Early teens is a very fragile time for children. And certainly, latency age (5 to 12 years old) is not a time to leave children all by themselves...The Academy of Pediatrics showed that [latchkey] kids were significantly more likely to get into drugs and sexual acting out and violent situations.*[21] Try to plan your schedule so that you are home when the kids get out of school. Sometimes we can be physically present but not mentally present because we are on the phone. When a child comes running in to tell you about his day, this could be the most important moment for mothering. This is the time when problems spill out. Avoid saying, *I'll talk to you in a minute.* Or, *Let's talk later.* Seize the moment when the child is ready to confide in you. Have cookies or some other snack ready. Then sit down together to talk about the day. If a child is not saying much, draw the child out. Teach the children to take turns relating their day so one does not monopolize mom. Then let the children rehash their day over dinner when dad can listen and give his input. Dr. Greenspan adds, *Just the awareness that the parent is physically close is very helpful...Children need this type of nurturing interaction and access to their parents on a daily basis. Yes, weekends are better than nothing but that's not meeting the basic needs of children.*[22]

Besides, when a mother spreads herself too thin as a professional and mother, someone or something is going to suffer. A working mother, the CEO of a hospital in Iowa, learned this lesson tragically. This woman, the mother of a seven-month old daughter and a four-year-old son, was in the habit of dropping her son off at the day-care center while her husband dropped off the baby at a sitter's home. When her husband's scheduled changed, the mother was to drop both children off so the baby was placed in her van. The woman dropped her son off as usual but became so engrossed in thinking about the demands at work that she forgot to drop off the baby. It was only after work when she went to pick up her son that she realized to her horror that her baby had perished in the 90-degree heat.

---

[21] *Ibid.*

[22] *Ibid.*

The Importance Of The Personal Touch

The personal touch of a mother is so important. Dale O'Leary,[23] writer and lecturer from Rhode Island, explains that it is the mother who teaches, cares for, and is the primary source of truth and wisdom for each of her children. Through daily interaction with a child, the mother names and gives values to each concept, idea and object. For example, it is the mother who teaches a child to say *daddy* as one of his or her first words. It's mom who explains the concept of *hot*, or what is *bad* or *icky*. It is mom who answers the questions of life and love. As Mrs. O'Leary emphasizes, the child sees the world through his mother's eyes because the mother gives it her values. As such, the mother is the primary evangelist of her family. If the mother is a committed, fervent Catholic, the child will naturally pick up that same fervor and commitment. Should our children be in the hands of other caregivers, they will pick up the values of that caregiver.

Should a mother fear the opinion of others, her children will succumb to peer pressure. It's that *trickle-down-effect*. Through daily living it is the mother who teaches the child to obey, *to dare to be different*...to stand up for the truth no matter the personal cost. It is the mother who teaches the children how to endure suffering and hardship that is part of daily life. By exhorting her children *to offer up* the sufferings and the disappointments, the sufferings of the children become not only bearable but acceptable. This along with instilling the virtue of temperance helps the child to cheerfully accept suffering. So teaching virtues is also a critical part of the mother's role since it is mom who teaches the children how to live Christ-like lives while bringing Christ to the world.

A mother who tries to make her children happy at any cost will raise children incapable of suffering. When unsolvable problems hit, and they will hit, the child unschooled in handling suffering will turn to drugs, alcohol, or suicide.

Likewise, it is the mother who trains her children in courtesy

---

[23] This information from the audio tape *The Vocation of Motherhood* by Dale O'Leary from R.B. Media, Inc.

and manners. It is she who teaches her children to greet people with a smile and a pleasant word, to say *thank-you, I'm sorry, please,* and insists that they write thank-you notes for gifts received.

Mothers, as the social directors of the family, have the opportunity to expose their children to other families who share the same values. Invite these families over for a picnic or plan some activity with the other family. This fosters friendships for our children with children who share their same values. It also reinforces the virtues and values that you are teaching your children. Developing friendships with people from different cultures is intellectually enriching besides being fun. If you do not host others in your home, you teach your children to become isolationists.

In the last chapter we discussed developing a Catholic culture. The mother, as the interior decorator of the home, teaches culture also by her tasteful interior design. There should never be anything garish or in bad taste in the home. Choose prints, paintings, figurines, and knickknacks that are beautiful. Why? Not only should your home be a peaceful oasis that refreshes each member of the family, but it should also educate your children in the love of beauty.

As wife and mother you are living the same vocation as Our Lady. Should you get discouraged with the mundane, recall that the Queen of the Universe did the same tasks as you do each day. She worked hard to make a pleasant home for the Child Jesus and St. Joseph. She planned delicious meals and cared for all the little details of running a home and raising a Child. Responsible for caring for the Son of God, just think how neat and clean her home must have been! When you imitate Our Lady's example your home becomes a living replica of that little home in Nazareth.

Caring for one's husband and children is also a great work of charity...a work of love. When you put love into your home, your husband will be eager to come home to you each evening rather than stopping off with friends at a bar. Your love will draw him like a magnet. In addition, through your love and work in the home you will *re-plant* a Christian society in our culture.

Unfortunately, the environment in which we live is not conducive to stay-at-home moms. Still, while the 1960's saw a massive exodus from the home, the daughters of that generation, in growing numbers, *are* staying home to care for their children. But these young women do not have it easy. *Many young mothers today are tormented by dissatisfaction with their role as housewife and mother, by wrong notions of self-realization, and by an inability to adjust to everyday tasks in the life of a woman. This breach in values can find expression in feelings that too much is expected of them... or an aversion towards daily household chores. Women and mothers have been so often made extremely uncertain regarding the tasks specific to their sex that emotionally they are no longer capable of affording their children proper attention.*[24]

This sort of inner rejection of the natural tasks of a woman and mother greatly endangers the emotional development of children who are vitally dependent on the full emotional commitment of their mothers. Moreover, the increasing spread of feminism and the battle of the sexes it advocates frequently poisons male and female relationships, preventing a relationship based on equality.[25]

The Issue Of Equality

What about the issue of equality? The wife, always the equal of her husband, is still under the loving and affectionate authority of her husband. This has been so from the time of creation. St. Thomas taught that *in the state of innocence, Eve was subject to Adam freely, in a kind of benevolent association.* [It would not have been a despotic authority]. *After the Fall, Eve was subjected more strictly to Adam, and less willingly.*[26]

In an age when people demand *freedom* to the point of license, being subjected to anyone is seen as irksome. Yet, in the scheme of things everyone has a head. St. Paul tells us **the head of every**

---

[24] "Imparting Values in the Family," *Op. Cit.*, p.7.

[25] *Ibid.*, p.6.

[26] *The Mystery of Sex and Marriage In Catholic Theology, Two In One Flesh, Part 2, Op. Cit.*, p. 33

man is Christ, and the head of the woman is the man, and the head of Christ is God (*1* Cor. 11:3-4). Every institution has a leader in which ultimate authority resides. The Holy Father heads the Church on earth. A president leads the government. A CEO heads each business. All clubs, organizations, and schools have one person who is in charge. Why should the family be exempt from similar leadership? St. Paul clearly explains this delicate balance: *Be subject to one another in the fear of Christ. Let wives be subject to their husbands as to the Lord; because a husband is head of the wife, just as Christ is head of the Church, being Himself savior of the body. But just as the Church is subject to Christ so also let wives be to their husbands in all things* (*Ephesians* 5: 21-24).

[Note attached to verse in the *Navarre Bible*: *i.e. in all things that pertain to the right relationship of husband and wife. Note well that the subjection inculcated in these verses is not a brutal or slavish subjection as to a tyrant, but that of the loved one to her lover, who is according to right order head of the family, as Christ is head of the Church.*]

Husbands, love your wives, just as Christ also loved the Church, and delivered Himself up for her...Even thus ought husbands also to love their wives as their own bodies. He, who loves his own wife, loves himself. For no one ever hated his own flesh; on the contrary he nourishes and cherishes it, as Christ also does the Church...[L]et each one of you also love his wife just as he loves himself; and let the wife respect her husband (*Ephesians* 5:21-33).

St. Paul teaches that the Sacrament of Baptism confers equality in the eyes of God but as in all units of society there is a hierarchy. The husband is the head and the wife is subject to him but rather than an infuriating subjugation, Baptism ennobles this marital bond so that the relationship is compared to Christ and His relationship to the Church. As Pope Pius XI wrote: *If the husband is the head, the wife is the heart.*[27] There is no place in such an arrangement for fear of despotism. St. Chrysostom emphasizes: *Thou hast seen the measure of obedience; hear also the measure of love. Wouldst thou have thy wife obedient to thee, as the Church is to Christ? Take then thyself the same provident care for her, as Christ takes for the Church. Yea, even if it shall be needful for thee to give thy life for her...refuse it not.*[28]

When St. Paul exhorts men to love their wives as their own bodies; he is talking about a sacrificial love, not carnal love. It must reflect the same intense type of selfless love that Christ has for His Church. Recall how in a earlier chapters we discussed how the Sacrament of Marriage used well cultivates holiness in each of the spouses. St. Peter counsels couples: ***Wives, be subject to your husbands, so that, even if any disobey the word, [God], they may, without any word, be won by the behavior of their wives, observing reverently your chaste behavior. Let not theirs be the outward adornment of braiding the hair, or of wearing gold, or of putting on robes; but let it be the inner life of the heart, in the imperishableness of a quiet and gentle spirit, which is of great price in the sight of God. For after this manner in old times the holy women also who hoped in God adorned themselves while being subject to their husbands. So Sara obeyed Abraham, calling him lord. You are daughters of hers when you do what is right and fear no disturbance.*** (*1 Peter* 3:1-6) [Note: in a mixed marriage Catholic wives are obliged to obey God's law regardless of pressure from non-Catholic or non-Christian husbands.]

St. Peter gives hope to wives married to unbelievers. Although they may not be converted to the faith through arguments or pleas, they may be converted by your interior goodness and example. Besides the example of St. Monica, we also have the example of Bertha, the daughter of King Charibert, a Frank. In 560 Bertha was given in marriage to Ethelbert, the heathen King of Kent, under the condition that Bertha would be free to practice the Catholic faith in England. Her father's insistence on this point introduced Catholicism to England. But it was through Bertha's example that her husband not only became a Catholic

---

[27] Pius XI, *Casti Connubii*, De. 31, 1930.

[28] D. J. Leahy, *A Catholic Commentary On Holy Scripture* (NY: Thomas Nelson and Sons, 1953) p.1124.

but also a saint. Bertha's example prompted St. Ethelbert to enact just laws, to end idol worship, and to convert two other kings to Catholicism.[29]

More recently we have the example of Elisabeth Leseur (1866-1914). Elisabeth married Felix Leseur, an aggressively atheistic husband. Seven years after their marriage Elisabeth abandoned the Catholic faith only to return two years later. As members of Parisian society, the couple traveled extensively despite her continuous illnesses. Unable to bring Felix back to the faith, Elisabeth used her sufferings and his taunts to quietly win his soul. Daily she recorded her spiritual journey in a diary. After her death in 1914, Felix discovered her diary. He was so moved by what he read that he returned to the Catholic faith. That alone was a miracle but more miracles were to come. In 1923 Felix was ordained a priest dedicating his life to spreading Elisabeth's doctrine throughout Europe. It was at his urging that the process for her canonization was opened. If you are in a similar situation, read Elisabeth's diary, *My Spirit Rejoices*.[30] It will open your eyes to the miracles God works when a person is obedient to the Will of God.[31]

St. Peter instructs husbands that they also have obligations toward their wives. *Husbands, in like manner dwell with your wives considerately, paying honor to the woman as to the weaker vessel, and as co-heir of the grace of life, that your prayers be not hindered* (*1 Peter* 3:1-6).

St. Peter adds that husbands are to be considerate (i.e. kind, thoughtful, not demanding nor demeaning) and honor their wives as *co-heirs of the grace of life*. He reminds men that if they treat their wives in such a manner, their prayers will be heard. If they don't, God will not answer their prayers. He will turn a deaf ear to them (*1 Peter* 3:7). If your prayers are not being heard,

---

[29] Rev. Hugo Hoever, SO Cist., Ph.D., *Lives of the Saints Illustrated Part I* (NJ: Catholic Book Publishing Co., 1999) p. 81.

[30] Elisabeth Leseur, *My Spirit Rejoices* (Mancehster, NH: Sophia Institute Press, 1996)

[31] Likewise, the good example of a husband can many times win the conversion of his wife.

consider your treatment of your wife!

With society in the stranglehold of feminism (*I am woman, I am strong*) St. Paul calling women a *weaker vessel* does not bode well. This is further accentuated when one compares how a woman handles childbirth and a man handles the common cold. Yet, St. Paul is correct. Women may be physically strong but let's be honest...men are emotionally more stoic. What wife isn't waiting at the door in the evening hoping against hope that her husband gets home early to solve the problems of the day? When he walks in the kids calm down, the broken appliances suddenly work, and he brings peace to her world of chaos. Husbands bring a silent strength, security, and a promise of hope in the most impossible situations. Covering the UN Conference in Cairo, Egypt, my first day there was a disaster. It began with being separated from my group in a country that the State Department warned was dangerous for tourists. Back at the hotel, I melted my curling iron, and then burned out an expensive, borrowed transcriber. Trying to keep calm, I decided to manually transcribe an interview that had to be faxed to various media outlets. It took five painful hours of tedious work. When the article was completed I immediately lost the file in my computer never to be retrieved. Traumatized by my terrible day I called my husband long distance. While it was impossible for him in Illinois to help me find my lost file in Egypt, he calmed me down and kept me persevering in the face of hardship. On the other hand, I have been able to observe my husband, Bob, handle ugly, tension-filled business situations with strength, valor and in a calm, charitable manner without succumbing to irritability. When a company he worked for went bankrupt, Bob was the court appointed trustee to manage the company while it was in receivership. When he was ordered to layoff all the clerical help, I offered to help answer phones and do the clerical work at his office. It was a horrible atmosphere in which to work. People not only stopped by to physically threaten him but he received threatening phone calls. Yet he never lost his composure or cheerful manner.

God created men and women with different strengths and temperaments to compliment our different duties and responsibilities. Rather than bemoaning this fact we should exalt in it. When each spouse lives according to God's plan we fit together like the pieces of a divine puzzle. The net results are a happy marriage and happy children.

Women, beware of falling into the three classes described by writer Emile Faguet: *those who are inclined to obey sometimes, those who never obey, those who always command.*[32] On the other hand, gentlemen do not be tyrants. Listen to the advice, wishes, and concerns of your wives then work together for the good of your families. For men in positions of authority in their work or profession this can be tricky. They are like the Centurion in the Gospels who told Jesus, *For I, too, am a man subject to authority, and have soldiers subject to me; and I say to one, "Go," and he goes; and to another, "Come," and he comes; and to my servant, "Do this," and he does it* (Matt. 8:9).

One harried-looking wife told me, *My husband has three secretaries to do his bidding but when he comes home it's only me and I'm exhausted from his demands.* In a **Wall Street Journal** article Ron Trancik *began finding it hard to stop giving orders when he got home. "My wife would remind me, 'You're not at work right now. You're not the director here. You're a father and a husband.'"*[33] Men, as you leave the cares of the office each day, also leave behind your authoritarian attitude. Take the example of Christ in Scripture as your leadership model at home. He motivated His followers with warmth and gentleness rather than demands. Over and over Jesus reiterates, **whoever wishes to become great among you shall be your servant; and whoever wishes to be first among you shall be your slave; even as the Son of Man has not come to be served but to serve and to give His life as a ransom for many** (Matt. 20:26-28).

Christ's example is the model for all Christian husbands and fathers. Use your drive home to shake off the cares of the day so

---

[32] *Christ In The Home, Op.Cit.* p.159.

[33] Sue Shellenbarger, "Fathers (Not Managers) Know Best," *The Wall Street Journal*, Sept. 12, 1991.

that you can greet your wife and children with a cheerful smile. Calmly accept any changes in your plans so as to accommodate your family. Your day does not end when you leave work. Rather the responsibilities change. At home you are called to give yourself to your wife and children. Like your wife's day, your day ends when your family is all tucked into bed. It is the time you spend with your children, not the gifts, that makes wonderful memories for them.

The cause of radical feminism is the ill-treatment of some women by some men, according to a spokesman for the Holy See at the UN Conference for Social Development in Copenhagen, Denmark. Personally, I feel that ill-treatment is not limited to the actions of some men but also to some women. Look at the atrocious situation in China. By law couples are permitted just one child. Female infants are being killed so Chinese families can have a son. Christians can likewise have negative attitudes toward daughters. A friend tells the story that when her first daughter was born, her in-laws invaded the hospital to see the baby. When the second daughter was born, her in-laws phoned their congratulations. When the third daughter was born there was a chilly silence. Like King Henry the VIII's wife, Catherine, she had failed to give the family a male heir. Although the father is biologically responsible for determining the sex of a child, God is also intimately involved in the process of creating each new life. By refusing to accept a daughter because a son is preferred is a rejection of God's will.

When talking about the ill-treatment of women we are not limiting it to physical, sexual, or emotional abuse. The most common ill-treatment is preferential treatment of men at the expense of women. When Patty went off to college she had to take the train back and forth to school. When her brother, Larry, went to college he was given a car *because it's a guy's' thing.* When Patty complained about the inequality she was told, *When you marry, your husband will get you a car.* Many times girls are expected to clean the house, while the boys are allowed to play. Although each individual child has to be treated according to his or her own needs, parents must be careful not to show favoritism based on the sex of the child. Allowances, privileges, and work assignments should be given related to the age of the child, not the sex. Boys can clean a house, iron and cook just as well as girls.

Whereas we tend to think we are an "enlightened" society some stereotypes such as male and female "ability" persist. Here are just some personal examples but most women could add their experiences as well. In junior high, my music teacher formed an orchestra. Although I won first place medals in violin competitions, the first chair was given to a male classmate. Outraged by the injustice, I demanded to know why. Sister kindly told me that, *Yes, you merit the first chair but boys usually have the first chair. Peter's feelings would be hurt if I gave the chair to you.* In college I founded a political action organization. Imagine my surprise when I was told to find a male to head it *because women can only play secondary roles in such organizations.* So I read "Letters to the Editors" in the student newspaper until I found a letter from a male who had similar political concerns. He was surprised by my call and request but agreed to head the new organization. Such discrimination is a thing of the past, right? Wrong. I found it very much alive when I prepared to attend the UN Conference on Population and Development in Cairo, Egypt. As I was organizing a news service to fax daily reports from Cairo to Catholic publications and family organizations, I phoned a Catholic gentleman, with a deep interior life, for some advice. When he heard what I was planning to do, he reprimanded me: *Mary Ann, you're simply a housewife. You can't do anything to help the pro-life cause in Egypt. Stay home and take care of your house!* God thought otherwise.

There is also the misconception that women are not as "intelligent" as men. Unjust and uncharitable attitudes toward female children and women trigger radical feminism, which in turn spawns disorder and dangerous reactions in society. Continually check your attitude toward your daughters and women in general so that you do not contribute to this problem!

Motherhood is not for wimps. It is a life of total self-sacrifice that comes equipped with countless joys. Unfortunately the daily cares can become tedious, making some women very negative toward motherhood if one does not have a supernatural outlook. Dr. Laura cites feminism in college and the complaints of her Italian mother about children and marriage that influenced her negatively toward both. It was only after watching a PBS special on conception, development and childbirth that she had her tubal ligation reversed and decided to marry.[34] By complaining of our vocation as wife and mother we not only give bad example but also could lead another to sin, especially our daughters, when they marry.

Blessed Escrivá tells wives and mothers, *[t]he job of a woman in her house is a social contribution in itself, and can easily be the most effective of all [jobs]...A mother can give her children a solid set of values and shape their character, and can make them, in their turn, other teachers, thus setting up an uninterrupted chain of responsibility and virtue.*

...A mother has three, five, ten or more children in her care and she can make of them a true work of art, a marvel of education, of balance and understanding, a model of the Christian way of life. She can teach them to be happy and to make themselves really useful to those around them.[35]

Husband And Father

"I do have a doctorate in education but much more important than my doctorate is my delight in kids...Nothing I've ever done has given me more joys and rewards than being a father to my five. In between these joys and rewards...has come the natural strife of family life, the little tensions and conflicts that are part of trying to bring civilization to children."
                                                                    Bill Cosby

The father is the founder of the family. His role is to set the family principles while the mother implements the principles. The father is the head; the mother is the heart of the family.

Amazingly, fathers, simply by being present provide a sense of

[34] This is related in *Parenthood By Proxy*, p. 3.
[35] *Conversations, Op. Cit.*, p.105.

security, support and strength through their ordinary actions to their children. Dr. Paul Vitz notes that manhood is a gift, a talent, and a true strength. Fatherhood nourishes, enriches and strengthens a man's personality. It brings about a sense of responsibility to man that helps to mature and deepen his personality. As the head of the family, the man no longer thinks about *me* but in terms of *them*. He thinks in terms of the future, the future of his family, the future of society. The love of a father for his child is a pure, unselfish love whereas romantic love at times is neither simple nor pure. (There is at times a hidden agenda when two adults are involved.)

Christian manhood emulates the servant/leader role of Christ. Following the example of Christ, who washed the feet of His apostles to exemplify service, the Christian father washes faces, hands, bodies, dishes, floors and clothes.

As head of the family, the father can be compared to the head of a small business. He needs to be there to handle the problems that arise. Since he is responsible for the family, he needs to be task orientated. At times he will be called on to cook, run errands, wait tables, and put the children to bed. James Stenson insists that *[t]he greatest challenge a man can face, by far, is that of raising his children well. Without exaggeration, it can be said that his success or failure at this constitutes his success or failure in life.*[36]

When fathers work long hours, leaving before the children awaken and coming home after the children are in bed, the children are taught a distorted view of motherhood and fatherhood since they are raised in a female-centered environment. The first priority for a father must be his family. Fathers cannot be workaholics. One father relates, *I feel like a stranger trying to get to know my own family...Ten years ago I told my wife and children to just wait until I get established, and then I could spend some time with them. Now that I want to get involved with them, I am finding they are more comfortable without me.*[37]

---

[36] James B. Stenson, "Fatherhood," Scepter Booklet #181/182 (NY: Scepter Publishers, 1989) p.6.

[37]"Fathers (Not Managers) Know Best," *Op. Cit.*

Prof. Jim O'Kane of Drew University, the father of five, cautions men tempted to be workaholics that someday the job will end but your family will continue long after the job. It is then that workaholics find that success is hollow. Prof. O'Kane gives the following tips to fathers:

- ✓ Have children. Go against the culture.
- ✓ Spend time with your children. Find opportunities for individual time with each child. Spend a weekend alone with each child. It makes for wonderful memories.
- ✓ Don't give your children too much money. A child does not need his/her own TV or the newest toys. Teach your children the spirit of poverty.
- ✓ Monitor what your children are learning in schools particularly in religion and sex education. If they are not being taught correctly take them out and teach them yourself.
- ✓ Let your children see you pray, go to Holy Mass, confession, say the rosary, attend retreats, and other forms of spiritual formation.

Author James Stenson warns parents: *You have one chance, and only one, to raise your children right...There it is, the choice that faces parents today: Pay now or pay later...Form your children well, or just let them be. Lead them to strong character and faith, or just keep them amused with an endless stream of pleasant sensations. Raise them as producers, or school them as consumers. Form their moral conscience, or let them be led by their passions and appetites. Teach them your religious faith as a rule of life,. or let them grow up living as if God does not exist.*

And the consequences of those choices are what parents see later in their children's lives...Adults who live as responsible Christians, or as technically skilled barbarians. Confident happiness in life, or substance abuse and promiscuity. Stable and happy family lives, or marriages broken apart. Well-formed and confident grandchildren, or wounded and lonely grandchildren—or even no grandchildren at all.

Along with all this, the final consequence of our choices: heaven or hell.[38]

Stenson adds, *as children approach young adulthood, they face an existential choice: religious faith or materialist faith. That choice seems to depend enormously on the religious leadership of their father.*[39]

Fathers have a tremendous impact on the self-esteem of their children when they are available for them. One father is greeted daily by his youngest daughter who gleefully arranges some type of entertainment for him each evening. It might be a play, a concert of made up songs or a skating exhibition. Although weary, he drops everything to watch her performances and finds himself more revived by her loving attention than if he hid behind a newspaper with a beer in his hand. A young mother reminisces that one of her favorite memories of Dad is going to the hardware store with him each Saturday and getting a hotdog. She's asked her husband to do the same with their little daughters.

Another father cut back his time spent at his law practice so he could be more involved with his children. An executive gave his two-year-old daughter her own briefcase. When he comes home from work they sit on the floor going through their brief cases together. Our sons-in-law, Michael and Jeff, take over their children when they walk in the door to give their wives a needed break. They relax after they bathe the children and put them to bed. Our son-in-law, Jeff, the missing groom on the cover, gets their three little ones up, dressed and fed before he leaves for work in the morning so that Mary Terese can shower and get dressed.

St. Thérèse writes more about the influence of her father than she does about her mother. Pope John Paul II's mother died when he was nine years old. Author George Weigel found that it was his father who most influenced the future pope. Weigel describes his father as a *gentleman of the old school and a man*

---

[38] *Lifeline. Op.Cit.,* pp. 7, 10.
[39] "Fatherhood," *Op.Cit.,* p. 32.

of granite integrity whose army career...was based on a combination of intelligence, diligence, dependability, and above all honesty. His outstanding characteristic...was that he was a "just man," and he believed he had a responsibility to transmit that commitment to living justly to his son.[40]

Charles Frank, a project manager for IBM and the father of three in New York, was strongly influenced by the example of his father, an auto mechanic with a strong Catholic faith. *He maintained a spiritual reading library at his garage for his customers. We can talk about the faith but unless we set the example by living the faith, our children will not practice the Catholic faith. If we practice charity with our wives, our children will imitate us when they marry. Real men change lots of diapers and they do it in front of the kids to give example. Real men are firm and consistent with discipline. Real men bring the kids to church knowing that the earlier they start attending Mass the better behaved the children will be sooner. Real men eat quiche on Friday. They are not wimps at work and macho at home. Real men realize that generations will be affected by their conduct today. They realize that they are responsible for the souls of their children. Finally, a Catholic man does not worry about his image because he lives for Christ.*

Human fatherhood has its origins in God the Father. The **Catechism of the Catholic Church** reminds us that *[t]he divine fatherhood is the source of human fatherhood; this is the foundation of the honor owed to parents.*[41] Likewise the authority of the father comes from God. How the father treats his children will have a tremendous impact on their relationship with God. A study was done on the effect of the father's faith on the faith of his children. It was found that if the father does not practice his faith, it will negatively impact his children even if the mother is a devout, practicing Catholic. On the other hand, if the mother is a fallen away Catholic or non-Catholic but the father continues to practice the faith, the children will usually be strong in their faith. Don't panic if your husband's a non-Catholic or a fallen

---

[40] George Weigel, *Witness To Hope* (NY: Cliff Street Books, 1999) p. 29.
[41] *Catechism of the Catholic Church* #2214.

away Catholic. It just means that you carry the full task of raising your children to be saints. With the grace of God and the many helps available to you, you can do it. But call on St. Monica. She understands your situation completely! While still a young girl, she married a much older man who was a pagan. Not only was her husband unfaithful, but he also had a violent temper. He shared none of her beliefs or values. Although he lacked virtues, Monica strove to develop them in herself. Her success is shown by the fact that she was one of the few wives in town not beaten by her husband. Her virtuous life and prayers for him were rewarded by his deathbed conversion. Monica had everything going against her. Yet despite her difficult situation, her three children, two sons and a daughter, are either beatified or canonized. Most of us are only familiar with her famous son, St. Augustine.

If your husband is a practicing Catholic use your feminine charm to persuade him to teach the children their prayers and catechism. Ask him to lead the daily family rosary, which is key for promoting peace and harmony within your home.

Father Mark A. Schulte, a diocesan priest of Springfield, Illinois gave a powerful homily on the topic of fatherhood that addresses many of the urgent issues facing men today. With his permission I would like to share with you his notes on this important topic: [42]

God the Father, the prototype for all fathers, sent His son Jesus to be the image, the revelation of Himself. Therefore the qualities of Jesus reflected in Scripture are the qualities of God the Father. These same qualities are to be imitated by all fathers. Some of the attributes of Jesus are love for the poor, the hungry, the downtrodden, and the marginalized. He is a shepherd who guards and guides His flock. He is gentle with women. But the most perfect image of the depth of the love that the Father has for his people can be seen in the passion and death of His only Son...From this we can see that the total sacrifice of self unto death is that true and ultimate image of a father.

---

[42] Novena to the Immaculate Conception, Nov. 30, 1999. Audio tapes of his homily available from R.B. Media,Inc.

But God has given us another man as a sublime example of true Fatherhood, St. Joseph. In the Litany of St. Joseph his qualities are listed as husband, guardian, head of the Holy Family, chaste and just, prudent and brave, obedient and loyal, patient, lover of poverty, model of workers, example of parents, pillar of family life. All fathers are called to posses these same qualities, and are indeed given them through grace by virtue of the Sacrament of Matrimony, when they are open to them.

Consider the men in the world in which we live. Consider those men whom the world might describe as the "stars" of our day. How many are chaste, just, prudent, and courageous? How many are true heads of the family, examples of patience, obedient to the laws of God? How many are true examples of parents, and pillars of family life? How many are truly striving to be holy as their Heavenly Father is holy? How many would you trust with your wife or daughter? How many would you trust to raise and train your children?

What has happened to our fathers? Many seem to be lost, disoriented, preoccupied with themselves, their own selfish interests, worldly affairs, and absent in various ways from the family. They are confused about who they are. Almost all family problems stem from this phenomenon.

The greatest crisis facing humanity today is profoundly theological because it is so closely associated with God the Father. It is the demise of true fatherhood itself or true leadership which itself is a fatherly role. In the words of Zechariah the Prophet (Zech. 13:7), the shepherd has been struck and the sheep have been scattered. The shepherd, the guide, has lost his way and as a result the sheep (the families) are wandering. This applies to fathers of families and to all men in general. This problem of false fatherhood that exists when men have not modeled the true image of God the Father, is not a new problem, it has been with us in varying degrees throughout history. It is only in our day that it has escalated and has become particularly acute.

We see that sin and death did not enter the world until Adam the first father sinned. Recall how scripture tells us that the sins of the father are visited on the children. God-fearing men see themselves as the first to be responsible for the condition of their families and family members. There are many good fathers in the world, not all are in crisis, but their numbers appear to be dwindling. Look at the statistics associated with broken families, unwed mothers, and abortion.

How has this breakdown in true fatherhood come about? From the very beginning, even before the creation of man, there has existed one great battle: the Devil, the father of lies, deceit, and deception vs. God the Father, the Father of truth. The Devil's great task is that of seeking to prevent souls from going to God the Father. Satan's most effective method is his attack on the true meaning of fatherhood.

Why this attack on fatherhood? In his hatred toward God and man, Satan seeks to destroy the divine institution of the family. He knows that in order to most effectively accomplish this destruction he must concentrate on that member of the family most responsible for its safety, the father. It was God who placed the father of the family as its shepherd, protector, and spiritual guide, having as it were its own individual "Joseph."

Through worldly distractions, and sin in general the Devil little by little seduces the father to abandon his fatherly qualities that were mentioned before. Above all the devil wants the father to lose his sense of self-sacrifice, that quality which most closely associates the father of the family to the image of Jesus, and binds him to the love and care of his family. Gradually the father begins to seek his own self-interest through selfishness. When the father of the family is no longer present (either physically or mentally because of TV, excessive sports or business) the family begins to fall apart, which in turn initiates other social and spiritual problems.

James Stenson notes that [c]hildren with serious character problems tend to have a father emotionally missing from the home. Father is either a tyrant (neglecting children's rights) or overly permissive (neglecting children's needs for firm, clear leadership).[43]

---

[43] James Stenson, "Fatherhood: The Dynamics of Character Formation Seminar" at Northridge Preparatory School.

Fr. Schulte emphasizes that *this distorted and false image of a father, portrayed by many fathers of our times, has as a result the* **destruction of the image of the earthly father,** *who is meant to model the image of the heavenly Father, and thus* **leads to the conscious loss of the image of the heavenly Father. Satan's attack is primarily directed against the Fatherhood of God.** *The end result is that those, whom the Father created, humanity, reject God the Father.*

Prof. Walter W. Benjamin, a professor of religion and applied ethics at Hamline University in St. Paul, Minnesota comes to the same conclusion as Fr. Schulte. In **The Wall Street Journal** he notes with concern the neutering of God: *Downgrading the fatherhood of God tragically carries over into the downgrading of fathers as necessary for families. Without a Heavenly Father, there are few norms that judge earthly fathers and hold them accountable for their behavior...*

By removing the father from heaven, are we unwittingly endorsing the breakup of the traditional family and maybe even contributing to the plague of domestic violence and teen pregnancy?[44]

Fr. Mark Schulte advises that *fathers must once again assume their God-given duties within their families. Each father must imitate the sacrificial actions of Christ for His Church. Fathers must be willing to strive with renewed vigor to acquire the fatherly virtues of St. Joseph. As Jesus gave every drop of His blood for His bride the Church, fathers must likewise give their entire being to their spouses and children. They must do this out of duty yes, but most importantly they must do it out of love. My dear fathers, I ask you, what wife, son, or daughter would not like to have this type of father in their home? It is their right to have him. It is your duty to give him to them.*

This renewal in fatherhood will have a most profound effect in both the public and private arena; the world will be transformed;

---

[44]Walter W. Benjamin, "Fatherless Heaven; Fatherless Children," *The Wall Street Journal.*

*the kingdom of God the Father will be expanded; souls will return to God; parishes will be given new life; and as we say during the elevation of the Holy Eucharist at Mass, **all glory and honor will be given to God our Almighty Father, forever and ever.***

Fathers, this renewal cannot be accomplished on your own. God has given you helpmates for a reason. The two of you are now one flesh. Wives, pray for your husbands and encourage them to fulfill the role that God has called them to. Theirs is a distinct vocation, one that only they can fulfill. If husbands happen to fail at times, and they surely will, continue to encourage them and pray for them. The Devil will attempt to deceive you into thinking that you should take your husbands' place as leaders of the family [and take on his responsibilities]. Do not try to replace your husbands with some other type of socially acceptable reconstruction of the family. Only God's plan for the family, built on the model of the Holy Family will work.

Fathers, for your children to be able to relate to God the Father as a warm, personal loving Father, they must have a warm, loving relationship with you. A strained or non-existent relationship with one's father makes it difficult to relate, to trust, and to pray to God the Father.

The Church has always stressed the value of the father in the family. Maximilian Kolbe became a saint by offering his life to save the life of a father in Auschwitz. During the Jubilee Year, eleven sisters of the Congregation of the Sacred Family of Nazareth of Nowogrodek were beatified because they too offered their lives in exchange for the lives of fathers captured by the Nazis.[45]

In a lighter vein, Bill Cosby, in his book **Fatherhood,** writes: *What is a father's role today? [H]is role is simply to be there, sharing all the chores with his wife. Let her have the babies; but after that, try to share every job around. Any man today who returns from work, sinks into a chair, and calls for his pipe is a man with an appetite for danger. Actually, changing a diaper takes less*

---

[45] "Martyrs of Nazism Save Lives Of Fathers of Families," *Zenit,* March 3, 2000, p.7.

time than waxing a car. A car doesn't spit on your pants, of course, but a baby's book value is considerably higher.[46]

Cosby continues: *[E]ven though your kids may not be paying attention, you pay attention to them from the very beginning, then you'll know the moment they start to swallow or sniff things that rearrange their brain cells...And with the attention...must be all the love you can give, especially in the first twelve or thirteen years. Then, when the kids start doing strange things under the guise of independence, they will always know that they are loved and that the lines are always open for them to send a message back to earth.*

This commitment...cannot be a part-time thing...He never must say, "Get these kids out of here; I'm trying to watch TV." If he ever does start saying this, he is liable to see one of his kids on the six o'clock news[47].

I make a lot of money and I've given a lot of it to charities, but I've given all of myself to my wife and the kids, and that's the best donation I'll ever make.[48]

In the *Afterward* of Crosby's book, Dr. Alvin F. Poussaint gives other insights into the topic of fatherhood. He begins by reassuring parents that there is no such thing as a perfect parent, each of us makes mistakes. If children are raised in a disciplined and loving family setting they can survive our blunders.

Since fatherhood begins at conception so should the support of the man for his wife who is undergoing physical, emotional and hormonal changes as the result of pregnancy. The responsibilities of fatherhood begin nine months before the birth of the child and continue throughout the father's life. There is never any time off for good behavior!

Adjusting to a new baby can be initially stressful for both parents. This is when fathers need to go into overdrive to help

---

[46] Bill Cosby, *Fatherhood* (NY: Berkley Publishing Group, 1987) p.61.

[47] *Ibid.*, p. 158.

[48] *Ibid.*, p. 85.

the new mommy who is physically weak and in pain from delivery or a c-section, emotionally on a roller coaster from out-of-whack hormones, and just plain exhausted. By helping to bathe, feed (in the case of bottle fed babies), diaper and rock the baby, the father begins to bond with his son or daughter. Dr. Poussaint remarks *that the new fatherhood movement sanctions such activities as "masculine." There is no cause here for men to worry about their manhood.*[49]

James Stenson adds that it is the mother's affection toward the father that reassures the baby that the father *is to be trusted, respected and loved. For his part, the father underscores this trust by playing with the infant...[I]t shows the child that Dad is both loving and powerful, a man of affection and competent strength.*[50]

The child increasingly turns to the father as the child reaches 16 to 17 months old. Between the ages of two to eleven children observe the different roles of mother and father. *Principally by example, the mother teaches order, attention to detail, steadfast emotional commitment, refinement, considerateness, patience. She is the force for stability and harmony. The father, also mainly by example, teaches long-range strategic planning, rational assessment of means and ends, courage, fair dealing with others, respect for lawful authority, and self-directed entrepreneurship. He is the force for purposeful activity, making one's way competently and confidently in the world.*[51] Stenson finds that when parents exercise mutual support the children acquire personalities that are well balanced.

The more a father bonds with his children and wife the more fulfilled, content, happy and satisfied he will be. As additional babies join the family, the father plays an important role in helping the other children adjust and accept the new baby. To dissipate sibling rivalry or jealousy he gives the other children extra attention while at the same time teaching them how to care for their new brother or sister. Neither parent should become so

---

[49] *Ibid.,* p.167.

[50] "Fatherhood," *Op. Cit.,* (booklet by James Stenson) p. 10.

[51] "Fatherhood," *Op. Cit.,* p. 11.

wrapped up in their infant that they neglect their own relationship. Remember, one's marriage endures long after the children leave home.

As children grow, children need more time with Dad according to Dr. Poussaint. This time should be spent playing games such as word, guessing, and number games; exploring nature; going on outings; doing chores; passing on skills; reading stories; praying together. This helps the childrens' intellectual, social, physical, and spiritual development. Tossing a ball in the backyard can help the child's coordination and motor skills. Little ones love to be tossed in the air and caught. Older children love to wrestle and rough house with their dads. They need this physical contact on a regular basis. Since involved fathers have a tremendous psychological effect on the development and personalities of their children, Dads need to avoid excessive outside commitments. For the same reason avoid placing your children in multiple outside activities. Not only is it stressful for parents to have their children in too many activities; it is stressful for the child. Besides, too much structure kills the child's imagination.

Dads, consult with your wife to select the right school for your children then follow-up on grades, homework and projects as well as attending teachers' conferences. Use dining out to teach your children manners and social skills. When trips to the store arise, use these occasions to teach them math and how to make change correctly. Fathers need not only to be available but also willing to discuss any topic with their sons or daughters, be it religion or topics related to chastity. By being cheerful and affectionate, your children will be comfortable coming to you with problems or questions.

During the teen years, Dad is especially important. Adolescents want to act like adults. They yearn for freedom. Since the father is the acknowledged expert in the outside world, they look to him for guidance. *Psychologists have noted that much of the posturing and verbal defiance of adolescents is really a testing and questioning of their father's standards. It's really an attempt to draw out into the open, explicitly and clearly, the implicit and unspoken convictions resting in Dad's experienced mind: "Where do we adults draw the lines, Dad? You're the expert and I need your guidance now!"*[52]

It is also the father who puts the finishing touches on the teen's conscience. *Psychology has substantiated that, though both parents must form conscience in small children, the formational role gradually shifts to the father as the children approach maturity. Dad is increasingly seen as the arbiter and model for objective, unsentimental standards of morality.*[53]

Consider the case of a young man who informed his parents that his girlfriend was moving in. He admitted to his parents that he was uncomfortable with the "live-in" arrangement. His highly educated parents listened. Although they were distressed, rather than discussing their opposition to the plan with him, they gave him their blessing. This is an example of a weak father who deforms rather than forms his son's conscience. His son came to him for a manly way out of this difficult situation but the father was a wimp. Contrast this case with the father who was throwing a family reunion at his farm. A couple of days before the party he learned that his nephew was bringing his "live in" girlfriend. The father called the nephew and told him that he was welcomed to come to the family party but his "live-in" was not to come. He further explained that his teenage granddaughters were coming and he did not want them exposed to the nephew's immorality and bad example. After talking to the nephew, the father called his sister and explained to her his stand. His position initially caused a family ruckus within his extended family but within his own immediate family a powerful lesson in morality was taught. His daughter reminisces, *while Dad is a highly successful businessman with tremendous accomplishments, the memory that stands out in my mind is the moral stand he took at the family reunion. He knew it would hurt his sister to take the stand but he did it anyway to protect the morals of his children and grandchildren. That is his most outstanding accomplishment in my mind.*

---

[52] *Ibid.*, p. 13.

[53] *Ibid.*, p. 14.

The father also plays an important role in teaching the young adult how to work; how to become more financially independent; and how to accept responsibility for his or her actions. Adolescent girls tend to take their father as a model for evaluating men. They usually marry males who are similar to their fathers or who they think are similar to their fathers. We have found this true in our family. When our two married daughters introduced their future husbands to us, they each prefaced the introduction with, *he's so like Dad.* After getting to know them, we discovered that our sons-in-law do share Bob's core values and virtues.

Charles Péguy describes fathers as *these great adventurers of the modern world.* And so they are. Not only are they willing to care for a wife, they must be open to all the children God wishes to send while working diligently to support their family through hard work. This requires **courage** combined with confidence in God. Fatherhood requires **patience** to deal with the various personalities of his wife and children, the crying babies, the moody teens, the boisterousness of the children, the mounting bills for schooling and illnesses. Dr. Paul Vitz, believes that fatherhood is the most important part of being a man because it demands a bond and a commitment. The father teaches the children to separate from the mother, to become independent, to learn self-control. (Sometimes mothers can become too controlling or too smothering.)

What happens if you are not around, Dad? Dr. Vitz finds that boys with absent fathers usually have a lower IQ (by about seven points) along with a distorted view of men. Since boys look to their fathers for maleness, if fathers are not available their sons gravitate toward the macho model of Rambo or the wimp model of a Woody Allan character. [54]

Dr. Vitz finds that fathers who are absent create a "father hunger" in their children. *Sometimes it's easier to stay at work than go home and deal with the kids.* This can result in sons

---

[54] This information is taken from two lectures given by Dr. Paul Vitz, "Christian Manhood: The Problems & Promises of Today," and "The Role of the Father in the Family," R.B.Media,Inc.

lacking social responsibility. Without normal interaction with their fathers, sons may become more aggressive. They may lack self-control. Subsequently there is high delinquency among this group. These sons tend to become involved in homosexual activities. Dr. Allan Schore also warns about the dangers of *father thirst* or *father hunger,* the unmet childhood need that can lead to same-sex attraction. [55]

These children are less trusting of others and have lower self-esteem. Researchers find that seventy percent of juvenile offenders grew up in a fatherless family. Single mothers have a difficult time dealing with male adolescents. [56] *The absence of a father figure leaves no one for them to model themselves after, no one to show them how to handle the pressures and temptations of adolescence.* [57]

Daughters are also negatively affected by absent or uninvolved fathers. Young girls can develop anxiety in regard to their self-worth when there is no male example in the home. They may become sexually promiscuous because they are searching for affection. David Blankenhorn reported in his book **Fatherless America** that a fatherless 15-year-old girl is three times more likely to lose her virginity before 16 than a teen who has lived with both parents. Daughters also develop less impulse control, less independence, less cognitive ability. *Kids will try to get their father's attention by taking drugs or getting pregnant.* Dr. Vitz believes that women's prisons are a testimony to the absence of fathers.

Not every child raised by a single parent is destined for trouble or poverty—but the risk is high. These children are 3 times likelier than those raised by two married parents to have a child out of wedlock themselves, twice as likely to drop out of high school, and 1.4 times more likely to be out of work. Seventy-two percent of

---

[55] *Affect Regulation and the Origin of the Self, The Neurobiology of Emotional Development,* Op. Cit., p.233.

[56] "Christian Manhood: The Problems & Promises of Today," and "The Role of the Father in the Family," *Op. Cit.*

[57] "Fatherless Heaven; Fatherless Children," *Op. Cit.*

teen-age murderers, 70% of long-term prison inmates and 60% of rapists come from fatherless homes.[58]

Rarely do children complain about the father's absence, instead the regret is internalized. Al Roker relates an instance when his two and a half year old daughter Courtney protested when he had to leave on a weekend for an assignment in D.C. The day he left she was clingy. As he tried to leave she grabbed his legs begging him, *Daddy, don't go!* When Roker reassured her that he would return tomorrow, with tears in her eyes she implored him, *But Daddy...I need you now.*[59] Your children need you now, too.

Sons who interact daily with their fathers can identify with males. They learn to control their impulses, they have a high need for achievement so they do better in school. These boys are less likely to become involved in delinquent activities.

Likewise successful daughters pattern themselves on their fathers. It is the father who through his interaction with his children brings support and order into their world. Fr. Plus, S.J. adds that in order to reinforce the control of the mother, the father needs **authority** over his children. His authority is likewise necessary because at times mom maybe too tired, too busy or too easy going to discipline the children.

In addition to authority, fathers need **insight** as to which virtues need to be developed by each child. This education in virtues hinges on the character and temperament of the child. Without insight the father will be at a loss to help his children. A man who has insight is levelheaded, is firm in important matters but flexible in the unimportant. He is prudent, wise, just, charitable, decisive and willing to change his opinion when given rational reasons. He is never obstinate or gruff

As regards some wives, Fr. Plus, S. J. encourages wives not to hamper their husbands through jealousy or selfishness. Some wives refuse to relocate when their husbands are offered

---

[58] Zenit, April 2, 2001.

[59] *Don't Make Me Stop This Car! Op. Cit.,* p. 162.

promotions or better jobs. Others pout when their husbands go on business trips to interesting places or have business dinners that exclude them. *A wife should stimulate and encourage but never paralyze.*[60]

James Stenson gives twelve traits of successful fathers:

✓ *Successful fathers have a sense of supportive partnership with their wife. They are neither domineering nor neglectful. They sincerely appreciate their wife's sacrifices, hard work, long hours, and loving attention to detail.*

✓ *Successful fathers think long-term about their children's future character as grown-up men and women. They think of inner strengths, not career choices.*

✓ *They frequently talk with their wife about the children's character strengths and weaknesses. Such men are conscious that their wife is probably more sensitive and insightful in these areas, and they respect her judgment...They realize how important it is for the children to see the parents united, especially in matters of discipline.*

✓ *These fathers frequently discuss things with their children. Such fathers listen to their children as well. They listen for what is unspoken and implied...They steer the children's judgment about people and affairs.*

✓ *Successful fathers keep television watching to a minimum. They realize that TV steals time from the family's life together. It squelches conversation.*

✓ *Successful fathers see discipline, not as punishment or mere behavior-control, but rather a means of building the children's self-control.*

✓ *Successful fathers are confident of their authority...[They] are not afraid of being temporarily unpopular.*

✓ *Most successful fathers seem to have a number of close friends. The home is open to guests: neighbors, relatives, colleagues from work, and friends from childhood. Such men also go out of their way to befriend adults who deal closely with their children: clergy, teachers, coaches, and parents of the kids' friends.*

✓ *Successful fathers frequently have a deep and active religious faith...This religious outlook seems to directly*

---

[60] *Ibid.*, p.163.

> affect the way these fathers discipline their children. They
> are neither tyrannical nor permissive, for both of these
> extremes are basically self-centered.
> ✓ Successful fathers teach their children to be "poor in
> spirit"...They work alongside their children at home, teaching
> the relationship between effort and results, along with the
> satisfaction of personal accomplishment. They are sparing
> in allowances. They make the children wait for things, and
> if possible, earn them. They give generously of time and
> money to the needy, and they encourage...the children to do
> the same. They don't fill the home with expensive gadgets
> and amusements.
> ✓ Finally, the most successful fathers always put their family's
> welfare ahead of their jobs. They know that their children
> can be seriously hurt through fatherly neglect...[61]

In addition to St. Joseph, pray to your favorite male saint for insights in raising your children. Call on St. Thomas More or St. Louis of France. Another possibility is Bl. Charles of Blois. His uncle was King Philip VI of France. As a military officer he knew well how to balance the priorities of God, wife, family, and career. He could well be called the John Wayne of the 14th century! He died with his boots on...in the midst of a battle. Another possibility is St. Leopold of Austria who lived in the twelfth century. He became the military governor of Austria at twenty-three years old. He married Emperor Henry IV's daughter and became the father of eighteen children. He knew his limitations and turned down the opportunity to become emperor. Blessed Joseph Tovini, an Italian who died in 1897, could be the businessman's patron. He was a notary, attorney, vice rector and professor of the College of Lovere. In time he became the mayor of Cividate, the provincial councilor for Brescia, as well as the founder of the Banca di Vallecamonica and the newspaper *Il Cittadino di Brescia*. The father of Pope Paul VI edited his newspaper. To help the poor he founded banks in Brescia and Milan along with a school, college, and educational programs. Three of his ten children became religious.

Let's not forget the courageous fathers and husbands who are

---

[61] "Fatherhood," Op. Cit., pp.34-39.

martyrs for the faith. Besides St. Thomas More there are the martyrs of Podlasie, Poland. In 1874 Czar Alexander II of Russia decreed that all Catholic churches in the Russian sector of Poland were to be absorbed by the Orthodox Church. Thirteen husbands and fathers, ranging in age from nineteen to fifty, knelt in the street in front of the church refusing to allow their parish to be confiscated. As they prayed and sang hymns, they kept repeating, *It is sweet to die for the faith* as they were shot by the Russian soldiers in front of their families.

Single Parents

The unsung heroines and heroes of our culture are single parents who have the difficult role of being both mom and dad to their children. Since raising children to be responsible adults is difficult without both parents available, God does not abandon single parents in their need. When a parent is lost through death, James Stenson encourages the surviving parent to *rely on the spiritual presence of their deceased spouse. The children are led to continue honoring him or her, and thus this loved one still abides in the family to influence the children's moral direction: "Your father (mother) would want you to act this way, and is watching over you from heaven."*[62]

Consider praying to St. Juliana Falconieri for guidance in raising your children. She knows well the loss of a parent. Her father died when she was but a toddler. It was her uncle, St. Alexis, one of the founders of the Servites, who helped her mother to raise Juliana. Bl. Marie of the Cross Jugan lost her father at sea when she was but three. St. John Bosco's father died when he was only two-years-old. Bl. Peter Friedhofen lost his father when he was only a year old. Bl. Teresa Michel lost her father when she was little. Bl. Rebecca De Himlaya lost her mother and was raised by a stepmother. St. Thérèse lost her mother as a pre-schooler. Her father and sisters raised her.

James Stenson advises divorced and single parents to not only forgive the erring partner but also to teach the children to forgive

---

[62]*Lifeline, Op. Cit.,* p. 41.

the erring father or mother. Despite the sorrows and wrongs committed by the other parent, help the child to love the parent. As Christians we are taught to *hate the sin, but love the sinner*.

If you suffer the trauma of divorce, call on St. Helena. While she is well known for discovering the cross of Jesus, it is not well known what a difficult life she led. The daughter of a British king, she was married to Constantius, a Roman officer. When Emperor Maximian named Constantius Caesar there was one condition. He had to divorce Helena so he could marry the daughter-in-law of the Emperor. So he did. St. Helena understands the heartache of divorce. Pray to her for advice and help.

Unwed parents can pray to St. Margaret of Cortona for help (1247-1297). She took a lover at seventeen. Upon his sudden death, she returned home with her son only to be forsaken by her father. St. Margaret will intercede for you and the needs of your child. Another patron is Bl. Ulricha Nisch of Germany. Illegitimate, the first six years of her life she was raised by her grandmother and godmother.

Parents who had their marriage annulled can pray for help to St. Theresa of Portugal. The daughter of King Sancho I of Portugal, Theresa married King Alfonse IX, of León, Spain. After several children, her marriage was annulled because of close blood ties. This left her in a terribly difficult situation.

Serious problems in your marriage? Turn to Bl. Seraphina Sforza. She was the victim of a vicious husband. When he tired of his marriage, not only did he have an affair, but he unsuccessfully tried to poison Seraphina. When the poison didn't kill her, he threw Seraphina out of his villa. Ask her for help if you suffer estrangement in your marriage.

The next hurdle is to accept the present circumstances without a victim mentality. Strive diligently to help your children to acquire sound consciences so that they will live upright lives. By instilling the Catholic faith and virtues, the flaws and mistakes in your marriage or situation will not adversely affect their future marriages.

With strong faith and hope, turn to God, Our Lady, St. Joseph, the saints and angels for help. The Holy Family can supplement what is missing in your family. On a natural level, find a role model for your children to replace the missing parent. It can be a grandparent, uncle, aunt, cousin, priest, friend, teacher or coach. In one large family the oldest son is the successful surrogate father. Tom Monaghan's father died when he about four-years-old. When he was in sixth grade he found a surrogate father in his parish priest. During the time he lived in a Catholic orphanage, Tom found a surrogate mother in Sister Beranda. Bl. Jane of Orvieto, Italy orphaned at the tender age of five, pointed to a statue of an angel, saying *he will look after me!* when children taunted her about having no parents.

Work

James Stenson reiterates that parents are not raising children but future adults. Work is the vital component in making a living. In **Laborem Exercens (On Human Work),** John Paul II points out that *[w]ork constitutes a foundation for the formation of family life...Work is a condition for making it possible to found a family, since the family requires the means of subsistence which man normally gains through work. Work and industriousness also influence the whole process of education in the family, for the very reason that everyone "becomes a human being" though, among other things, work, and becoming a human being is precisely the main purpose of the whole process of education.*

Obviously, two aspects of work in a sense come into play here: the one making family life and its upkeep possible, and the other making possible the achievement of the purposes of the family, especially education.

...[T]he family constitutes one of the most important terms of reference for shaping the social and ethical order of human work...In fact, the family is simultaneously a community made possible by work and the first school of work, within the home, for every person.[63]

---

[63] John Paul II, *Laborem Exercens*, 1981. #10

Since work is part of every person's existence, it is important to discuss the type of work Dad does. In an agrarian society, little children watch their parents work side by side in the farm fields. Older children are needed to pitch in and help, to work together for the common good of the family. This work situation allows the children to see their father dealing with serious problems such as drought, floods, broken equipment, financial reverses, and difficult people. Matt Brum, a high school student in Ottawa, Illinois, writes, *ever since I was about five I've known that being a farmer means being at the mercy of the weather...I spent a lot of time in the fields, and it hurt to see our effort wasted when the corn started to go from "stress" in the middle of July. No alfalfa grew after July either. My dad kept his head up and made jokes about it. He'd say, "I have food and shelter, so I can't complain." I realized he was right. That drought and my dad taught me to have faith and to remember that we are all at the mercy of God.*[64]

John and Sharon Monier of Sparland, Illinois relate that *at mealtime it's not unusual for one of the children to add at the end of grace "and please, God, make Daddy's combine work."*[65]

While children see a stay-at-home Mom at work, they rarely see Dad at work. Dads, take your children to see where you work, with whom you work, and what your work entails. Children need to see how their father deals with stress, difficulties, unreasonable people and deadlines. Without at least a visit to where Dad works the children cannot understand the magnitude of Dad's responsibilities. Talk about the father's work over dinner. When Dad's at home the children only see him relaxing or doing odd chores around the house. If Dad travels a lot consider getting the book ***The Business Traveling Parent (How to Stay Close to Your Kids When You're Far Away)*** by Dan Verdick. Verdick has some fun ideas.

Many companies, when interviewing for an executive position also interview the wife and family. If the children have an idea

---

[64] Matt Brum, *We Are Family* (Peoria: Office of Family Life, Diocese of Peoria, 1992) p.45.

[65] John & Sharon Monier, *We Are Family, Op. Cit.*, p. 35.

of their father's work it will help them should they be in an interview situation. When my husband took his current job our family went through the interview process. It was rather stressful not knowing what our three daughters might say. Everything went well until we parted company with the CEO and his family after dinner. As they turned to leave our third grader piped up in a loud voice, *Well, **did** Dad get the job?*

Part of our responsibilities as parents is to teach our children our intention for working, why we work and how to work. Our intention in working is to do everything for the honor and glory of God—from picking up a piece of paper on the floor, to making dinner or doing specific professional activities. By saying the "Morning Offering" all of our actions become prayers that we send nonstop to God throughout the day.

Why do we work? Fathers, out of love, work to support their families. Mothers, out of love, work in the home to care for the physical needs of the children while shaping their characters. In addition she cares for the home and keeps the social calendar. The children, out of love, work in the home/in the family business to contribute to the common good of the family. The family working together contributes to the betterment of society.

How do we work? We work to the very best of our capabilities since we are offering our work to God. No half-hearted, poorly done work is acceptable. There should be attention to detail since we are doing our work for the love of God. One day I asked my youngest daughter to clean the bathroom. She did a good job except for the shower stall. There was still some mildew in the tile cracks. So I asked her to redo it. After her second attempt, she was told to redo it again until it was done correctly. On the third attempt it looked wonderful. It was years later that I learned that she finally painted the mildew with "white-out" liquid paper! Well, it worked. The idea here is that if we offer our day to God we keep redoing a task until it is done to the very best of our ability. We cannot offer God mediocrity. Little ones can offer their work to the Baby Jesus, older children to the Child Jesus.

When our two older daughters were in their teens I asked them to clean while I was working on another project. The two huddled together than audaciously confronted me saying, *Cleaning the house is your work. We are no longer going to do it!* Without missing a beat I simply explained, *my job is to teach you to do my job. Get the house cleaned!* Grumbling under their breath they beat a hasty retreat. Our goal as parents is to teach our children to be as independent as possible at each stage of the children's development. This job begins about a year after birth and continues throughout the lives of parents and children.

When our eldest daughter was in kindergarten, we were invited to her friend's home for lunch. It was an eye-opening experience. Besides the kindergartener, the mother had a first grader and a baby. It was amazing to see the responsibilities these two little ones had and how capable they were in doing each task. The first grader, a little boy, made breakfast for the family every morning. Rather than fixing cereal, he made either scrambled eggs or blueberry pancakes complete with bacon or sausage. He and his younger sister could clean the house (dusting, straightening, and vacuuming), clean the bathrooms, and do the dishes and laundry. Both were able to help with the baby.

Motivated by this family's example we taught our daughters how to do the same tasks. We found that children thrive when there is structure in their day. By having set chores and activities planned each day the children know what to expect, what is expected of them, which in turn makes them feel secure. Granted, when you teach children a chore, they do not have the eye or the fine motor skills to do things as well or as swiftly as you can do them. The temptation is to do the chore yourself to get it done. But that would be depriving your child of growing in character and responsibility. By having set chores for each child, children are taught responsibility. But problems can surface when you ask a different child to do the chore of his sibling. The child will usually retort, *That's not my job!* When this occurs use it as an opportunity to teach the virtues of generosity and spirit of service by explaining that everyone must pitch in to help when someone is not able or not available to do his job. Rotate job assignments so everyone learns how to do everything.

Mary Ann Presberg, of Lake Forest, Illinois, is the mother of twelve. From her home she ran a professional daycare center based on teaching children virtues. She observed how quickly children learn skills and right behavior if parents have the patience to spend time with the children. By spending one time period or one day on a specific behavior, the child learns and then effortlessly repeats the behavior in the future. If a parent does not take the time to teach the correct behavior, there is continual chaos rather than order in the family. The key is the practice of the virtue of patience by a parent until the child develops the procedure or right behavior. Once the routine is established, family life becomes happier and easier. Mrs. Presberg suggests having a daily plan along with setting a daily goal for each child rather than letting the day control you.

Playing is part of the work of children. Unfortunately many of the toys are simply flashy but do not trigger children's imagination. Haven't you had the experience of buying a child a great toy only to have the child play with the box it came in? Select toys that fuel the imagination. Then teach the child how to play. Playing does not come naturally to children. That is why children love toys that mimic the activities of their parents. They see how their parents work so they naturally imitate them by playing with tea sets, toy kitchens and workbenches. Get down on the floor with your child to play store, house, mailman, restaurant, cars, or dolls until the child understands how to play alone. Fights erupt when children do not know how to play, problem-solve, or share. Try to calmly work with each child in these three areas. While the children are playing introduce them to classical music or show tunes. This has a soothing or upbeat influence on them.

Mrs. Presberg recommends purchasing Lincoln Logs or building blocks for your children. The logs have a specific way to lock in or the building comes tumbling down. She finds this activity more stimulating to the child's brain than Legos. Introduce older children to marbles, jacks, yoyos, tops, erector sets, sewing, knitting, crafts, art, flying a kite, catching butterflies or lighting bugs. Patiently teach them how to do each activity.

Children who are two years old can learn to cut and paste if you spend time showing the child how to do each step. Children have a thirst to learn. Should a child have difficulty doing an activity, help him so that he does not become discouraged. Never criticize a child's effort. Instead be encouraging by telling them that they can do it correctly in time. *Let's just try to do this over. You are getting better. Let's try again.*

Mary Ann taught the children to understand beauty and the importance of doing things well. She does not believe in complimenting a child for doing something ugly since this would be insincere. If a child cannot draw she suggests helping the child to cut out pictures from old magazines. Teach your child how to cut, use paste, and then how to paste the item down neatly. Children do not have innate abilities in these areas. Each step must be patiently taught, but once taught the child is able to progress on his own.

To stimulate your children's imagination, keep a box of supplies that contains colored and different textures of paper, pens, wash-off markers, pencils, chalk, finger-paints, modeling clay, crayons, paste and scissors for art projects. Have another box of dress-up clothes or props for the children to play with. They can create plays based on favorite books, stories, or movies. Older children can make hand puppets and put on a show for the younger children. Presberg suggests letting the children invite characters from a story to lunch some days. For example, if the children are reading **Peter Pan**, let the children discuss who could be and could not be invited to lunch. Captain Hook should not be invited because he has not proven that he is a nice person. This teaches the children to discern the difference between good and bad actions, good and bad people and what their attitude should be toward good and evil.

Teach the children to care for their toys and to treasure books. Toys are not to be thrown, intentionally broken nor books torn. Have a set place in your home for the children to play. Insist that the children keep their toys in that area. Have a toy box or container for all the toys. At the end of the day teach your child to put the toys away. This teaches the virtue of order. At Christmas time teach the children the virtue of generosity by asking each to give one of his toys to a poor child.

As the children grow older, introduce them to activities that are not organized such as croquet, badminton, horseshoes, bocce, jump rope, volleyball, and a neighborhood game of softball or baseball. Games such as checkers, chess, Chinese checkers, and cards are not only fun but also intellectually challenging.

Encourage children to play outside so that they can get some exercise. They can skate, swim, run through the sprinkler, have races, ride bikes, play games such as Red Rover, Steal the Bacon, Spud, It, Hide and Seek or play in the snow. At times persuade them to find a quiet spot in your yard to simply read a book.

As for chores, children as young as 12-17 months can learn to put their toys back in a toy chest. As they put them back count the items. This will help them to learn their numbers. Colors can be taught by asking them to put all the red toys back, then the blue, etc. Toddlers can help set the table and help empty the dishwasher. They have the ability to put items on the table or back into the refrigerator. They love to throw anything in the garbage. They can run and get a diaper or other objects that you need. They can put their dirty clothes in the hamper and fold washcloths along with other simple items.

Small children become easily confused so give only one direction at a time. If you ask a toddler to do two or three things at the same time the child becomes overwhelmed and will most probably do nothing.

Children between two years and three can dress themselves if the clothes are simple to put on and laid out the night before. They can carry items upstairs and put them away. If you lower the clothes rack in the closet, children can hang up their clothes, or consider purchasing a child's clothes tree for them to hang things on. Children this age can learn to sweep the floor, empty wastepaper baskets, set the table, clean-up a little mess with a cloth, start to do dishes by washing them off and putting them in the dishwasher. (We went through a set of inexpensive china with each daughter.) Fold larger towels and items. They can get out the cereal for breakfast.

By three they can answer the phone, put canned goods away, and dust. They can clean a bathroom sink, dry dishes and do simple yard chores. A child this age can also make a bed if it is not against a wall. He has the dexterity to smooth the sheets and pull up a comforter. Depending on the development of motor skills, the child can put a pillow in a sham. They can also strip a bed. Take them to pick strawberries and blueberries. Let them help you bake. Children this age are eager to help. Don't discourage them by preferring to do it yourself or expect too much from them in terms of perfection.

At four a child can help to sort the wash and make a peanut butter and jelly sandwich, and keep his bedroom clean.

By five children can work the washer and dryer. They can make simple foods and are great for running errands. Have them water plants outside, pull weeds, and help watch younger siblings when you are doing a task in the home. Ask them to help you carry items into the house from the store.

At six years old, a child should make his own school lunch the night before. He should also be fairly proficient in all of the earlier tasks just discussed.

It is also important for Dad to start teaching both the girls and boys simple repairs around the house even if it is beyond their present capabilities. Children enjoy "working" with their fathers. They can drag small tree branches; or lug tools for you. Explain the purpose of each tool then show them how it works.

By eight, children can do gardening chores, shovel snow, help remove wallpaper and even do simple painting. As the children grow keep teaching them various skills appropriate for their age and ability such as how to use a screwdriver and hammer.

Fourth graders can begin baking and cooking by themselves. A ten-year-old should be able to iron clothes and linens, sew on buttons as well as cook a breakfast, lunch and dinner.

A child who is able to handle the above responsibilities has enough maturity by the age of eleven or twelve to be a capable babysitter for smaller children. Next, teach your children how to entertain by setting a table with china, crystal, and linens. Enlist them to be your waiters and waitresses at your parties. Demonstrate before hand how to take beverage orders then serve them; how to pour coffee, pass food, and remove dirty plates and glasses. This will train them to serve others besides family members.

By junior high your children should be able to put on a dinner, run your household, run to the store on their bike, paint and repair items.

Children are not born with these abilities programmed to appear at the suggested ages. Parents, using patience, perseverance and motivation have to teach these tasks and techniques. To learn any skill, it takes time, practice, and a few mistakes are necessary. It may take years before a bed is perfectly made or a child cheerfully does his chores. It may take some broken plates before Suzy gets the knack of washing and drying dishes, but if that is what it takes, then, in justice to Suzy, her parents must help her learn this and other tasks.

Parents sometimes complain that their children are lazy and shiftless, but in the same breath they explain how their children wanted to do a task but *they were making a mess* or *it is easier to do it myself.* Yes, it is easier and faster to do it oneself but the child cannot learn that way. If you do a task your child can do, your child is not learning to be an independent and responsible person. A parent who does everything for his child from dressing him in the morning, to making his school lunch, to making his bed is neither an effective nor loving parent. Such a parent is teaching his child to be dependent and irresponsible rather than independent and responsible. Parents who feel that it is too much of a "hassle" to demand that their children help around the house should not be shocked when the child graduates from high school without any skills then proceeds to lounge around the house until someone gets him or her a job.

To be a good parent today involves being constantly on top of the situation at home. House rules can help a parent implement this training. For example: Rule #1—a child does not leave the home until the chores are completed and done well even if it takes three attempts to get the tub cleaned properly. Rule # 2—beds must be made before breakfast, etc.

By teaching your children skills as they grow, children experience a sense of accomplishment, self-worth, self-esteem, and satisfaction in being able to contribute to the common good of the family. They also become dependable, helpful, thoughtful individuals. I was reminded of this fact recently when I was a guest in the home of the Wrobel family in Carmel, Indiana. The oldest son, a sixth grader greeted me at the door and told me his mother was at the grocery store. He took my suitcase, leading me to his room to freshen up. When I came down to the family room he asked if I would like something to drink. He and his siblings then entertained me until his parents returned. Their parents had formed these children well.

When unforeseen events occur, if the children are well trained, everyone can jump in to help. Theresa Fagan, the mother of eight, recounts how she was just about to get into the shower before a business dinner engagement when her husband announced that a couple was coming by to pick them up. *Are they coming in? Yes.* Immediately she marshaled the children to put the house in order. By the time she was dressed and came down to meet the couple, her home was in perfect order.

When our youngest daughter was in junior high, I was 70 miles away giving a talk when she called to tell me that a business associate was unexpectedly in town and would be coming for dinner that night. After my initial panic, we discussed possible menu options. By the time I arrived home, the house was in perfect order; the table was set with silver, crystal, china and a simple floral bouquet that she designed. It was amazing to see her ability in handling everything so well, at such short notice, on her own. Her dinner was delicious. When Mary Terese was seventeen she calmly took over all the cooking and setup when

Mother Angelica was a guest in our home. This prompted Mother to jokingly issue her an invitation to consider joining her order!

When children develop such skills, through your coaching, they can handle any situation that arises calmly, with self-assurance. Getting married and setting up a home seems natural to them. When parents, on the other hand, do everything for their children because it is easier or with a mistaken idea of love, they end up casting their children into adulthood with no experience. So many young men and women have no training in how to make simple house repairs, balance a checkbook, cook, do laundry or iron. No wonder there are so many boomerang young adults. Once they taste the effort of independence they decide it is easier just to move back home and let Mom and Dad take care of the work and problems. St. Zita, a domestic worker in the late 13th century used to say *a servant is not pious if she is not industrious; work-shy piety in people...is sham piety.*[66] To become saints, our children must be willing to work, to do their work well as they offer it to God.

Pat Slattery, a journalist and farmer lists his family chores on a blackboard. *"The kids like doing these things. They like the feeling of accomplishment."* He recently volunteered to work a couple of days with Habitat for Humanity...and took his eight-year-old son Gabe with him. *"There were several other fathers there with their sons and I enjoyed observing the father-son relationship in the midst of this kind of outreach activity.*

"I'm also really a believer in the concept of family enterprise where every member has the opportunity to contribute to the financial well-being of the family by doing work in the home and together. We have been going to various fairs at which we sell homemade pork sandwiches. I would eventually like to see each of the kids in charge of our family's participation in one of these fairs each year...Kids outlook on work...should come from observing and sharing their parent's work."[67] Mr. Slattery believes that work is important because it builds character rather than just preparing a child for a career. It also teaches children the

---

[66] *Lives of the Saints Illustrated Part I, Op. Cit.,* p. 167.

importance of taking over responsibilities so that their parents have some time to do apostolate, which is simply making God known and loved by others. My first book, **You Can Become A Saint!** was truly a family affair. Without Bob and our three daughters taking over most of the household tasks I would never have had the time to write the book.

Love, Kisses, Hugs & Deeds

In happy families love is lavished on family members with kisses, hugs, signs of affection, loving words and deeds throughout the day. Mom and Dad kiss and hug good-bye in the morning along with any children who are awake. In the evening when Dad trudges home weary from a difficult day of work he is greeted at the door with hugs, kisses and squeals of delight from Mom and the children (Mom doesn't have to squeal). At bedtime there are more hugs and kisses after night prayers. During the day affection is liberally sprinkled on all the children. Pats on the head, a tickle here and there, and a squeeze all lift the heart. The words *I love you* need to be spoken frequently to each family member but not simply words but words spoken from the heart. When affection is only internalized but never expressed children feel unloved. One elderly woman, the baby of a family of eight, never recalls any sign of affection from her mother. She chokes up as she recalls how as a child when she played house she wanted to *be the child that was loved.* Her mother loved her dearly but her reserve nature did not permit her to express that love through hugs, kisses, squeezes, etc. If we are not outwardly affectionate toward our children, they may not be able to express affection toward their spouses and children.

While it's easy to lavish affection on dimply babies, adolescents need hugs and kisses even more—even if they do pull away from you. Teens hunger for affection. If they do not get it from you they will search for it from a gang, a peer or a boyfriend or girlfriend. It is dangerous to have the attitude that *they know I love them. I don't have to keep telling them or hugging them.* Wrong! Giving constant shows of affection is more necessary

[67] Greg Pierce, "Faith and Work," *Catholic Times,* Sept. 16, 1990, p. 9.

than three meals a day. Show appreciation, delight and excitement in your children's accomplishments and goodness. Compliment them when they look nice or do something well. Turn to them when you need help. Everyone loves to be needed. Show your children that they are valued.

No matter what happens during the day, our children and spouse need to know that you indeed love the "sinner," just hate the sin. Never hold grudges or give the silent treatment. Love swiftly gets over hurts. It is self-love that sulks. Teach each child to revere the dignity of the other children and you as parents. Never permit a child to say *I hate you* to you or to another child. Those words crush the heart.

In Patrick and Therese Fagan's Maryland home, if a child makes fun of another child, the offending child has to do a chore. Teach your children to say *I'm sorry.* When we babysat for three of our grandchildren, ages three to 15 months, it was precious to hear them apologizing to each other often during the day.

Teach your children to express concern when someone is hurt. If the person is a child, your child can give a hug, a toy or book for the child to play with or simply talk the child into smiling again. Concern should be shown to anyone injured or sick by running errands or reading a story to the patient, making get well cards, waiting on the person by bringing something to eat or drink or playing a quiet game with the invalid.

Do the children listen to each other and you? Or are they too busy talking to listen? Train your children in listening skills. Teach them not to monopolize conversations. Their adult friends will be grateful to you. Interest in the thoughts of other people is an aspect of love.

Train your children to welcome visitors by greeting them at the door with excitement and smiles. Explain to the children when they are young as to what their duties are as host and hostess. Show them how to include other children in their play routine, by sharing toys, by offering and serving their guests refreshments. Before visitors arrive, role-play with your children their duties and responsibilities toward their guests. Lay down rules before the guests arrive so the children understand what behavior is acceptable and which behavior is not. Then if a child-guest wants to run in the house or throw a ball inside, your child can explain the house rules.

Family love becomes self-interest if it excludes our extended families, which include grandparents, uncles, aunts, and cousins. Love is deeper than occasional hugs. It means staying in touch, making time to get together on the holidays and special family occasions, it's helping out relatives in time of need, it's daily prayer for extended family members. It means doing things with grandparents. Favorite memories of our daughters include going to Sunday Mass and brunch as a family with their maternal grandparents each Sunday morning. Sunday afternoons many times were spent with their paternal grandparents and cousins.

Children love to hear family stories and family history. Keep photos of relatives around the home pointing out who the people are to the children. Some families keep photo albums that the children can leaf through at their leisure. One father composed a family history for both sides of the family. Then he put together a photo album with a page devoted to each family member showing the different stages of his/her life.

Love means helping out without pay when needed. When grandparents need help send the kids over. If a relative needs help with a new baby send one of your teens to help. Teach the teens to offer to sit gratis for a young couple that needs a night away from the kids.

At times we can get so caught up in our own lives and problems that we become unwilling to complicate our lives further by helping out extended family members. Remember, sanctity means heroic virtue practiced daily, even in the most disappointing or difficult circumstances. One friend and her daughter had plans to go diamond mining with another mother and her daughter. She was so excited about the trip because this was something she always wanted to do. Then the day before she left, her mother was rushed to the hospital. The woman canceled her trip to stay with her mother. Besides canceling vacation plans, sometimes we have to modify them to help a relative. A business opportunity may be missed because we have to help care for someone who needs our help. It may mean making a meal for a new mom at the worst possible time for us. As Mother Teresa of Calcutta wrote, *What counts is not the amount of our actions but the intensity of love with which we do each one.*[68]

Is our love truly heroic that we can actually give ourselves completely for another like Christ did for us? John Paul II reminds us that the sacrifice of Christ *inspires us...to give our lives for God and our brothers without reserve...[up to the shedding of blood], as did so many martyrs.*[69] When we are reluctant or unwilling to love heroically, or grudgingly do the action, we cause turmoil within ourselves that spills over into misplaced aggression toward other family members. A lack of love causes suffering, hurt feelings, and estrangement. It is difficult to imagine the importance of heroic love until you are at the receiving end. When I had sudden major surgery at a time when my husband was quite ill our daughters stepped in to help although they all live quite a distance away. Mary Kate's husband, Michael, although unable to take vacation time, took a half-week off to care for their four children so Katie could be with me through the surgery and at the hospital. Mary Terese, husband Jeff and their ten-month-old baby came down to bring me home from the hospital, and help me recuperate at home. Her husband had taken his vacation time to help us out. It was a hardship for both young families yet they loved with a sacrificial love.

Loyalty, trust and solidarity are also aspects of love. Children live love when as adults they are loyal and foster closeness to their parents and siblings. When a child becomes an adult but separates himself or herself from his family, that child never really learned to love. As parents we have to teach our children when they are small that after God and spouse, family comes first. Teens tend to put their friends first. If children are not trained before their teens in the importance of family solidarity, they will

---

[68] "Secret of Sanctity: Live Every Day As Though It is The Last," *Zenit* March 14, 2000.

[69] John Paul II, Audience July 1, 2000.

take the mindset of friends over family with them throughout life. This is a growing problem. Tens of thousands of elderly people (and not so elderly) are abandoned by their adult children because they never taught their children to love them.

Trust is likewise part of love. As our children can trust us to be honest, our children must also be trained in honesty. When a child lies, the child not only breaks our trust but also shows a lack of honor and love for us. Lying is something that needs to be punished immediately and in a memorable fashion so that the action is not repeated. American author, Willa Cather, wrote an interesting short story on the mushrooming ill-effects of lying entitled "Paul's Case, A Study In Temperament." I encourage you to read the story. Her story begins by setting the stage: *This was a lie, but Paul was quite accustomed to lying; found it, indeed, indispensable for overcoming friction.*[70] As Paul's story unfolds we find that his lies have led him to live a life of fear. *Even when he was a little boy, it was always there—behind him, or before, or on either side. There had always been the shadowed corner, the dark place into which he dared not look, but from which something seemed always to be watching him—and Paul had done things that were not pretty to watch, he knew.*[71] Escaping his past he found *[t]he mere release from the necessity of petty lying, lying every day and every day, restored his self-respect. He had never lied for pleasure, even at school; but to be noticed and admired, to assert his difference...It was characteristic that remorse did not occur to him.*[72]

Who wants the shame of being known as the parent of a dishonorable adult? In the video *The Winslow Boy*, the fourteen-year-old son is accused of stealing a postal order. He was found guilty by his school and expelled. The father asked the boy if he was guilty or innocent. The boy insisted he was innocent. On the word of his son, the father staked his income, his savings, all he possessed and his health to clear the son's name. As the court

---

[70] Willa Cather, *The Willa Cather Reader* (Philadelphia: Courage Books, 1997), p. 415.

[71] *Ibid.,* p. 429.

[72] *Ibid.,* p. 433.

case dragged on, the rest of the family members were likewise called to make heroic sacrifices. Would you be willing to stake everything you possess on the word of your child?

Successful Parents

"Praise not any man before death, for a man is known by his children."
(Ecclesiasticus 11:30).

Successful parents raise considerate, responsible future adults in a manner that promotes happy and fun memories of Mom and Dad. It's memories of coming home from school to the aroma of chocolate chips or cinnamon rolls baking in the oven. It's a snowball fight with Dad after the walk is shoveled. It's Sunday excursions or visits to relatives. It's the rained out picnic on the beach when the family sang songs under an umbrella until the rain passed.

In an earlier chapter we discussed the importance of happy memories for spouses to keep the marriage thriving. To keep our family thriving we also have to provide warm happy memories for our children. When an eighth grader learned her family was moving out of state she was devastated. To pick up her spirits her mother decided to throw a surprise birthday party at school during the lunch hour. The mother took her youngest daughter out of school at noon for an hour. She dressed her as Miss Piggy complete with snout. "Miss Piggy" brought in two-dozen purple helium balloons along with an ice cream snack for each of her sister's classmates. The party pulled the older daughter out of her doldrums and provided lots of funny memories for the family.

Along with providing warm memories, James Stenson finds that successful parents have specific characteristics. They include:

✓ **Both** parents are dominant: each takes responsibility for proper role; each respects the other's leadership. Children see united effort in making the family work. Each child has only one mind and one conscience, and therefore needs one consistent set of directions emanating from both parents. Manipulative children take advantage of disunity between parents. Successful parents do not permit this to happen.

✓ Parents encourage children to overcome "feelings" for sake of a higher good. Parents realize that "no" is also a loving word, that feelings pass but that lessons of right and wrong remain. They show children that long-term happiness is more important than short-term gratification.

✓ Both parents have outside interests and friends. Both have religious faith that leads to dutiful practice.

✓ Parents distinguish between children's judgment and children's integrity: though they may mistrust judgment, they trust children's sense of honor.

✓ Parents do not permit what they do not approve of. They give example to children that what is wrong is unacceptable, that age is irrelevant to ethical propriety.

✓ The father takes increased interest in his children as they approach adolescence. He is not afraid to show, and speak about, his struggles and shortcomings. He talks about his own youth and his present life outside the family. The children know what he does in the outside world, and why.

✓ There is relatively little television watching. Both parents have a respect for learning, and both encourage discriminating reading.

✓ The children have real responsibilities in the family's life. They are held accountable, and praiseworthy, for their contributions.[73]

✓ Each spouse frequently shows the children his or her respect for the spouse.

✓ The parents have a clear-cut idea that they are raising adults, not children. They realize that the kids need correction and leadership to grow up.

✓ They treat their children the way God treats all of us. They combine firmness with understanding. They lay down the law, but affectionately and with forgiveness.

---

[73] Fatherhood: The Dynamics of Character Formation , *Op. Cit.*

✓ *They make each child feel needed at home. Each child contributes some effort, however small, toward making the home a successful team enterprise.*

✓ *The parents show the children their own responsibilities in action. They show responsibility toward God and His law, toward the Church, toward employers, toward the needy, toward guests and friends.*

✓ *Parents talk a lot with their children. They go out of their way to find out what their children are thinking.*

✓ *Successful parents seem to realize that they have one chance—and only one—to raise their children right. They know they have only the first 16 to 18 years of a child's life to prepare that young person's earthly and eternal happiness.[74]*

To succeed in living the above points, one needs to place God at the center of the family. Monsignor Cormac Burke observes, *Holy families are the most special need of our times. They can be formed only by couples who are truly trying to be saints. Only in such families will good be stronger than evil, and able to overcome it. Only from such families will that good spread which can save the world; for only the Saints are strong with the "strength of God."*

The problem with our modern world is that it wants to be happy by getting, not by giving; something that runs counter to the basic rules of human living. In the end we cannot and should not want to ignore the fact that happiness—also the happiness which marriage promises—is not possible without generosity and sacrifice. Blessed Escrivá often said "happiness has its roots in the shape of a Cross." It is the rule and apparent paradox of the Gospel: only by 'losing' and giving ourselves—the essence of love— can we begin to find ourselves and, even more than ourselves, find the happiness we are made for.[75]

---

[74] James Stenson, Audio tape "How Successful Parents Raise Responsible Adults," R.B.Media, Inc.

[75] "Love and the family in today's world," *Op. Cit.*, p. 27.

You've Only Just Begun!

As this concludes the first book in the series on how to **Raise Happy Children,** I hope it has given you a few ideas to help you deepen your marriage relationship along with your interior life. I would encourage you now to read the next in the series, **Raise Happy Children...Raise Them Saints!** and then **Raise Happy Children...Teach Them Virtues!** Consider these books as three parenting courses: one on marriage and family life; the second on how to teach and live the Catholic faith; and the third on how to teach and live the various virtues at different ages. (See the appendix for a listing of the topics covered in each book.)

St. Paul reminds us: **God is not mocked. For what a man sows, that he will also reap. For he who sows in the flesh, from the flesh also will reap corruption. But he who sows in the spirit from the spirit will reap life everlasting. And in doing good let us not grow tired; for in due time we shall reap if we do not relax. Therefore, while we have time, let us do good to all men, but especially to those who are of the household of faith** (Galatians 6:7-10).

Besides, as Blessed Escrivá points out, *The more generous you are for God, the happier you will be.*[76] So raise happy children through a happier marriage!

 *Additional Helps*

✓ Sit down with your spouse and draw up "house rules."
✓ Assign your children specific chores. Consider which skills they need to learn for their age then devise a specific plan to teach them those skills.
✓ Rent the videos *The Winslow Boy* and *Meet Me In*

---

[76] *Furrow, Op.Cit.,*no. 18.

St. Louis for your family. Discuss afterwards how these two families showed their love, loyalty and trust for each other.

✓ Read **Christ In The Home** by Raoul Plus, S. J. This book is excellent! It can be downloaded at:
www.ewtn.com/library/FAMILY/CHRISTH1.TXT

✓ Non-Catholic spouse? Read **My Spirit Rejoices** the diary of Elisabeth Leseur (Sophia).

✓ For a fun look at parenting read Bill Cosby's book, **Fatherhood**.

✓ Read **Lifeline, The Religious Upbringing of Your Children**, by James Stenson (Scepter (800)322-8773) and form a dicussion group with friends to discuss it.

✓ Audiotape sets you may find helpful from R.B. Media include: "Parenthood and the Formation of Children," "Marriage: Covenant of Love," "Marriage & Parenthood," "Rebuilding the Family," "Focus On The Family," Fatherhood, Motherhood & Family Life," "The Importance of the Father in the Family," "How Fathers Pass The Faith On To Children," "Successful Families In The '90s," "Toward A More Human Society." Check out www.rbmediainc.com for a detailed explanation of each set.

Appendix

Table Of Contents For

Raise Happy Children...
*   Raise Them Saints!*

CHAPTER 1
THE DO'S AND DON'TS OF PARENTING

Study the parenting techniques of the parents of St. Thérèse, Bl. Padre
Pio, Bl. Escrivá, St. Maximilian Kolbe, St. Thomas More, St. Jeanne-
Francoise de Chantel and Alice of Montar. (All of Alice's children are
either beatified or canonized.) See how their techniques contrasted with
the example of the parents of the visionaries of La Salette, who were
never canonized. Learn the formula for raising your children saints.

CHAPTER 2
THE STORY OF TWO LIVES:
*   THE ROLE OF FAITH IN CHARACTER*

The character of a child is strongly influenced by faith. Learn how the
Catholic faith/the lack of the faith changed the similar lives of billionaires
Tom Monaghan, the founder of Domino's Pizza and Ted Turner, the founder
of CNN.

CHAPTER 3
TEACHING THE FAITH...
TO YOUR CHILDREN

There are numerous saintly families in the Church. Yours can be one too! Learn how to begin to raise your child a saint before birth! Discover the importance of naming a child. Find out fun ways to teach the faith pre-school - high school years and beyond. Study how to teach your children the importance of the Bible, guardian angels, the lives of the saints, prayer, and Holy Mass. Tips are given on how to teach your child the value of self-sacrifice, to differentiate between "wants" and "needs."

CHAPTER 4
HOW THE SACRAMENTS HELP
YOUR CHILDREN TO GROW HOLY!

Using the example of the saints and the parents of saints, explore the importance of the seven sacraments. Why is baptism necessary? When should a baby be baptized? What is the responsibility of godparents? At what age should a child make his First Confession? What should the child know? What age should a child make his First Communion? Learn how to develop love for the Eucharist in your children. Explore the gifts of the Holy Spirit, fruits of the Holy Spirit and how these gifts influence your childrens' daily lives in the Sacrament of Confirmation. Discover how to prepare your children for the Sacrament of Matrimony. Learn how to guide your children in their choice of a future spouse. The power of the priesthood is explored in Holy Orders. Tips are given as to how to encourage vocations in your family using the examples of the parents of saints. The Sacrament of the Sick is explained.

CHAPTER 5
WHICH METHOD OF EDUCATION
IS BEST FOR YOUR CHILD?

Parents are the primary educators of their children. Learn why the saints and parents of saints put such effort into the education of their children. Learn how to select the right school or educational method by considering the pros and cons of educational choices: public, Catholic, private Catholic and home schooling.   What are the rights and specific duties of parents in the matter of schooling? Consider the problems of the overprogrammed child. Discover the impact of negative outside influences on your children: computer, TV, radio, reading material, movies, music, food allergies. Study how to teach your children to live the spiritual and corporal works of mercy.

Table of Contents For

Raise Happy Children...
Teach Them Virtues!

The development of children ages 8 to 12 is explained along with the importance of developing the above virtues during this stage of childhood. How to specifically teach each virtue is explained as well as how to continue the growth of these virtues in teens.

CHAPTER 4
HOW TO TEACH THE VIRTUES OF TEMPERANCE, MODERATION, MODESTY, CHASTITY, SOCIABILITY, FRIENDSHIP, RESPECT FOR OTHERS, SIMPLICTY, AND PATRIOTISM

What's in store during the rebellious teen years? This chapter studies ages 13 to 15. Why do teens rebel? Learn what the awakening of intimacy means and how to deal with it. Discover how to exercise authority through consistency, flexibility and personal prestige with your teens. Why do teens crave independence, uniqueness and attention? Why is there a generation gap? Why are these specific virtues so important for teens? How are they taught? What can you do when your teen falls in love? These questions, along with others are addressed in this chapter.

CHAPTER 5
HOW TO TEACH THE VIRTUES OF PRUDENCE, FLEXIBILITY, UNDERSTANDING, LOYALTY, AUDACITY, HUMILITY, AND OPTIMISM TO TEENS

The final stage of adolescence, 16 to 18 years, is considered along with how to develop the critical virtues of prudence, flexibility, understanding, loyalty, audacity, humility and optimism that teens need for holy, productive and happy lives.

CHAPTER 6
HAPPINESS & JOY

What is happiness? How is it related to hope? How does one develop the virtue of cheerfulness? What is joy and how can our children and we possess it? These are the topics covered in the concluding chapter of the series.

Bibliography

Altajeros, Professor Francisco.
"The Denial of Happiness." Spain, 1982.
"Pain and Love in Education." Spain, 1982.
Angelica, Mother. *EWTN Family Newsletter.* April 2000.
Anthony of Padua, Sermon I, 226.
Apostolate of the Little Flower. 1998.
Aquinas, St. Thomas. *Summa Theologica*
  In duo praecepta caritatis et in decem praecepta decalogi.
  Summa contra Gentiles.
Araujo, Dr. Ana Maria. "Some Aspects of Marriage." Spain, 1992.
              "The Stages of Married Life," 1987.
Augustine, St.. *De diversis quaestionibus.*
              De moribus Ecclesiae Catholicae.
              In Ioannis Evangelilum tractatus.
              Sermons 65, 169, and 260.
Benjamin, Walter W. "Fatherless Heaven; Fatherless Children." *The Wall Street Journal.*
Black, Anne Lewis and Dennis McCafferty. "The Age of Contentment." *USA Weekend.* 1998.
Blocker, O.F.M., Hyacinth. *Walk With The Wise.* 1950.
Bolinski, Jayette. "UIS student: Nightclub dress codes cloak racial bias." *The State Journal Register.* Illinois, May 12, 2001.
Bossis, Gabrielle. *He and i.* Quebec, 1969.
Browder, Sue Ellen. "The Power of Marriage." *Women's Day.* 1999.
Brum, Matt. *We Are Family.* Peoria, IL, 1992.
Buchholz, Dr. Annemarie and Dr. Eve-Maria Föllmer. "Imparting Values in the Family," *Current Concerns.* Zurich, 2000.
Budnik, Mary Ann. *You Can Become A Saint!* Springfield, 2001.
Burke, Msgr. Cormac. "Love and the family in today's world." *Homiletic & Pastoral Review,* 1995.

Cantalamessa O.F.M.Cap., Raniero. *The Mystery of God's Word.* MN, 1994.

Catechism of the Catholic Church. Boston, 1994.

Cather, Willa. *The Willa Cather Reader.* Philadelphia, 1994.

Chaput, O.F.M., Archbishop Charles J. *Of Human Life: A pastoral letter to the people of God...on the truth and meaning of married love.* Denver, 1998.

Chrysostom, St. John. *In 1 Epistolam I ad Corinthios homiliae.*
    In Matth. Hom. 49.

Cosby, Bill. *Fatherhood.* NY, 1987.

Covey, Stephen R. *The 7 Habits of Highly Effective Families.* New York, 1997.

Daneil-Rops, H. *The Church of Apostles and Martyrs.* NY, 1960.

D'Ascoli, OFM, CAP., Emidio. *Family and Marriage.* Chicago, 1961.

Del Val, Cardinal Merry. *Memories of Pope Pius X.* Maryland, 1951.

De Sales, St. Francis. *Thy Will Be Done: Letters to the Persons in the World.* 1995.

Detroit Free Press, March 20, 1999.

Drake, Tim. "She Gave Her Life That Her Child Might Live." *Celebrate Life.* Stafford, 2000.

D'Souza, Dinesh. *Ronald Reagan, How an Ordinary Man Became an Extraordinary Leader.* NY, 1997.

DuPlantis, Jr. P. D., Lloyd J. "The Pill, A Human Time Bomb." *Celebrate Life, May-June 2001.*

Elliott, Peter J. *What God Has Joined...The Sacramentality of Marriage.* NY, 1997.

Escriva de Balaguer, Blessed Josemaría.
    Christ is Passing By. New York. 1982.
    Conversations With Msgr. Escrivá. Dublin, 1969.
    Friends of God. New York. 1981.
    Furrow. New York. 1987.
    The Forge. New York, 1988.
    The Way. New York, 1954.
    The Way of the Cross. New York. 1982.

Eymard, St. Peter Julian. *The Real Presence.* Ohio, 1939.

Falconi, Robert. "If you want to move up, don't dress down." *Financial Executive,* 1996.

Falk, Barbara. *Family Leadership: A Woman's Perspective.* Audiotape, Springfield, IL

Fernandez-Carvajal, Francis and Peter Beteta. *Children of God.* NJ, 1997.

Fowler, Suzanne. *The Light Weigh.* Kansas, 1998.

Garrigou-LaGrange, Rev. *The Three Ages of the Interior Life.*

Gerrard, Thomas J. *Marriage and Parenthood, the Catholic Ideal.* New York, 1911.

Gregory, St. of Nissa. *Homilia I de pauperibus amandis et benignitate complectendis.*

Gutierrez, Terri and R. John Freese. "Benefit or Burden? Dress Down Days." *The CPA Journal*, 1999.

Hardon, SJ, John A. *The Catholic Family In The Modern World.* MN, 1991.

Harvard Women's Health Watch. August, 2000.

Hass, Dr. John M. "Marriage and the Priesthood." NY, 1987.

Hoever, S.O. Cist.,Ph. D., Rev. Hugo. *Lives of the Saints.* NJ, 1999.

Hoffman, Fr. Frank. "The Christian Influence on Culture," Niles, IL, 2000.

Howard, Jr., Father Joseph C. "In vitro fertilization and surrogate motherhood," *Celebrate Life,* May-June 2001.

Human Life International Newsletter. Front Royal, VA 1998

Isaacs, Dr. David. *Character Building, A Guide For Parents And Teachers.* Dublin, 1984.

"Communication and Decision Making In Matrimony," 1985.

"Conditions for Giving and Receiving In Marriage," 1990.

"Conditions for a Developing Relationship in Marriage," 1990

Course on Happiness and Suffering In The Family. Chicago, IL, 1990

Course on Marriage Relationships. Spain, 1992.

Kahlenborn, MD, Chris. *Breast Cancer, Its Link to Abortion and the Birth Control Pill.* Dayton,Ohio, 2000.

Kelly, Katy. "Child docs to parents: Stay home and save your kids," *U.S. News & World Report*, Oct. 30, 20001.

Kowalski, St. Maria Faustina. *Diary, Divine Mercy in My Soul.* MA, 1987.

Landis, Debra. "Kids According to Katz." *The State-Journal Register.* Springfield, IL, 1992.

Leahy, D.J. *A Catholic Commentary On Holy Scripture.* NY, 1953.

Leaper, Debbie. "The Dollars and Sense of Image." *People and Productivity*, 1999.

Leifeld, Wendy. *Mothers of the Saints.* Ann Arbor, 1991.

Leseur, Elisabeth. *My Spirit Rejoices.* NH, 1996.

Lewis, C.S. *The Problem of Pain.* New York, 1962.

Los Angeles Daily News, April 27, 1997.

Mc Astocker, SJ, David P. *The Joy of Sorrow.* New York, 1936.

McCullough, David. *John Adams.* New York, 2001.

McGinley, Laurie. "Heart and Soul: Stem-Cell Debate Consumes A Charity." *The Wall Street Journal,* June, 2001.

Messenger, Ph.D., Rev. E. C. *The Mystery of Sex and Marriage In Catholic Theology, Two In One Flesh, Part 2.* Maryland, 1948.

Montalban, Ricardo. "In The Heart Of Tinseltown, A Faith Lived Deeply." *BE Magazine*, 2000.

Morice, Henri. *The Apostolate of Moral Beauty.* St. Louis, MO. 1961.

Noffke, O.P., Suzanne. *Catherine of Siena, The Dialogue.*

Olson, Barbara. *Hell to Pay.* Washington, DC, 1999.

O'Leary, Dale. *The Vocation of Motherhood* audiotape. Springfield, IL.

Owen, Richard. *The London Times,* May 8, 2001.

Parente, OFM, Cap., Fr. Alessio. "The Family: A Three Part Essay." *Echoes of Padre Pio's Voice,* 1998.

Pero-Sanz, Rev. José M. "Maturity." *Palabra* #214 May, 1983.

Pierce, Greg. "Faith and Work." *Catholic Times.* Springfield, IL, 1990.

Plus, SJ, Raoul. *Christ in the Home.* New York, 1951.

Pope John Paul II. Address. October 25, 1978.

Address. November 8, 1978.

Address. November 15, 1978

Address. November 22, 1978.

Address. October 26, 1983.

Address. Beatification in Slovenia. 1999.

Address. Kiel Center Address to Youth. 1999.

Address. Dedication of New Museum Entrances. 2000.

Address. January 1, 2000.

Address. July 1, 2000.

Dies Domini (On Keeping the Lord's Day Holy). 1998

Dominus Iesus. 2000

Familiaris Consortio. 1981.

Laborem Exercens. 1981

Reconciliation and Penance. 1984.

Pope Paul VI. Audience, August 22, 1963.

Humanae Vitae.

Octogesima adveniens.

Pope Pius XI. *Divini illius magistri.* 1929.

Casti Connubii. 1930.

Pope Pius XII. *Christmas Radio Message.* December 24,1953.

Women's Duties in Social and Political Life.

Purcell, Mary. *The Halo On The Sword.* Maryland. 1952.

Raspberry, William. "Teaching Youngsters to Volunteer." *State-Journal Register,* 1991.

Rebuttati, Art. *Matrimonio,* in *Nuovo Digesto Italiano.* Turin, 1939.

Reich, Howard. *Chicago Tribune.* 1988.

Rogers, C.R. "The Necessary and Sufficient Conditions of Therapeutic Personality Change." *Journal of Consulting Psychology,* 1957.

Roker, Al, *Don't Make Me Stop This Car, Adventures in Fatherhood.* New York, 2000.

Rosemond, John. *Better Homes and Gardens.* April, 1991.

Russell, Claire. *Glimpses of the Church Fathers.* London, 1994.

Martens, VHM, Sr. Mary Christine. "Léonie Martin: The Forgotten Sister of

St. Thérèse." *Apostolate of the Little Flower.* San Antonio, 2000.

Sager, Carole Bayer. *Playing Our Song.* Casablanca Record and Film Works, Inc., 1979.

Sancrasagra, Mithre J. "As People Live Longer, World's Economies Feel The Strain."

Schent, Rev. Dick. Retreat. Valparaiso, Indiana, 1998.

Schiffman, James R. "Teen-agers End Up In Psychiatric Hospitals In Alarming Numbers." *The Wall Street Journal. 1989.*

Schlessinger, Dr. Laura. *Parenthood By Proxy.* New York, 2000.

Schore, Allan N. *Affected Regulation and the Origin of the Self, The Neurobiology of Emotional Development.* NJ, 1994.

Schulte, Rev. Mark. *The Father of Truth* audiotape. Springfield, IL, 1999.

Scupoli, Lawrence. *The Spiritual Combat.* NY, 1978.

Sheed, F.J. *Marriage and the Family.* New York. No date.

Sheen, Archbishop Fulton J. *Peace Of The Soul.* New York. 1951.

Shellenbarger, Sue. "Fathers (Not Managers) Know Best." *The Wall Street Journal.* 1991.

Sheridan, Bishop Michael J. Homily. June 26, 2000.

Spotlight, "Unteaching Toddlers." Washington, D. C. May 7, 2001.

Spurgeon, Devon. "Author's Divorce Pits Her 'Rules' Against Reality." *The Wall Street Journal,* 2001.

Stenson, James B. *Upbringing—The Religious Upbringing of Your Children.* New York. 1999.

"Fatherhood." New York. 1989.

"Fatherhood: The Dynamics of Character Formation Seminar at Northridge Prep School."

How Successful Parents Raise Responsible Adults, audiotape, Springfield, IL.

Stetson, Rev. Bill. Homily. Chicago, IL. 2000.

Trese, Leo T. *More Than Many Sparrows.* Chicago, 1958.

Trochu, Abbe Trancis. *The Cure D'Ars.* Rockford. 1977.

The Topeka Capital-Journal. "Are we too casual?" 1997.

Vatican II. *Apostolicam actuositatem.*
 Gaudium et spes.
 Optatam Totius.
 Presbyterorum ordinis.

Vitz, Dr. Paul. *Catholic Manhood: The Problems & Promises of Today* audiotape. Springfield, IL
 The Role of the Father In the F amily, audiotape. Springfield, IL

Vollmer, Ambassador and Mrs. Alberto. "Paternity and Maternity, Human and Christian Values." Seminar comments.

Von Hildebrand, Dr. Alice. "Women At Work." New York. 1985.

Vitullo-Martin, Julia. "A Joyful Noise." *Wall Street Journal,* December 15, 2000

Webster's New Collegiate Dictionary. Springfield, MA. 1980

Weigel, George. *Witness To Hope.* New York. 1999.

Weldon, Michele. "Out of the Shallows." *Chicago Tribune.* 1991.

Womble, Jeffery. "Dress the Part," *Fayetteville (NC) Observer-Times.* 1997.

Zenit.   January 21, 2000.

        March 3, 2000.

        March 7, 2000.

        March 14, 2000.

        February 20, 2001.

        February 22, 2001.

        February 27, 2001.

        March 14, 2001.

        March 11, 2001.

        March 12, 2001.

        March 22, 2001.

        April 1, 2001.

        April 2, 2001.

$\mathcal{INDEX}$

𝒰

Understanding, virtue of 17, 164, 176, 193, 206-207
Unity 63, 66-69, 157-158, 165, 180, 188

𝒱

Values 165, 186, 204-205, 213, 223, 262
Vatican II 113-114, 118, 123, 129
Veracity, virtue of 124
Vermeer, Johannes 31
Vianney, St. John 8, 27, 120, 126
Vice 108, 118, 131, 149
Virtues 12-14, 17, 22, 29, 36, 45, 61-62, 69, 90, 92, 105-152, 177, 186, 203, 215, 223, 242-243, 258, 261, 305
Vitz, Dr. Paul 258, 272, 285-286
Vocation 16, 157, 192, 192, 203
Vollmer, Ambassador and Mrs. 249-250
Von Hildebrand, Dr. Alice 199, 258

𝒲

Waite, Dr. 96
Waugh, Evelyn 32
Weldon, Michele 209-210
Wisdom, virtue of 121
Wives 40, 128, 203, 209, 253-271
Women's Duties in Social and Political Life 253
Work, virtue of 159, 200, 258, 292-303
Works of Mercy, 29, 219, 230, 257
Worship 159
Wrobel 301

𝒴

Young, Loretta 50, 51, 53

𝒵

Zenit 30
Zita, St. 302

YOU CAN BECOME A SAINT!

by
Mary Ann Budnik

"The best kept secret in the world is that God created you to be a saint! Since your vocation is your path to holiness, learn how to use it to become a saint!"

You Are Called To Be A Saint!

Sainthood isn't optional. We are all called to holiness by virtue of our baptism. Pope John Paul II told us New Orleans in 1987: "The world needs...saints. Holiness is not the privilege of a few; it is a gift offered to all."

But Aren't Saints Special People?

No! Robert Louis Stevenson writes: *The saints are the sinners who keep on trying.* Saints are people like you and like me. *No one* is born a saint. Saints become saints by the way they live their lives. Our sanctity depends on how we use our free will to cooperate with God's grace. With the grace of God, our determination, and applying what the experts consider the A B C's of becoming a saint, we can all grow in holiness. Mary Ann Budnik writes in a simple to understand, conversational tone...as though the author was chatting one on one with you over a cup of coffee.

What Topics Are Covered?

Topics include the universal call to sanctity; the various types of graces and how they effect our souls; the theological virtues, moral virtues and natural virtues and how we can obtain them; a plan for growing in holiness; how to sanctify daily work; how to order your life; the role of your guardian angel; mental prayer and its necessity; the importance of daily spiritual reading and scripture reading; what to read to grow in holiness; the problem of sin, the commandments, and the sacrament of penance; the power of Holy Mass and the Blessed Sacrament and why we need them; how to develop devotion to Our Lady and her rosary; why suffer?; how to perseverance in striving for holiness; along with fascinating examples from the lives of the saints.

"To read this book is to change your life." **St. Louis**
"This book has made such an impact on my life." **Wichita**

YOU CAN BECOME A SAINT! WORKBOOK

WHAT MAKES THIS WORKBOOK UNIQUE?

The workbook, to be used in conjunction with the book YOU CAN BECOME A SAINT!, is laid out as a 16 week course. While it follows the original book, it also supplements that material by drawing on Holy Scripture, the *Catechism of the Catholic Church*, the latest writings of the Holy Father, the Fathers of the Church, the saints and renowned Catholic writers.

The 8 1/2 x 11 inch book has 228 pages. Each chapter takes the reader step by step along the narrow path of holiness by utilizing the material in the original book along with the introduction of new material. At the end of each chapter, concrete steps and additional readings are suggested. A weekly calendar entitled "Schedule God Into Your Day" is provided so that the reader can individualized his/her plan to grow closer to God. YOU CAN BECOME A SAINT! WORKBOOK is enhanced by graphic artist Frank J. O'Connell's illustrations.

Fr. John A. Hardon, Theologian and Consultant for the Holy See writes: "*The author stops at nothing to take the reader through the path to holiness step by step so that no one with a spark of the true faith can follow her directives without growing in sanctity. What is most remarkable about this book is its down-to-earth practicality...[H]oliness is not only possible, but easily accessible to anyone who is willing to pay the price...Mary Ann Budnik['s] book is a masterpiece of practicality.*"

WHO CAN USE THIS WORKBOOK?

Since YOU CAN BECOME A SAINT! has an imprimatur, the book along with the workbook, can be used by individuals or by groups. Groups presently using the workbook include parish study groups, Marian groups, Bible groups, R.C.I.A., adult and young adult ministry, high school religion classes and homeschoolers. Those who already own the book will want to purchase the workbook to use along with the book to go deeper into their interior life. Copies of the book sell for $16.95 plus $4.50 for UPS. Discounts available for quantity orders. To order, send check or money order to R.B. Media, Inc., 154 Doral, Springfield, IL 62704 or call (217) 546-5261, Fax (217) 546-0558 or check out our website: www.rbmediainc.com

Looking For Peace?
Try Confession!
by
Mary Ann Budnik

Why is there so much turmoil in my life and in the world? How can I find peace and happiness in the midst of the craziness all around me? I don't do anything bad, why go to confession? Why tell my sins to a priest? What are mortal sins? Where is confession mentioned in the bible? It's been so long since I went to confession, I'm not sure what to do. Do I have to confess face-to-face? What do I confess since I'm a pretty good person?

These questions and more are answered in Mary Ann Budnik's latest book, **Looking for Peace? Try Confession!**

God, in His divine mercy, gives us the *gift* of the Sacrament of Reconciliation to restore peace, joy, and happiness to our souls, our relationships and to the world in general. Learn how to use this gift well!

"**Looking for Peace? Try Confession!** by Mary Ann Budnik should be read by every priest and believing Catholic...It will inspire the faithful to go to confession frequently, because by receiving this sacrament, we obtain that peace of soul which is so desperately needed in our confused and anxious age."
John A. Hardon, S.J.
Theologian, consultant for the Holy See and author

The book has an imprimatur so it can be used as a text-book for doctrinal classes.

To order books:

Quantity	Title	Unit Price	Amount
_____	You Can Become A Saint!	$14.95	_____
_____	You Can Become A Saint! Workbook	$16.95	_____
_____	Looking for Peace? Try Confession!	$11.95	_____
_____	Raise Happy Children Through A Happier Marriage? (Book 1)	$14.95	_____
_____	Raise Happy Children... Raise Them Saints! (Book 2)	$14.95	_____
_____	Raise Happy Children... Teach Them Virtues! (Book 3)	$14.95	_____

Name: _____

Address:_____

City:_____

State: _____ Zip:_____

SUBTOTAL: _____

Tax* _____

Shipping** _____

TOTAL: _____

*Illinois residents add 7.25% tax. Shipping is $4.50 for one book. Please add $1 for each additional book.